Praise for *The Turnaway Study*

"A remarkable piece of research. . . . The Turnaway Study will be understood, criticized, and used politically, however carefully conceived and painstakingly executed the research was. Given that inevitability, it's worth underlining the most helpful political work that the study does. In light of its findings, the rationale for so many recent abortion restrictions—namely, that abortion is uniquely harmful to the people who choose it—simply topples."

—Margaret Talbot, *The New Yorker*

"Foster's findings are particularly relevant now, as the coronavirus pandemic, the economic downturn, and ongoing efforts to restrict abortion access have made the procedure even more difficult for many to obtain."

—Melissa Jeltsen, *HuffPost*

"*The Turnaway Study* . . . provides definitive evidence that abortion access strongly enhances women's health and well-being, whereas denying abortion results in physical and economic harm. Based on a ten-year investigation, the book combines engaging, in-depth stories of women who received and were denied abortion care along with study data from 50 peer-reviewed papers published in top medical and social science journals."

—Carrie N. Baker, *Ms.*

"Foster has succeeded in producing a book that will be indispensable to policy makers, lawyers, and advocates as they conduct evidence-informed work to promote reproductive justice and improve the lives of women and children. *The Turnaway Study* is a call to action to trust women; a reminder that women make thoughtful decisions about their bodies, families, and future."

—*Contraception*

"Required reading for anyone concerned with reproductive justice."

—*Kirkus Reviews* (starred review)

"Foster's clearheaded account cuts through the noise surrounding this contentious issue. Policy makers and abortion rights activists should consider it a must-read."

—*Publishers Weekly*

"Foster listens to the 'turnaway women,' and lets their stories, even more than her own scholarship, disrupt the accepted moral and political narratives that regulate access to abortion."

—*Library Journal*

"If you read only one book about democracy, *The Turnaway Study* should be it. Why? Because without the power to make decisions about our own bodies, there is no democracy. There is no freedom and justice without reproductive freedom and justice."

—Gloria Steinem

"Dr. Foster brings what is too often missing from the public debate around abortion: science, data, and the real-life experiences of people from diverse backgrounds. Dr. Foster's book offers the first in-depth look at the impact of being denied abortion on mental and physical health, economic well-being, relationships, and families. This should be required reading for every judge, member of Congress, and candidate for office—as well as anyone who hopes to better understand this complex and important issue."

—Cecile Richards, cofounder of Supermajority,
former president of Planned Parenthood,
and author of *Make Trouble*

"*The Turnaway Study* demonstrates the power of narrative in illuminating why women seek abortions. I have always been a feminist, and I believe we have a responsibility to safeguard reproductive rights for women everywhere—and for future generations. In this book, statistics and stories meet to reveal the consequences of denying women this service, as well as what happens when they receive it. *The Turnaway Study* is an essential read."

—Isabel Allende, author of *A Long Petal of the Sea*
and *The House of the Spirits*

"Dispelling so many of the prevailing myths about why women seek abortion, this compelling, carefully researched, and unique study makes clear how public policies can so powerfully harm women as they make this deeply personal decision. The moving stories of real women will help illuminate for all of us—both pro-choice and anti-abortion advocates—how restrictive policies can damage the lives of women and their families and why no woman should be turned away when she seeks an abortion."

—Judy Norsigian and Jane Pincus,
coauthors of *Our Bodies, Ourselves*

"Discourse and dialogue about abortion are far too often a fact-free zone, filled with emotion and ideology and bereft of the wisdom of social science. Foster has been at the forefront of changing this destructive dynamic. She has spent years studying the impact on real people and real lives of being able to access abortion services. Her work challenges how we evaluate morality in public policy—it's a must-read."

—Ilyse Hogue, president of
NARAL Pro-Choice America

"Our reproductive realities were the victims of fake news before the term existed, which is why Dr. Foster and her team's work is ever more essential. With rigor and honesty, this book is an important and clarifying contribution to a reality-based conversation about abortion."

—Irin Carmon, coauthor of *Notorious RBG:
The Life and Times of Ruth Bader Ginsburg*

"The stories and findings in *The Turnaway Study* are captivating and confirm what abortion funds have witnessed from their help lines for decades. Hundreds of thousands of people calling for help across the country are navigating too many barriers to the care they need. This book illustrates that the process of obtaining an abortion is entirely too complicated and the outcomes of being denied an abortion are unjust."

—Yamani Hernandez, executive director of
the National Network of Abortion Funds

"The loud discourse around abortion, framed in the language of politics, religious beliefs, and women's changing social roles, is so intense that sometimes people don't take the time to discover the who, what, when, and why of actual people making decisions and having real health and social outcomes. Dr. Foster has created an indispensable resource for scientists, policy makers, doctors, and legislators who are seeking facts to inform their opinions."

—Dr. Stephanie Teal, professor of Obstetrics and Gynecology, Pediatrics, and Clinical Science at the University of Colorado School of Medicine and former president of the Society of Family Planning

"*The Turnaway Study* reflects the ultimate in scientific methodology on this contentious subject. The rich, accurate information resonates with the poignant personal accounts. Here is the complete abortion book, both informative for health professionals and accessible to lay readers."

—Dr. Nada L. Stotland, professor of Psychiatry at Rush University and former president of the American Psychiatric Association

"Dr. Foster has contextualized the groundbreaking Turnaway Study using the stories of the people who are the most central to the abortion debate but whose experiences are generally overlooked: people who have abortions."

—Monica R. McLemore, PhD, MPH, RN, FAAN, associate professor of Nursing at UCSF, and chair for Sexual and Reproductive Health at the American Public Health Association

THE TURNAWAY STUDY

Ten Years, a Thousand Women,
and the Consequences of Having—
or Being Denied—an Abortion

DIANA GREENE FOSTER, PhD

SCRIBNER

New York   London   Toronto   Sydney   New Delhi

Scribner
An Imprint of Simon & Schuster, Inc.
1230 Avenue of the Americas
New York, NY 10020

First Scribner trade paperback edition June 2021

For information about special discounts for bulk purchases,
please contact Simon & Schuster Special Sales at 1-866-506-1949
or business@simonandschuster.com.

The Simon & Schuster Speakers Bureau can bring authors to your live event.
For more information or to book an event, contact the Simon & Schuster Speakers
Bureau at 1-866-248-3049 or visit our website at www.simonspeakers.com.

Interior design by Erich Hobbing

3 5 7 9 10 8 6 4

Library of Congress Cataloging-in-Publication Data is available.

ISBN 978-1-9821-4156-1
ISBN 978-1-9821-4157-8 (pbk)
ISBN 978-1-9821-4158-5 (ebook)

Note to Readers: Names and identifying details have been changed
and first-person interviews have been condensed and edited for clarity.

To the women of
the Turnaway Study

Contents

CONTENTS

Introduction

Ten women sit in a clinic waiting room. They have come from as far as three hundred miles away, made many calls to find this place, and passed shouting protesters on the way in. One is a woman holding her husband's hand. Another is a college student with her boyfriend. There's a woman on her phone, checking in with the roommate who is watching her three-year-old child. Another woman is also on the phone, telling someone where she is and what she is about to do. There's a woman who looks miserable and sick. Two of the women are nervous—worried about being judged for getting here late. Although most of the women are in their twenties, two are teenagers, each accompanied by a friend. The final woman, clearly upset by the protesters outside, is leafing through a book of journal entries written by others. One by one, they are called in to find out if they got to the clinic soon enough.

Did the time it took for these women to realize they were pregnant, to have conversations with partners or parents, to decide what to do, to gather enough money, to figure out where to go and how to get there—did it delay them until it was too late?

Will they receive an abortion, and what they hope will be a second chance?

Or will they be turned away?

Every day, all over the United States, this scene repeats itself—in a hospital in San Francisco; in a small clinic in the middle of Maine;

in the only clinics in North Dakota and South Dakota; in a clinic in Texas on the border with Mexico; in a clinic in a Manhattan high-rise; in a big facility in Chicago; in Atlanta, Boston, Little Rock, Seattle, Louisville, Albuquerque, Tuscaloosa, Dallas, Pittsburgh, Tallahassee, Cleveland, Phoenix, Portland, Los Angeles, and in hundreds of other clinics and hospitals across the country. Every year, thousands of people are denied abortions because they show up too late in pregnancy.[1]

This book is about what happens to women who come in just under a clinic's deadline and receive a wanted abortion, and what happens to those who arrive at the very same clinics just a few days or weeks later in pregnancy and are turned away. It is also a book about the state of abortion access in our country and the people whose lives are affected by it.

Because politics drives abortion access in the United States, the cutoff—the point in pregnancy after which one is unable to get an abortion—depends on where you live. Over the decades since the 1973 landmark case *Roe v. Wade*, which allowed states to ban abortion only after viability and never if necessary to preserve maternal life or health, the Supreme Court has permitted states to impose a huge range of restrictions on abortion and what is required to get one.[2] Conservative statehouses have passed countless regulations, keeping abortion legal but rendering it all but inaccessible for many Americans who don't have the resources to travel great distances to less restrictive states. Forty-three states ban abortions for most women after a certain point in their pregnancy.[3] A third of states currently ban abortion at 20 weeks' gestation. And in 2019, at least 17 states introduced legislation that would ban abortion at six weeks into pregnancy or even earlier.[4] The bills became law in Georgia, Kentucky, Louisiana, Mississippi, and Ohio but immediately faced legal challenges that postponed their implementation. And regardless of where each state draws the line, many clinics won't terminate a pregnancy beyond the first trimester, and many more don't go all

2

the way to their state's legal limit because of a lack of trained providers, the presence of various laws restricting abortion facilities, or a desire to avoid attention from protesters and politicians.

The fact that many of the state abortion gestational limit laws have already led to lawsuits is by design. Lawmakers and anti-abortion activists have crafted these laws specifically to challenge *Roe*, hoping to provoke a lawsuit that will end up before a Supreme Court newly stacked in favor of allowing laws that ban abortion. In 2016, President Donald Trump's fiercely anti-abortion running mate and now vice president, Mike Pence, pledged on the campaign trail, "If we appoint strict constructionists to the Supreme Court of the United States, as Donald Trump intends to do, I believe we will see *Roe versus Wade* consigned to the ash heap of history, where it belongs. I promise you."[5] In their first term in office, the duo has turned that pledge into a genuine possibility. With the addition of Justices Neil Gorsuch and Brett Kavanaugh, the Supreme Court may now have enough conservative votes to reverse that 1973 precedent on abortion rights—that is, to reject the Supreme Court's measured approach and instead allow states full discretion to ban abortion outright.

Since *Roe v. Wade*, abortion has dominated our political discussions in the United States. Political and legal efforts to restrict access to abortion have never been more intense than they have been in the past decade. Rhetoric and policy proposals have expanded from punishing abortion providers to imprisoning patients. Recently, 207 members of Congress signed a letter to the Supreme Court asking the justices to uphold in Louisiana a restrictive law similar to one the Court ruled unconstitutional in Texas in 2016.[6] But the letter goes further, urging the Court to take the opportunity to reconsider whether abortion rights are protected by the Constitution at all.[7] In other words, access to abortion is in greater jeopardy than it has been since *Roe* was decided more than forty-five years ago.

Many restrictions on abortion are passed with the justification that they make abortion safer, or prevent women who might experience regret and psychological harm from getting an abortion. The political debate about abortion has shifted in the last few decades. Instead of focusing on the rights of fetuses versus the rights of women, anti-abortion advocates and lawmakers have tried to reframe the abortion debate as a women's health issue, suggesting that abortion hurts women, leading to depression, anxiety, and suicidal thoughts. Where evidence is lacking, policymakers have routinely invented it. In 2007, Supreme Court justice Anthony Kennedy, writing the majority opinion upholding a ban on one abortion procedure performed later in pregnancy, seized an opportunity to weigh in on the emotional and mental state of women who have abortions. He wrote, "While we find no reliable data to measure the phenomenon, it seems unexceptionable to conclude some women come to regret their choice to abort the infant life they once created and sustained. Severe depression and loss of esteem can follow."[8] Clearly, in 2007, there was a serious need for reliable data on the consequences of abortion.

Just one year earlier, Dr. Eleanor Drey, the medical director of the Women's Options Center at San Francisco General Hospital, said to me, "I wonder what happens to the women we turn away." I'm a researcher at the University of California, San Francisco (UCSF), in the Department of Obstetrics, Gynecology and Reproductive Sciences. Dr. Drey and I had collaborated on a study about what delays women seeking abortion into the second trimester. People seeking later abortions, although they represent only a small percentage of those seeking abortions, face the most legal restrictions, social condemnation, and logistical hurdles. According to data from the Centers for Disease Control and Prevention, the vast majority (over 90%) of people having abortions in the United States are in the first trimester, within 13 weeks after the first day of their last menstrual period.[9] About 8% have abortions between 14 and 20 weeks. And only a fraction—just over 1%—have abortions when they are more than 20 weeks pregnant.

Dr. Drey and I wanted to understand what causes people to delay getting an abortion, given that later abortions are usually more expensive, more time-consuming, harder to get, and, outside California, often heavily legally restricted. What we found is that the leading reason women get abortions in the second trimester is that they didn't realize they were pregnant—more than half of the two hundred second-trimester patients in our California study did not know they were pregnant until they had already passed the first trimester mark.[10] Many of these women never experience pregnancy symptoms. When a woman realizes she is pregnant and she decides she really doesn't want to be, if she is past the first trimester, the logistical barriers to getting an abortion—the cost of the procedure, the time off required, the need for transportation and perhaps child care for existing children—multiply. The more the pregnancy progresses, the higher the price climbs, as the medical procedure becomes more complex, and the nearest available clinic willing or able to provide it gets farther away. Often, this causes a snowball effect. By the time she finally gets to a clinic, it might be too late.

After my conversation with Dr. Drey and our work on *why* women seek abortions in the second trimester, I wanted to know what happens to them: both the women who get the abortions they want, and the women clinics turn away. Do they remain in a relationship with the man who got them pregnant? Are they able to take care of the children they already have and, if they are denied the abortion, a new baby as well? Do they have the kids they want to have later? Do those who get the abortion come to regret it? Do those who are turned away regret having a child? In comparing women who receive wanted abortions to those who are denied, I saw the potential to answer the hotly debated question *Does abortion hurt women?* And, on the flip side, *What are the harms from not being able to access a wanted abortion?*

I called it the Turnaway Study because "turnaways" is what Dr. Drey calls women who are too far along in their pregnancies to receive an abortion at her hospital. For me, that phrase also resonates with a whole set of issues that surround women's decision-making around pregnancy. Women seeking abortion are turning away from the possibility of imminent motherhood, and it's also what they may have to do to their non-child-related plans if they are denied the abortion. Turning away is what society does to women when we debate the moral status of fetuses without considering the lives of women who would become mothers. It's what our government does to women and children when low-income women, unable to get an abortion, are not given enough child care, food, and housing assistance to raise their children without the constant fear of not having enough.

The Turnaway Study was the first of its kind to investigate how abortion affects women by comparing those who get an abortion and those who want one but don't get it. Before our study, the little data previously used in the debate over whether abortion hurts women came from studies that compared women who had abortions to women who gave birth, whether or not they had considered having an abortion first. The problem with this comparison is that women are more likely to choose to give birth when times are good—when they are in good relationships, when they are financially stable, when they feel ready to support a child. On the other hand, women are more likely to choose to have an abortion when times are not so good—when their relationship is rocky, their health is poor, and they don't have enough money to cover rent and food. So if you compare women who have abortions to women who have births, there will be differences that have little to do with the experience of getting an abortion but instead reflect the circumstances of whether a pregnancy is wanted or unwanted.

The book you are reading is the culmination of my quest for answers, a quest that became a ten-year-long exploration of the experiences of women who have, or try to have, abortions in the United States. More than 40 researchers—project directors, interviewers, epidemiologists, demographers, sociologists, economists, psychologists, statisticians, nurses, and public health scientists—collaborated for more than a decade to carry out this study. We recruited just over a thousand women seeking abortions at 30 facilities across the U.S., including those who received an abortion early in pregnancy, those who barely made it in time but received an abortion, and those who were a little too late and were turned away. We sought to interview each woman every six months over five years to learn how receiving versus being denied a wanted abortion affects a woman's mental and physical health, her life aspirations, and the well-being of her family. We published almost 50 academic papers in leading medical, public health, and sociology journals. Our design and subsequent data have been met with widespread attention and acclaim, cited by prominent media outlets, and profiled in the *New York Times Magazine* as the "most rigorous" study to look at whether women develop mental health problems following an abortion.[11] Laying out the findings of the largest study of women's experiences with abortion in the United States, this book represents the first time that the results of our in-depth ten-year investigation have been collected in one place. In order to bring these findings further to life, I have also gathered the stories of ten women from the study, told in their own words, of how they came to need an abortion and what happened to them after they did or did not receive one.

In these pages, I document the emotional, health, and socioeconomic outcomes for women who received a wanted abortion and those who were denied one. Before our judges and policymakers consider eroding abortion rights or criminalizing abortion, I want them—and the voters and others responsible for elevating them to power—to understand what banning abortion would mean for women and children.

I didn't design this study thinking about politics, or even about women's rights. I came to this work with a desire to document both positive and negative aspects of abortion and carrying a pregnancy to term. I imagined that having a baby after an unwanted pregnancy is likely to be both a burden and a joy. Even though abortion is a choice women make in response to their own life circumstances, I believed it was also possible that having an abortion might cause significant distress, and potentially guilt or regret.

As I formulated our survey questions, I tried to measure all the ways in which abortion might improve women's lives and all the ways in which it might cause harm. I wanted to hear from women who were actually experiencing what the rest of us debate in the abstract.

This is a book about scientific research. But because the research subject is abortion, it is also a book about politics, policy, and the lives of women and children. As a scientist, I realize that science will never resolve the moral question of when a fetus becomes a person, nor will it answer the legal question of when, if ever, the rights of a fetus should outweigh those of the person whose body carries it. But our moral and legal opinions should be based on an accurate understanding of our world. And lack of data severely hampers our understanding of abortion. The Turnaway Study offers a unique opportunity to examine the effect of abortion on women's lives, and the immediate and far-reaching consequences of laws that restrict access to it.

A Note about Terminology

I use the word "women" to describe the participants in the study. Some people who are assigned female at birth and later identify as male or nonbinary also experience unintended pregnancy and seek abortion care. However, our consent form specified that the target study population was pregnant women, and, to my knowledge, no trans men participated. Many of the issues I identify would likely resonate with trans men and nonbinary people who become pregnant. All the additional ways in which being a trans man makes access to reproductive health care more difficult are not captured by this study but are important topics for future research.

I use the more accurate word "people" to describe those who get abortions outside the study. However, I believe that the reason that contraceptives are so difficult to get, decision-making ability is doubted, and politicians feel they can weigh in on the most fundamental of decisions about one's body is precisely because the vast majority of people needing abortions are women. Sometimes, I use the word "women" rather than the more inclusive "people who need abortions" to highlight the misogyny and root cause of the problem.

A Note about Statistics

My research team conducted almost eight thousand interviews of nearly one thousand women over eight years. The credit report and death records searches included over 1,100 women. The field of statistics has powerful methods of analyzing such large data sets to account for any variation in outcomes by recruitment site, to analyze repeated measures for the same woman over time, and to compensate for much of the bias that could come from women dropping out of the study over time, and, when differences exist, adjust for baseline differences between the study groups. If you, like me, find this exciting, please read our scientific papers, many of which are available on our website, www.turnawaystudy.com. For this book, I have summarized differences by presenting a simple comparison of percentages, usually comparing women who gave birth after being denied an abortion because they were just over a clinic's gestational limit to those just under the clinic's limit who received an abortion. If I mention a difference, the conclusion is not that two percentages differed at one point in time. Instead, it means that our statistical models showed that the whole trajectory of the two groups differed over time in a way that is unlikely to have occurred by chance. The percentages merely give you a sense of the magnitude of the difference. The graphs represent the trajectories of these two groups.[1] I present data for the first-trimester sample when the results are substantively different from the sample of women who received abortions just under the clinic gestational limits, most of whom were in the second trimester.

11

CHAPTER 1

The Turnaway Study

I n the summer of 1987, President Ronald Reagan addressed the leaders of the right-to-life movement during a gathering in Washington, DC, and did what Republican presidents have been doing ever since abortion become legal in the United States.[1] He promised to fight to overturn *Roe v. Wade*, the 1973 Supreme Court decision that continues to rankle the Grand Old Party's religious-right base all these decades later.

"I will not rest until a human life amendment becomes a part of our Constitution," Reagan promised, referring to the name given to various proposed constitutional amendments introduced since 1973 that would have granted legal personhood to embryos and fetuses and effectively criminalized all abortions, sometimes without exceptions. To date, no such proposal has gone far in Congress, and Reagan clearly didn't expect it to go far in his last years in office. Before the anti-abortion leaders ceased their applause, Reagan quickly turned the conversation to incremental attacks on abortion. "At the same time," he said, "we must continue to search for practical steps that we can take now, even before the battle for the human life amendment is won."

Reagan listed four steps his administration had taken, steps he believed represented "powerful examples of what can be done now to protect the lives of unborn children." The third step on his list, however, did not address those "unborn children," but rather the need for proof that abortion harms women.

"Growing numbers of women who've had abortions now say

that they have been misled by inaccurate information," he said. "Making accurate data on maternal morbidity available to women before an abortion is performed is an essential element of informed consent. I am, therefore, directing the Surgeon General to issue a comprehensive medical report on the health effects, physical and emotional, of abortion on women."

That task fell to Surgeon General C. Everett Koop, an acclaimed pediatric surgeon who very publicly opposed abortion. The doctor had written a book and produced short films arguing that abortion would inevitably lead to forced euthanasia for seniors and people with disabilities.[2] He had previously toured the country giving multimedia presentations on the evils of abortion. This is the man who was charged with finding evidence that abortion harms women. Reagan and his religious-right constituents hoped that Koop's report would provide the basis for abortion to be legislated accordingly.

However, Koop could find no such evidence. And it wasn't for lack of trying. As he would write in his final letter to President Reagan a year and a half later, the surgeon general reviewed more than 250 studies pertaining to the psychological impact of abortion.[3] He interviewed women who'd had abortions and talked to dozens of medical, social, and philosophical groups on both sides of the debate.

Koop surprised his initial critics with his commitment to science and public health, even in the face of religious and political opposition, when he ultimately concluded that the existing data, showing either that abortion was harmful or that it wasn't, were rife with methodological problems: "I regret, Mr. President, that in spite of a diligent review on the part of many in the Public Health Service and in the private sector, the scientific studies do not provide conclusive data about the health effects of abortion on women."

In Koop's 1989 letter to President Reagan, he called for more and better research of abortion's effects, specifically a five-year prospective study analyzing all the many outcomes of sex and reproduction, including the psychological and physical effects of trying but failing to conceive; having planned and unplanned, wanted and unwanted pregnancies; and delivering, miscarrying, or aborting pregnancies. His call for better research would go unfulfilled for twenty years.

Until, that is, 2007, when my team of social scientists decided to take on a portion of what Koop had envisioned: to study the outcomes of both birth and abortion for women with unwanted pregnancies. Abortion is a medical procedure so controversial it decides elections and ruins Thanksgiving dinners. Yet it is also extremely common—between one in four and one in three women in the U.S. will have an abortion during their lifetime.[4] But being common does not make it easy to study. We needed to overcome the methodological pitfalls that had discredited all the earlier studies Koop had reviewed. In particular, we needed to avoid comparisons between women who have abortions and those who have wanted pregnancies. After all, the set of circumstances that in some cases makes a pregnancy unwanted—such as poverty, poor mental health, or lack of social support—might be the primary stressor that causes poor outcomes, rather than the abortion itself. And given the difficulties brought to the fore when a woman discovers she is pregnant but doesn't have the job, housing, family support, or other resources required to raise a child, it may not only be the unintended pregnancy that causes distress, but the life reckoning that comes when making the decision to have an abortion.

An unbiased study would focus on women who share the same circumstance of becoming pregnant and not feeling able or willing to have a baby. Pregnant women like Jessica, a 23-year-old mother of two whose previous pregnancies had exacerbated her serious health problems and who was married to a man she described as abusive and whom she wanted to leave. Or Sofia, who at 19 was in what she called a "rocky" relationship and whose family had just been evicted from their home. Then we would compare the outcomes—physical, psychological, financial, romantic, familial—of women who got the abortions they wanted, like Jessica, to women who were turned away because they were too far along, like Sofia.

Our study design is what social scientists call a natural experiment, where randomness in access to a program or a service allows researchers to compare people who received it and people who didn't. A classic example is a lottery that determines which people get health insurance, as was done in Oregon in the rollout of an expansion in Medicaid.[5] Obviously, it would be unethical to randomly deny women wanted abortions for the sake of science. But women are denied abortions all the time in the United States—sometimes because they cannot afford one and, sometimes (for at least 4,000 women per year) because there are no clinics nearby that perform abortions at their gestation.[6]

The strength of the Turnaway Study's design is that women just above and just below the gestational limit are women facing the same circumstances—sometimes just a few days determines whether a woman can access abortion. Any divergences in their outcomes are likely a result of whether they received their wanted abortion. Over the course of three years, 2008 through 2010, we recruited more than 1,000 pregnant women from the waiting rooms of 30 abortion facilities in 21 states. Facilities set their gestational limits to reflect their doctors' level of comfort and ability, as well as to comply with state law. Because most of the facilities we chose have limits in the second trimester but more than 90% of women in the U.S. have abortions in the first trimester, we also recruited first-trimester patients, who would represent a more typical abortion experience. At each site, for every woman denied the abortion, we recruited two women who received an abortion just under the gestational limit and one who received an abortion in the first trimester.

We interviewed these women by phone twice a year for up to five years—through both easy and difficult recoveries from abortion and birth. We asked about their emotions and mental health, their physical health, their life goals and financial well-being, and the health and development of their children. For those denied abortions, we followed some who continued their search for another clinic that could provide their abortion. The great majority (70%) of those turned away carried the pregnancy to term, and we asked them about their childbirth and subsequent decisions about parenting. We examined nearly every aspect of how receiving or being denied an abortion affected these women's lives and the lives of their families. We gathered data about why women want to end their pregnancies and how hard it is to get an abortion in the U.S. We had study participants take us back to the day of their abortions, to the protesters they encountered, to the ultrasound images of embryos or fetuses that some state laws required their doctors to offer to show them. We wanted to learn how these experiences affected women's long-term emotions about their abortion. We documented their physical health and how it changed with pregnancy, abortion, and birth and in the years that followed. We analyzed the role of men in abortion-related decision-making and how the outcome of the pregnancy affected women's romantic relationships. A team of UCSF researchers used the latest statistical techniques to analyze data from thousands of interviews, often collaborating with scientists across the country.

Launching the Turnaway Study

I would not have been able to carry out the Turnaway Study on my own. As you will see, I had help from many other people from the beginning. In 2007, when I first conceived of the study, Sandy Stonesifer was working as the assistant to the chief of the family planning division at San Francisco General Hospital. I needed to conduct a pilot study to see if women faced with the news that they would not be able to get an abortion would be willing to sign up for a study about their outcomes. Sandy offered to run down the hall to the Women's Options Center to try to recruit women deemed too late to receive an abortion. When the pilot proved successful, Sandy took over the job of managing the study and finding other abortion facilities that would help direct their patients and their turnaways to our small study team. So Sandy and I embarked on a series of abortion-clinic tours. We visited a clinic in Fargo, North Dakota, in the middle of a massive snowstorm in February. Come sweltering July we were touring clinics in Texas. Clinic staff welcomed us out of the snow and heat and into their communities. Many clinic workers seemed enthusiastic about our mission to understand the experiences of both the women they serve and those they're unable to serve. Everyone we visited was proud of their clinic.

Some clinics were architecturally beautiful, like one in Atlanta that featured a high-peaked trellised wooden ceiling above its waiting room. Others were rather spare, like one in a converted auto mechanic shop in the Midwest. A few clinics we visited displayed feminist-themed décor—posters urging patients and accompaniers to vote or telling them that "good women have abortions." Most of the clinics we toured seemed like ordinary health care clinics designed by the same architect who designed all the public schools I attended as a kid in Maryland—who apparently believed that no kid should get to see natural light while at school. But in the case of abortion clinics, the fortress is designed to keep protesters out instead of occupants in. Security is a big deal in these buildings. Some abortion doctors wear bulletproof vests to work.[7] At the time we did these tours, between 2007 and 2010, violence at clinics was less common than it was in the 1980s and '90s, when blockades and violent attacks on clinics and providers surged in America.[8] Most facilities we went to were just busy medical clinics. Roughly half of those we visited had protesters, but the protesters usually just stood there peacefully and did not talk to the women going in.[9] Only a few facilities had loud and aggressive protesters.

In the ten years since we toured the clinics, incidences of harassment, threats, and violence have increased substantially.[10] Clinic bombings and shootings occur, and sometimes they're fatal. Most recently, in 2015 three people were murdered at a Planned Parenthood clinic in Colorado Springs, Colorado.[11] But the fact that the national media most often pays attention to abortion clinics when there's a mass shooting or a bombing creates a misperception that abortion facilities are constantly under violent attack. The media focus on protesters contributes to the perception that abortion is a political act rather than the provision of routine health care.

Sandy left after a couple of years to bring her excellent management skills to Washington, DC, and I recruited Rana Barar, a Columbia University–trained expert in reproductive health research management, to direct the increasingly complicated study logistics. She expanded the number of recruiting clinics and oversaw a growing team of interviewers and database developers that collected data from 7,851 interviews. We eventually chose 30 recruitment sites that had the latest gestational limit within 150 miles—if a woman was too late for one of these clinics, no clinic nearby could provide her abortion. At each site, one staff person was responsible for approaching women and asking them if they would be interested in participating in a nationwide study of women seeking abortion services. Many of these designated recruiters were initially skeptical that someone who was denied care would stick around long enough to hear about a study and, more to the point, that they would agree to anything, given that they were being turned away. It was the recruiting success of Dr. Drey's Women's Options Center, where 70% of women agreed to participate, that gave the point people at the other clinic sites the courage to approach women. As Tammi Kromenaker, the point person in Fargo, North Dakota, would tell women, "It's your chance to have your story heard."

The Women of the Turnaway Study

The women who agreed to participate in this study closely resemble the profile of women who get abortions nationally.[12] Just over a third (37%) were white and not Latina, just under a third (29%) were African American, one in five (21%) were Latina, 4% were American Indian, and 3% were Asian American. Similar to abortion patients nationwide, more than half of the women (60%) were in their twenties at the time of the abortion. Almost one in five (18%)

were teenagers, and just over one in five (22%) were 30 or older. Half were living in poverty, although women seeking abortion later in pregnancy were more likely to be poor—40% of those in the first trimester and 57% of those who sought abortions just above or below the clinic gestational limit.[13] There are economically privileged women in the study as well. Roughly a quarter of the study participants were middle-class or wealthier, had private health insurance, and reported that they often or always have enough money. Women of all ethnic and economic backgrounds seek abortions.

They came from more than 40 states across the country to the clinics in 21 states where we recruited, from Maine to Florida, Washington to Texas. Sixty percent had children, and 45% had experienced a prior abortion. Sixty-one percent were in a current romantic relationship with the man with whom they became pregnant; 39% reported that the man was a friend, ex-partner, or acquaintance, or that they had no relationship with him. One in five women reported a history of sexual assault or rape; 11 women (1%) were pregnant as a result of rape.

Where the women in this study differ from the national profile of women getting abortions is in how far along many of them were in their pregnancies. Again, roughly 90% of women in America who have abortions do so in the first trimester (13 weeks and under), and only 1% do so after 20 weeks of pregnancy. But in the Turnaway Study, 25% of the women were in the first trimester, 30% were between 14 and 19 weeks, and 45% were 20 weeks or later. This gives us extremely important data on the most politically vulnerable and least socially accepted abortion patients.

I decided to exclude from the study women who were terminating pregnancies because of a known fetal anomaly or because of their own severe immediate health risks. My rationale was that the law allows providers to terminate pregnancies after viability in cases like these. Therefore, if I had recruited these patients, I probably would have had to remove them from the analyses because they might only end up in one study group—those getting their wanted abortions and not in the group of women who were denied. This would defeat the concept of the study design, where women are similar on both sides of the gestational limit. In retrospect, I wish I had included them, if only to analyze their data separately. Very little is known about women's experiences and the emotional consequences of terminating a wanted pregnancy for reasons related to fetal or maternal health. Based on previous research showing that women who aborted wanted pregnancies due to fetal anomaly anticipate more difficulty coping immediately after the abortion, women might have more distress after an abortion for fetal anomaly or maternal health than after aborting an unwanted pregnancy.[14] But before we leap to saying that abortion for those reasons results in poor outcomes, we would want to know about distress and coping after carrying such a pregnancy to term. It would also have been interesting to look at whether those women had subsequent, healthier pregnancies and how their emotional health fared in the long run. Further study is needed in these areas.

Our Findings

We find no evidence that abortion hurts women. For every outcome we analyzed, women who received an abortion were either the same or, more frequently, better off than women who were denied an abortion. Their physical health was better. Their employment and financial situations were better. Their mental health was initially better and eventually the same. They had more aspirational plans for the coming year. They had a greater chance of having a wanted pregnancy and being in a good romantic relationship years down the road. And the children they already had were better off, too.

We find many ways in which women were hurt by carrying an unwanted pregnancy to term. Continued pregnancy and childbirth is associated with large physical health risks, so great that two women in our study died from childbirth-related causes. Many others experienced complications from delivery and, extending over the next five years, increased chronic head and joint pain, hypertension, and poorer self-rated overall health. In the short run, women experienced increased anxiety and loss of life satisfaction after being denied an abortion, and those with violent partners found it difficult to extricate themselves after the birth. Over the next several years, women who were denied abortions experienced economic hardships not experienced by women who received their wanted abortions.

Abortion opponents often accuse women seeking abortions of being misinformed, irresponsible, or amoral. In fact, as the Turnaway Study results make clear, women make thoughtful, well-considered decisions about whether to have an abortion. When asked why they want to end a pregnancy, women give specific and personal reasons. And their fears are borne out in the experiences of women who carry unwanted pregnancies to term. Women seeking abortions worry that they cannot afford to raise a baby, and we find that women denied abortions are more likely to live in poverty. They worry that their relationship isn't strong enough to support a child, and we find that relationships with the man involved dissolve regardless of whether they carry the pregnancy to term or have an abortion. They worry about not being able to take care of their existing children, and we find evidence that women's children do worse on several measures of health and development when women carry an unwanted pregnancy to term than when they receive an abortion. The Turnaway Study brings powerful evidence about the ability of women to foresee consequences and make decisions that are best for their lives and families.

Women's Stories

In this book, you'll see how women's lives are changed when they receive a wanted abortion and when they are turned away. The consequences reach far beyond one pregnancy to shape the direction of their lives and their children's. The data—measurable quantitative outcomes faced by women who receive abortions versus women who are denied them, such as symptoms of depression, income levels, and cases of hypertension—don't tell the whole story. To get a deeper understanding of the lived experiences of the women in the study, you need to hear from the women themselves. My colleague Heather Gould conducted in-depth interviews with 31 women—28 who were randomly selected from those who had completed five years of interviews, two who had placed children for adoption, and one who had completed the surveys in Spanish. You'll hear from most of these 31 women (referred to by pseudonyms) and in particular ten whom I have selected to tell their whole stories. I picked them for the strength of their voices and the breadth of their experiences.

In their own words, these women will tell you about their unwanted pregnancies. Some will recount the abortions they were able to have, whether early or late in their pregnancies. Others will tell you about the babies they birthed, which some chose to parent and others chose to place for adoption. You'll hear from a woman who is smart and ambitious but also young, barely 20 when we first meet her, and rationalizes that a two-year joint cell phone contract should lock her in a relationship with a man who fills their home with cigarette smoke and aggravates her crippling asthma, who hurts her and who forces her into sex. As you will see, it takes facing the reality of an accidental pregnancy to set her on a more independent path. You will hear from the partygoing store clerk turned Christian-café owner whose life changes when she falls in love with her steakhouse waiter. She's too far along for an abortion in her city. She could travel more than 250 miles to get a later abortion; in fact, her family insists she do just that. But she resists and experiences isolation, depression, and, eventually, happiness, with the birth of her son. These stories and the many others included here show that our reproductive lives are complex. Women who have abortions also have wanted pregnancies; women who place children for adoption later decide to raise a child.

Ten women cannot represent the nearly one million people who have abortions each year. But the ten stories from women in the Turnaway Study do give some insight into the personal experiences of women seeking abortion. I have changed their names and identifying details, but the words are theirs, taken and condensed from the interview transcripts. The stories appear between chapters, presented in order of increasing gestational age at the time each woman enrolled in this study. It's probably not a coincidence that the woman with the earliest abortion also has one of the least complicated stories. Not being poor, sick, unsupported, or conflicted about her decision probably helped Amy seek an abortion earlier than the other women you'll hear from. I think Amy's is the ideal story to start with because she shows that unwanted pregnancies can happen to anyone. Amy is nurturing, funny, kind, and feels grateful for her "extravagant, wonderful ordinary life." It doesn't take a life in crisis to need an abortion. Over 30-plus years of trying to avoid pregnancy, accidents can happen. They can even happen more than once. Amy's situation is happy and stable, and having an abortion helped her preserve that. The abortion is a part of how Amy handled her life and planned her family. She and her husband had a child already, and they didn't want another. She'd tried adoption once and knew it wasn't for her.

Amy's experience is an example of what the bioethicist Katie Watson calls, in her excellent book, *Scarlet A*, an "ordinary abortion."[15] Abortion-rights advocates often hold up the extreme cases—the woman with a violent partner, the woman with a life-threatening illness, the 14-year-old girl raped by a relative, the woman whose fetus wouldn't survive more than a few moments after birth. The motivation might be to try to evoke sympathy for someone in such dire circumstances. But the message communicated may be that abortion is an extreme remedy for an extreme situation. Instead, as Amy shows, abortion can be a normal part of planning a family and living a meaningful life. Extreme cases do occur and should also receive our sympathy, but the story of abortion is overwhelmingly one of people in ordinary circumstances wanting to have some control over their bodies, their childbearing, and their lives.

AMY

*I just couldn't imagine starting over and doing it
all again. I would be depriving my first child
by having to support a second one.*

I was born in Texas, and I lived there with my mom and my dad.
My mom worked in a nursing home. My dad was a mechanic.
They divorced when I was a little kid. My parents are remarried
and have their own families now. So we're still here in Texas.

When my parents got divorced, it really wasn't the best time
for a kid. So I don't really remember a whole lot other than my
grandparents, who had a farm. You know, there was lots of animals.
But my parents were both very good parents. I can remember they
were good.

My husband and I, we've been together since high school. We
had just got married when I became pregnant. When we found out
that I was pregnant with our first child, our only child, I was 17,
and we had considered adoption. Well, we had picked out a family,
and she actually went there for about two weeks until we changed
our mind. We had thought, you know, if we couldn't give her the
life that she deserved, then we'll give somebody else the opportunity to. We had signed the papers and everything that we were
supposed to do. And she was with the family. It was so sad. I tried
to separate the postpartum blues from my own emotions. And
then I realized it's not postpartum. This is our child. We need to

get her back and raise her even if we have to struggle or we have to sacrifice different things. We'll make it work. So we got her back.

We were just living the American dream and just living one day at a time and trying to raise a daughter the best we could. We talked about having more kids when our daughter was younger. My husband would say, "You know, we should have one more." And first I was like, "Yeah, well, when she's four." And then I was like, "Okay, when she's five or when she's six or when she's seven." And then it just became—there's really no point in starting over. She's in school and there was no time, no room, no money, no nothing for an extra mouth to feed. Every marriage has its challenges. Was it anything out of the ordinary? No. We were just like any other married couple, I guess.

I was living with my husband and my daughter when I became pregnant again. At that time I was coaching figure skating and my daughter was ten. I was working, and living life, and stuff happens and there you are. We have to make decisions.

We weren't struggling, but we had recently bought a house. My daughter was a figure skater, which was quite expensive. It was a good chunk of money each month to do that. And we were planning to send her to a private school. I felt like I wanted to give one kid everything that I possibly could. I couldn't fathom giving two children all the things that I wanted to be able to give one.

When I found out I was pregnant again, I had mixed emotions. I was kind of scared, like, okay, what are we going to do? Sad because I already knew that I never wanted any more children.

My husband was—he had mixed emotions as well. He couldn't believe that it had happened, because even though we had the one child, she was pretty much a miracle baby because my husband cannot have children, and here we were expecting another. When he was a teenager, my husband had a medical issue. And when he got finished with his surgeries, they told him the likelihood for him to have any children would be slim to none. So our first one was a surprise because we never thought that he would ever be able to have children. So when we found out that I was pregnant the second time, it was a lot to deal with.

I remember I told my husband on his birthday that I was pregnant. And he had asked me, he said, "Well, what are we going to do?"

So, on this new pregnancy, we already knew what the options were. We already knew that adoption wasn't going to work. That just wasn't in our blood. So we looked at the route of the abortion. And that just fit our plan better. When I went to my doctor, who I'd been seeing for the past ten years, she knew that I never wanted any more children, so she gave me a pamphlet, and I had to call and set up an appointment.

There were some protesters outside the clinic. There weren't very many, and it didn't faze me. I knew what I wanted to do, and I'm a pretty strong-willed person. So they weren't going to change my mind. But I guess if some people were uncertain about their decision, then it could have affected them. But I just went on in. In the clinic, I was super nervous. One, you don't want to see anybody that you know. So you just hold your head down and just get through it. We saw all types of different people there. But the staff was wonderful. They were—after you have the abortion, you're kind of out of it a little bit, but I remember everybody being really nice and making sure that everything was taken care of properly. They kind of commended me on my bravery and were understanding and made me feel like I was making the right choice for me. When I left, everything was fine, and it was a rock lifted off my chest.

I don't think that the abortion has affected anything since then negatively. And honestly I'm not even sure if it's been positive, either. I think it was just something that I knew that had to be done, and we went about our lives. My husband owns his own business, and I'm working in a field that I love. I work as a medical assistant now. I remember when I was younger I would take a toy medical kit and pretend to listen to the heartbeats of my stuffed animals. So early on, I kind of had an idea that I liked health care. And here I am doing it, you know, three decades later. Our daughter has grown up with everything that I could've, would've, should've given her. You know, we have a house. We have a family. It's a good life. I'm happy where I am. My daughter is a teenager. She's a pretty big highlight of my life. I basically think that everything that I've ever done, ever worked for has been for her. So every moment, every day that I get to spend with her, is a highlight. Raising a teenage daughter, I'm so blessed because she's such a good kid. It's an ordinary life, but it's an extravagant, wonderful ordinary life.

I never wanted any more children after I had our daughter, but she is dating a boy who came from very little. We've basically taken him in on our own and, you know, supported him as much as we can. And so it's funny that I never wanted any more children, but here I am helping out another one. So it's so funny. I tease him, "You're the son that I never wanted." But he's a good kid.

When I did the studies every six months or so, they'd be like, "How often do you think about the pregnancy?" And I said, "Only when you call me." It wasn't something that plagued me or I thought about really much at all because I just knew that it was something that had to be done. So we just kept living.

If I hadn't had the abortion, I'd basically be starting over, because this child would be, like, in kindergarten, first grade, and we'd be doing the same thing that we've already done. I just couldn't imagine starting over and doing it all again. I would be depriving my first child by having to support a second one. And I guess being an only child myself I was really selfish, and I'm still selfish. I just want to give one person everything that I can. We'd have to buy a different house. We'd need a bigger house. Now we get to go on vacations. We're sending our daughter off to Mexico this summer. Just things that I don't think would be possible with a second child.

I'm glad that I did it. I don't think that it's a bad thing at all. I think it's definitely a woman's choice. That's what I decided along with my family, and it was the best choice for us. I had the support of my husband, but I believe that it is always a woman's choice. I don't necessarily believe in it as a form of birth control, but it is—it's still a woman's choice.

My goal right now is sending the kiddo to college—a good college. Get her in and make sure she's prepared for her own future. I want to continue to be happy. I mean, really that's what anybody wants: Everybody just wants to be happy. And as long as we have that, I think that, to me, is a bright future. Happiness and having a supportive backbone is a pretty good goal for me.

Amy, a white woman from Texas, was 28 years old and six weeks pregnant when she had an abortion.

CHAPTER 2

Why Do People
Have Abortions?

A 2012 episode of *Fault Lines*, Al Jazeera English's long-running documentary series about fractious political issues in the U.S., brings viewers into the loud and jarring world that is America's abortion debate.[1] It starts with a scene of teenagers performing a "die-in" on the Venice Beach boardwalk in Los Angeles to represent survivors of the "American abortion holocaust." But the scene that strikes me the most in this episode, called "The Abortion War," doesn't take place on the pavement with the protesters but, rather, inside the halls of the Ohio legislature.

No-nonsense correspondent Zeina Awad interviews Jim Buchy, an Ohio state representative at the time, in his office. The Republican Greenville native had recently cosponsored a bill that would have banned abortion at the first detection of cardiac activity, typically possible as early as six weeks' gestation, in the embryonic stage of pregnancy. At this point, many women are only just beginning to suspect they are pregnant, and many more, particularly those with no symptoms, have no clue.

This Ohio bill failed at the time, but it launched a wave of states trying to pass so-called heartbeat bills. In 2013, two states—Arkansas and North Dakota—successfully passed and were the first to adopt such bans. Courts eventually blocked these laws, because bans on any abortion before viability directly violate *Roe v. Wade* and subsequent Supreme Court decisions. But that was just the beginning. In 2019, more than a dozen states (including, this time, Ohio), passed heartbeat bills—not coincidentally after the U.S. Supreme Court gained two new conservative justices—each proposed in the hope that the Supreme Court would reexamine the constitutional basis of abortion rights.[2]

In the *Fault Lines* episode, Buchy at first speaks very self-assuredly about abortion policy. He believes in the "sanctity of life," and he favors laws that will "reduce or eliminate abortion." But he pauses when Awad asks him, "What do you think makes a woman want to have an abortion?"

Buchy swishes air around in his mouth. He squirms in his chair.

"Well, there's probably a lot of reas— I, I'm not a woman, so I can't—" He chuckles, his awkward attempt at a joke eliciting no reaction from the stone-faced Awad. "I'm thinking now. If I'm a woman, why would I want to get . . ." Buchy looks searchingly up toward the heavens for some kind of response. "Some of it has to do with economics," he offers. "A lot of it has to do with economics. I don't know. I've never— It's a question I've never even thought about."

It's a question he'd never even thought about.

In the decades-long battle over abortion rights, this one moment completely captures the disconnect between the politics of restricting abortion and the lived experiences of women who want one. This man who had taken such a strong stand against abortion had never actually considered the women whose lives he was affecting—it had never occurred to him to wonder why they would want a procedure he abhors.

But I almost can't blame Buchy. If he forms his opinions based on newspapers, he could read an awful lot of articles about abortion and never learn anything about what makes women want to have one. My colleague Katie Woodruff, a public health social scientist, studied this lack of attention to women when she was a doctoral student at the University of California, Berkeley.[3] She read two years' worth of articles that mentioned the word "abortion" in the *Washington Post*, *New York Times*, and Associated

Press. And you know what? There are a lot of them—on average, one a day. In the sample Dr. Woodruff reviewed, most articles merely mentioned the topic of abortion, usually as an example of a hot political issue. Only 32 out of 783 articles (4%) actually referred to a real-life woman who experienced an unwanted pregnancy. I've noticed that when one of my academic articles is featured in the news, the accompanying stock photo is often an image of a very pregnant woman's torso—a big belly with the woman's head literally cut out of the frame. Never mind that most women have abortions before their belly shows they are pregnant and that all the people who choose to have abortions actually have heads. Although I suspect the use of torso pictures is an attempt to shield stock-photo models from stigma, it aptly reflects the way that the idea of women as decision-makers is often excluded from the conversation entirely.

Clearly, one can be a well-read consumer of news and still have very little insight into the issue of abortion.

As noted earlier, between a quarter and a third of women in the U.S. will have abortions during their lives. So there's a strong chance that at least one of Buchy's friends, relatives, colleagues, or neighbors has had an abortion. Of course, chances are much slimmer that one of them will ever pull Buchy aside and explain their decision to end an unwanted pregnancy. Women who have abortions generally don't talk about them, and they generally don't talk about abortion with people who oppose it. Another doctoral student from UC Berkeley, Sarah Cowan, now a sociology professor at New York University, actually studied this.[4] She found that Americans who don't think abortion should be legal are far less likely to hear about someone's abortion than Americans who support abortion rights. So it is possible for people to spend a lot of time weighing the moral status of fetuses against a woman's bodily autonomy while never considering the woman's perspective. And let's face it: most politicians with the power to restrict abortion are male and do not relate to the experience of being a woman.

I witnessed this phenomenon in my own neighborhood. My

experience of having young kids is that being with moms of kids the same age provides a lot of camaraderie and reassurance. Just over ten years ago, I was at a gathering of mothers whose children went to the same daycare. A new mom joined the group, and I don't know what led to this comment (probably someone pointed at me and said, "That woman studies abortion"), but I heard her say across the room, "I don't know how anyone could kill their baby." Then, silence. We all heard it but nobody engaged with her comment. She was the first to leave the gathering, maybe half an hour later. As soon as the door shut behind her, the stories poured out. One woman told us about having an abortion in high school and how she felt so grateful that she had that abortion so she could go on to have two intended pregnancies as an adult. Another told the sad story of her recent 24-week abortion for a very wanted pregnancy. Her doctor had explained that her baby would likely die soon after birth due to severe genetic anomalies. At the time, she was devastated but also overwhelmed with gratitude for the doctor who ended the pregnancy, sparing her from having to stay pregnant for another four months and deliver a child who would suffer for its entire short life. Then a third woman told the group she'd been raped as an 18-year-old growing up outside the United States. In her home country, abortion is illegal except in cases of rape, so she had managed, with the confidential help of her own doctor, to get a legal, safe abortion in a hospital. Three abortion stories among maybe eight of us, and the woman who made the "baby-killing" statement that spurred the conversation never heard any of it. She left possibly thinking we all shared her perspective.

If you think nobody you know has had an abortion, more likely nobody you know has *told you* about their abortion. It is extremely unlikely that the kind of people you know are just not the kind of people who have abortions. People from all walks of life, racial and ethnic groups, political affiliations, and religions have abortions.[5]

So why *do* women choose abortion? We asked each woman in the Turnaway Study the same open-ended question: *What are some of the reasons you decided to have an abortion?* We wanted the study participants to feel free to give any reason, and as many as they wanted. We then grouped the answers by general themes, such as financial reasons, partner-related reasons, or the need to focus on existing children. For example, both Kiara and Brenda were included in the category of women who chose to abort for financial reasons. Twenty-six-year-old Kiara, who received an abortion in Kentucky, was "barely making it as a single mother with just one child, let alone two of them." Brenda, at age 24, was turned away in New York, and said she was in "no position at all to even think about raising a kid" and "could not afford diaper number one."

Table 1

**Reasons Women Seek Abortions
in the United States, 2008–2010**

	Percentage (*n*=954)
Not financially prepared	40%
Not the right time for a baby	36%
Partner-related reasons	31%
Needs to focus on other children	29%
Interferes with future opportunities	20%
Not emotionally or mentally prepared	19%
Health-related reasons	12%
Wants a better life for the baby than she could provide	12%
Not independent or mature enough for a baby	7%
Influences from family or friends	5%
Doesn't want a baby or to place baby for adoption	4%
Other	1%

Source: Biggs MA, Gould H, Foster DG. Understanding why women seek abortions in the US. *BMC Women's Health*. 2013 Jul 5;13:29.

As I noted earlier, I have dozens of academic papers' worth of data to share with you. But let's focus now on one particular paper about why women have abortions, led by my colleague Dr. Antonia Biggs, a social psychologist. When we look back at this paper, one of the first published on Turnaway Study data, we find that the reasons women give for wanting an abortion strongly predict the consequences they experience when they are denied that abortion. Table 1 shows the frequency of specific reasons for abortion.

There's Usually More Than One Reason

When she was in high school, Martina's conservative parents forbade her from holding hands with her boyfriend. So she felt she couldn't tell them when, at 22, she became pregnant with a younger man, who was already a father, and a lousy one, she thought. Martina was determined to finish college, to terminate the pregnancy, and to never let her parents find out. The idea of disappointing them tortured her and made her abortion experience desperately sad and lonely. Comfort came in the recovery room while reading stories from women before her who had chosen to terminate their pregnancies. She was surprised by the breadth of their experiences. "Everybody's situation is unique," Martina learned. "And a lot of the reasons behind getting an abortion are not what people think." She is right about the singularity of each woman's abortion situation. And at the same time, patterns emerge when we look at the data for almost a thousand women.

About two-thirds of the women we interviewed gave us more than one reason why they wanted to end their pregnancies. As it turns out, Representative Buchy is right, too. About 40% of women in our study said they wanted an abortion because they did not think they had enough money to raise a child—or another child, if they already had children. Of all the reasons given, money was the most common. Not surprisingly, many women reporting financial reasons separately reported that they already didn't have enough money to pay for basic living expenses like food, housing, and transportation. As you'll see later in this book, women are right to be concerned. When we followed these women over time, we found that those denied abortions were much more likely to end up living in poverty than the women who got their abortions. However, although 40% said they didn't have enough money, a small percentage of women (6%) gave *only* financial reasons for wanting to end a pregnancy. One 42-year-old woman said about her reasons for abortion, "[It was] all financial." But then she goes on to give a list of other reasons: "Me not having a job, living off death benefits, dealing with my fourteen-year-old son." The fact that few women give *only* financial reasons for seeking an abortion indicates to me that even generous support for women and children is not likely to result in a dramatic reduction in abortion rates.

The second most common reason women gave was that it wasn't the right time for a baby. For some, like Jessica, whose story you'll read after this chapter, it's a matter of practical circumstances. At 23, Jessica found herself pregnant just five months after giving birth to her first child. But it wasn't just the fact of already having a newborn to take care of that helped cement Jessica's decision to abort the new pregnancy. The young new mom was also experiencing a deterioration in both her health and her relationship with her husband.

"It was one of those 'pick between possibly maybe being okay while pregnant—possibly maybe—or dying,'" Jessica told us. "Knowing my husband, if something happened to me, he wouldn't take care of my kids. He doesn't take care of them now. He's in jail again. I couldn't just fathom. I had to be selfish, I guess you'd say."

For other women in our study, bad timing meant they did not feel emotionally ready for a baby, like the woman who said, "Emotionally, I couldn't take care of another baby." The design of our study enabled us to find out what happened to women when they had babies they didn't feel emotionally ready to have. We learned that women who got the abortion they wanted and then went on to have a child later reported feeling more closely bonded to their child than the women who were forced to carry the unwanted pregnancy to term. I'll share more of those results in chapter 7, which is about children.

Men—or, more specifically, bad relationships with men—represent another very common reason for ending a pregnancy, one given by almost a third of women. Many of the women seeking abortion in our study were in romantic relationships they felt were too fragile to support a child (or another child). In fact, many of these relationships were already breaking down, and some of them had turned toxic or abusive long before the positive pregnancy test. We found that within two years after seeking an abortion, more than half of the women—both those who received an abortion and those who were turned away and had a baby—had broken up with the man involved in that pregnancy.[6] More on that in chapter 8.

A majority (60%) of the women in our study were already mothers, half of whom reported that they wanted an abortion to be able to take care of the children they already had. One woman after another told Turnaway Study interviewers that they needed to care for their current children and could not imagine being able to draw on any more personal energy, let alone physical and financial resources, for a new child. A 31-year-old white woman from the Midwest told how she was seeking this abortion so she could care for her sick child. "My son was diagnosed with cancer. His treatment requires driving ten hours, and now we found out we need to go to New York for some of his treatment. He relies on me."

This mother's story is only one of many heartbreakers in the Turnaway Study. More typical stories have to do with women wanting to be good moms to their existing children. You heard from Amy from Texas, who sought an abortion because she wanted to be able to give her daughter "everything that I possibly could." Unlike Amy, who was happily married and not worrying about money, Destiny, a 30-year-old African American woman from Florida, was a single parent to a two-year-old when she discovered she was pregnant. She was working two jobs, including running her own business, while trying to complete a college degree. The man she became pregnant with was not planning to help her, so she opted to terminate the pregnancy to focus on her toddler. But she was one week too late. A family member had offered to adopt Destiny's baby but eventually rescinded the offer. So Destiny had no choice but to raise two children on her own.

Next, a large proportion of women—one in five—reported that having a new baby would derail life plans and career goals. I'll discuss how receiving or being denied an abortion affects a woman's life course in chapter 6. The short answer is that being denied a wanted abortion curtails women's aspirational plans over the next year, and it affects their chances of having a wanted pregnancy later.[7] While the impact of abortion denial on educational attainment remains uncertain, the effect on income and employment is clear. Women who were able to receive an abortion were more likely to stay employed and live above the federal poverty level.[8]

For years, and in the absence of conclusive data, politicians and anti-abortion activists have posited that abortion likely causes depression or some form of mental health harm. So it is interesting that for almost 20% of women, concern about their emotional stability and mental health is what made them choose to have an abortion in the first place. "I have a lot of problems, serious problems," said a nineteen-year-old Latina from New Jersey, who already had one child as well as a history of depression and physical abuse. She decided her best option was to terminate her pregnancy. "I'm not prepared for another baby," she said. We found no mental health harm from receiving an abortion, but we did find short-term increases in symptoms of anxiety and lower self-esteem among women who were denied an abortion.

Women also sometimes elect to end an unwanted pregnancy because they have concerns about their own health. As discussed, the study excluded women whose pregnancies posed imminent health risks to their own life. Still, for about one in eight women in the Turnaway Study, a health concern, even if it wasn't a life-threatening crisis, was a reason for choosing abortion. The first-person account you'll read next is from Jessica, whose health problems were greatly exacerbated by pregnancy. Another woman who completed an in-depth interview, Margot, a white woman from Washington State, told us that her longstanding kidney problems motivated her to have an abortion when she found herself single and unexpectedly pregnant in 2009. She was at the time dating a man who was unstable and verbally abusive. She considered leaving him and having this second child on her own, but it was her health situation that was really the deciding factor. "My kidneys started failing when I was fifteen years old," Margot explained. "I would get severe kidney infections and kidney stones and stuff. And when my son was born I had complications with him. I had been on bed rest for over six months of the pregnancy. And then I had to have specialists there when he was born because they didn't think I would make it through the delivery."

Few women, about 5%, reported wanting an abortion because of concerns about the health of their fetus. But the Turnaway Study is not a good source of information about abortion for reasons of fetal anomaly since as we've discussed, we specifically excluded women from the study if they were terminating wanted pregnancies as a result of fetal diagnoses.

Alcohol, Tobacco, and Drugs as a Reason for Abortion

One in twenty women in our study (5%) reported choosing abortion in part because of alcohol, tobacco, or drug use at the beginning of their pregnancies. (They're included among those reporting health-related reasons in Table 1 on p. 35.) Many women, like Brenda, whom you will meet later, drink alcohol before they realize they are pregnant, especially when they are not trying to conceive. We wanted to find out whether women are seeking to terminate otherwise wanted pregnancies out of fear that their substance use had harmed their fetus. Dr. Sarah Roberts, a public health researcher and expert on alcohol and drug use during pregnancy, joined the Turnaway team to find out whether public health and medical recommendations to abstain from drugs and alcohol were causing women to abort wanted pregnancies for fear of having damaged their fetus, or for fear of prosecution for exposing an in utero child to drugs.

In the past twenty years, hundreds of pregnant women across the U.S. have ended up behind bars because either they or their newborns tested positive for controlled substances.[9] This trend has picked up in the last two decades with the rise of both the opioid crisis and the "personhood" movement. Anti-abortion politicians and activists have tried to establish a legal standing for embryos and fetuses in myriad legal contexts—including adding "personhood amendments" to state constitutions—as a way to create a legal precedent for personhood in order to eventually abolish abortion.[10] Voters have overwhelmingly rejected these personhood amendments at the ballot box, in part because of the organizing of reproductive-justice advocates and the impact these laws would have on certain types of birth control and fertility treatments like in vitro fertilization.[11]

Dr. Roberts learned that most women who reported using alcohol, tobacco, and drugs were using substances at a level where there was some cause for concern about fetal development. Of those who cited alcohol or drug use as a reason, half reported binge drinking or symptoms of problematic levels of alcohol use. Two-thirds smoked cigarettes. Half used drugs (20% marijuana only and 30% other drugs). While there are definitely harms that could result from the level of substance use reported by women in the study, it is a personal call whether the risk of these harms or the severity of these harms would warrant terminating a wanted pregnancy. However, there is no evidence from the Turnaway Study that threats of prosecution for substance use during pregnancy or recommendations to abstain from all substances during pregnancy are leading women to terminate otherwise wanted pregnancies. Nearly all (98%) pregnancies where the woman reported alcohol or drug use as a reason for abortion were undesired pregnancies at the time of conception. In other words, women who report substance use as a reason for abortion have legitimate cause for concern that their level of substance use could cause poor outcomes if they carried the pregnancy to term, but they are not seeking abortions for that reason alone.

Pressure to Have an Abortion

Let's turn to one of the least common but potentially most concerning reasons to have an abortion. The idea that women are pressured into having an abortion—that they don't know what they are doing or that someone is coercing them into it—looms large in the public imagination and has been used to justify a range of parental consent laws, state-mandated counseling information, and required waiting periods for abortion.[12] The Turnaway Study finds that coercion is uncommon among women seeking abortion. Five percent report that family or friends played a part in their decision. This can mean that they felt that having a baby would negatively affect their family or that they are seeking an abortion in order to keep family or friends from finding out about the pregnancy. A small number of women (1%) reported actual pressure from family or friends to have an abortion. Some of these women may feel like they were coerced into the decision, against their own will. For others, reporting that the decision was someone else's may be an attempt to share the responsibility for having made the decision to end a pregnancy. As one 17-year-old black woman from Ohio told us when asked why she was seeking an abortion, "My mother convinced me to get one." All the abortion facilities where we recruited women for the study have policies and procedures in place to screen women to make sure they are making the decision of their own free will. This means that the facilities where we recruited may have declined to provide abortions for some women who reported being pressured or coerced into the decision before they got an opportunity to sign up for our study. This low percentage of women reporting that the decision was primarily someone else's is consistent with national figures, indicating that the practice of screening women who may not be making the decision of their own free will is widespread, or that the incidence of women being coerced into seeking abortion is low to begin with.[13]

Why would someone wait until the second trimester?

Second-trimester abortions, as we've learned, are rare, but they are among the most stigmatized of abortions. Perhaps as a result, the type of abortion restrictions that garner the greatest public support are gestational limits. If *Roe* is overturned, a national gestational age limit prior to viability could be passed by Congress. Part of the reason for a lack of support for abortions at later gestational ages has to do with fetal development—many people feel that as a fetus grows, so too grows its claim to personhood.

Though much hatred and stigma are aimed at people who seek out abortions after the first trimester (and at the doctors who perform them), very little was known about why some people have abortions after the first trimester. Thanks to the Turnaway Study, we now have a much clearer understanding.

Our study design relies on comparing women who fall just below and just above clinic gestational limits, most of which are in the second trimester. (As I noted in the last chapter, our study also included a sample of first-trimester patients.) Having such a large sample of women seeking second-trimester abortions for unwanted pregnancies enabled us to answer questions that hadn't been answered before. For starters, why would anyone wait so long to get an abortion?

Spoiler alert: they're not waiting. The question above makes an assumption that turns out to be wrong. Some women just don't learn early on that they are pregnant. In rare cases, women find out they are pregnant when they are about to give birth. There was even a documentary television series created about the phenomenon. *I Didn't Know I Was Pregnant* premiered in 2008 and ran for five seasons; each episode featured one or more women who did not realize they were pregnant until they were about to deliver.[14] Although there has been much more voyeuristic media attention than medical attention paid to the topic, it is clear that pregnancy symptoms do not manifest the same way in all women.

The idea that everyone spends the first trimester throwing up from "morning sickness" is clearly not true. Women who don't react strongly to the hormonal changes of pregnancy might not be tired or nauseated. While a lack of nausea and fatigue might be a blessing for a woman with a wanted pregnancy, for others it can be the cause of late recognition of pregnancy, especially for women who already have irregular periods or spotting because they are young, are obese, are using hormonal contraceptives, or have recently given birth.

Two of the women profiled here, Camila and Sofia, each assumed that the regularly appearing blood in their underwear was menstrual blood. It's not uncommon to "spot" during early pregnancy, and for women who don't expect to be pregnant, spotting can seem like a light period. Other women never have regular periods, like Brenda, whom you'll meet later. Michelle, an eighteen-year-old Latina from California, didn't recognize the symptoms of pregnancy for many months, until it was too late for an abortion. She told us, "I never have had periods regularly ever. When I had morning sickness, my boyfriend at the time had the flu. I wasn't aware of the body changes that I was going through. They weren't familiar to me, so I couldn't really tell what was going on until finally I realized that pregnancy must be the only answer."

Other women in our study did not notice any physical symptoms and also didn't discover they were pregnant until it was too late for an abortion. That happened to Penny, a twenty-six-year-old white woman from New Jersey. She had been very aware when she was pregnant with her two previous children—she was regularly nauseated; she could see her body's physical changes. But with her third pregnancy, Penny wasn't gaining weight, she was still getting her period every month, she never felt the urge to vomit, and she never noticed any fetal movement. Her ob-gyn castigated her when she finally sought care. She still remembers his harsh words: "Don't be surprised if the baby has something wrong with him." The doctor was upset with Penny for continuing to smoke cigarettes and take over-the-counter medication and for not receiving prenatal care earlier. But really, Penny had *no idea*. Her doctor later apologized to her when he performed the ultrasound and discovered how far back her uterus was, and that the fetus was quite small.

Failing to recognize pregnancy because you're not experiencing symptoms is not the same as denying said symptoms. Of course, some women do report being in denial—often young people, like 19-year-old Jada from Illinois, whom you will meet later. "I was in love," Jada says, talking about her high school boyfriend. "I really didn't even think about the fact that I would get pregnant. . . . For so long my friends were asking me was I pregnant, because I guess they saw the changes in me, but I didn't see it." Jada fully admits now that she didn't *want* to see those changes. "I was almost—I was, like, twenty weeks, and I didn't even know because I was in so much denial."

Some women who are in denial about their pregnancies will have a miscarriage. (10–20% of pregnancies end in spontaneous miscarriage.)[15] But when the pregnancy does not end on its own, being in denial can greatly increase the difficulty of getting an abortion.

Taking Time to Decide

In the Turnaway Study, the vast majority of women having early abortions as well as women having later abortions (at or after 20 weeks)—80% of first-trimester patients and 94% of later abortion patients—reported that something slowed them down from getting an abortion earlier in pregnancy.[16] One of my colleagues, the public health scientist Dr. Ushma Upadhyay, examined pathways to getting an abortion and found that early and later abortion patients were equally likely to say that not recognizing pregnancy slowed them down (43%) but, as I discussed earlier, women seeking later abortions were much farther along when they discovered their pregnancy than women seeking first-trimester abortions—12 weeks, on average, compared with just five weeks. People assume that women who have later abortions were just sitting around trying to make up their mind. It is true that a third (37%) of women report that taking time to decide whether to have an abortion slowed them down, but we're talking about a number of days, not even a week, on average. We found no significant difference between women seeking first-trimester versus later abortions in how long it took to decide. See Figure 1.

Figure 1

Time from Last Menstrual Period to Getting an Abortion

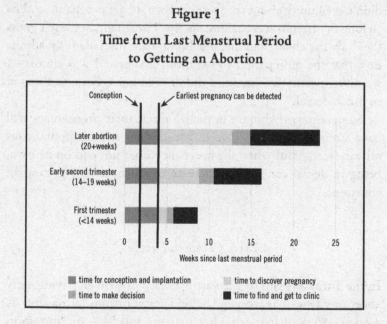

For some women the decision to have an abortion is straightforward—30% of the women in our study said it was somewhat or very easy to decide to have an abortion, and 14% said the decision was neither easy nor difficult.[17] For just over half of women, it is a difficult decision—29% reported it was somewhat difficult, and 27% reported that it was very difficult. Deciding to have an abortion can be difficult, but it is certainly not always difficult. And let's take a moment to note that a decision that is easy to make isn't necessarily a thoughtless decision. It may simply be abundantly clear to the woman what the right choice is given her circumstances.

Once women have made the decision, there is no need to make them wait before they can have the procedure. Based on women's own reports about the soundness of their decision-making, which you'll read about in chapter 4, the Turnaway Study shows that women don't need the government to tell them how long to think about whether or not to terminate a pregnancy. Mandatory waiting periods are one of those laws that sound good (everyone should get time to think about such a critical decision) but have unintended consequences in raising the cost and causing abortions to happen later in pregnancy than women want them.

Why are women becoming pregnant if they don't want to have a baby?

With all these compelling reasons not to carry an unwanted pregnancy to term, one has to wonder why these women became pregnant in the first place. I've made the case that women have good judgment and make thoughtful decisions about their pregnancies, based on the Turnaway Study findings. But you may be wondering why you should trust their judgment on whether to end a pregnancy, when one could argue they seem to have shown a lapse in judgment by unintentionally starting one.

Where to begin? First, contraception and abortion are often viewed as women's issues and seen as women's problems. But the reality, of course, is that women cannot conceive on their own. Still, in American society we tend to think of accidental pregnancy and its consequences as a woman's fault and ultimately her burden.

In September 2018, Mormon mother of six Gabrielle Blair took to Twitter, fed up after a lifetime of "listening to men grandstand about women's reproductive rights."[18] In Blair's view, men do not merely *share* the responsibility of unwanted pregnancies; they deserve the bulk of the blame. Blair argues that many men refuse to use condoms consistently (because condoms dull sensations) even though condoms are inexpensive, available everywhere, and work instantaneously—in direct contrast to women's contraceptive options.

"Unwanted pregnancies can only happen when men orgasm irresponsibly," writes Blair, in a thread that has been retweeted more than 100,000 times. "Many men keep going as is, causing unwanted pregnancies with irresponsible ejaculations and never giving it thought. When the topic of abortion comes up, men might think: Abortion is horrible; women should not have abortions. And never once consider the man who CAUSED the unwanted pregnancy. If you're not holding men responsible for unwanted pregnancies, then you are wasting your time. Stop protesting at clinics. Stop shaming women. Stop trying to overturn abortion laws. If you actually care about reducing or eliminating the number of abortions in our country, simply HOLD MEN RESPONSIBLE FOR THEIR ACTIONS."

I appreciate Blair's attempt to redirect the burden of blame, stigma, and punishment that traditionally redounds entirely on women. But with the exception of cases of rape, contraceptive sabotage, and sexual coercion, women do have some agency in decision-making around sex and contraception. I am not saying that the solution is to share blame equally. Instead, we need less blame all around, more sex education, and much better contraceptive options.

Consistently using contraception from one's first time having sex to menopause—taking a break just to conceive and gestate a couple of intended pregnancies—is a major endeavor. Contraception is expensive, and it requires a lot of diligence, forethought, and, in many cases, tolerance of side effects. Exactly what sort of commitment does it require to prevent pregnancy for a heterosexual woman who begins having sex at eighteen, starts menopause around age forty-five, and wants to—when she's ready—have two kids? She would have to take 6,844 contraceptive pills, use condoms every time for perhaps two thousand acts of intercourse, replace her 975 patches or 325 vaginal rings in a timely fashion, or have four to six intrauterine devices (IUDs) inserted and removed. Table 2 shows my estimates of the sheer quantity of contraceptives required and the number of unintended pregnancies expected, despite contraceptive use, for a woman who is sexually active her whole adult life and uses one method throughout. Of course, most women use more than one method over a lifetime, so she will also have to make regular medical appointments to arrange for the appropriate prescriptions or procedures, and regular trips to the pharmacy to keep up her supplies. All of this assumes she has uninterrupted access to health insurance and can afford the copayments. Most unintended pregnancies in the United States are caused not by contraceptive failure, but by gaps in contraceptive use.[19] Even for the woman who uses contraceptives consistently, there would still be significant chances of becoming pregnant. Over a reproductive lifetime, she might still become pregnant as many as two times on the pill, four times with condoms, and seven using withdrawal.

Let's talk about a concern frequently raised by many who are supportive of abortion rights but worry that such a right will be overused—that women might be using abortion as their primary method of family planning. Well, if a woman wanted to use abortion as a regular method of family planning from first sex to menopause, she would need to have about 30 first-trimester abortions or 25 second-trimester abortions over her lifetime. That is what using abortion as a method of birth control would entail. If you are talking about someone who has had fewer than ten abortions, consider them an unlucky or perhaps an inconsistent contraceptive user, not a user of abortion as their sole method of family planning.

Table 2

Family Planning Methods Needed from First Intercourse to the End of Menopause to Have Only Two Children Over One's Lifetime

	Estimated number needed	Unwanted pregnancies expected (despite use of the method)
Contraception as a method of family planning		
Condoms	Over 2,000 condoms	0.5–3.8
Copper IUD	4 IUDs	0.2
Hormonal IUD	6 IUDs	0.1
Implant	9 implants	0.0
Oral contraceptives	6,844 pills	0.1–2.0
Contraceptive patch	975 patches	0.2–2.5
Contraceptive ring	325 rings	0.1–2.0
Injectable contraceptives	100 shots	0.1–0.8
Withdrawal	Over 2,000 times	1.0–6.8
Abortion as a method of family planning		
Early medication abortions	30 abortions	30
Second-trimester abortions	25 abortions	25

Source: These estimates are based on published contraceptive failure rates and frequency of intercourse data by age.[20]

Note: Estimates assume a woman is sexually active throughout her reproductive years and uses just one method of family planning over that time period.

In real life, most women in the United States do use contraception, usually a variety of different methods over several decades. Many women who have sex with men start with condoms, get on the pill during their first steady relationship, try lots of methods but never like any of them entirely, sometimes go without using a method, have a pregnancy scare that turns out to be or not to be a pregnancy, maybe have an abortion or a miscarriage or two, have a kid or two or three, and finally, maybe, get a tubal ligation. That's how it often goes, but the range of experiences is vast. For me, it was condoms, pills, a pregnancy scare that was only a scare, more pills, diaphragm for a bit, an IUD, a heartbreaking miscarriage, my first child, an IUD, my second child, and then more IUDs while I wait for menopause. The women profiled in this book have experienced miscarriages, other abortions, births following intended and unintended pregnancies, problems getting a supply of pills, and difficulty finding a method that didn't exacerbate health conditions. Then there is Melissa, whom you will meet between chapters 6 and 7, who tried to get a tubal ligation after giving birth to each of her second through fifth kids. The excuse for why it was not done was that the hospital had lost the paperwork, or that she hadn't given her approval in time. But the truth, which even Melissa doesn't realize, is that she was giving birth at Catholic hospitals where sterilization is not provided because it conflicts with the hospital's religious doctrine. The only way to get a tubal ligation is to go to a non-Catholic hospital. Which she eventually does, but not before having three more births and an abortion.

Reasons for Unprotected Intercourse

Most women in our study (64%) were using a contraceptive method in the month they conceived—37% barrier methods like condoms and diaphragms and 27% hormonal methods like the pill, patch, or ring.[21] For just over a third (36%), the pregnancies occurred because the woman and her partner were not using any method of contraception. What might surprise you is that many of the women who used contraception inconsistently or not at all just didn't think they would get pregnant. In their defense, it's actually not easy to become pregnant from a single act of intercourse. The likelihood of conception per each act is about 3% if a woman doesn't know where she is in her menstrual cycle.[22] If the sexual act falls within the six-day period leading up to ovulation, the likelihood is about 10% and then 0% for the rest of the month. Most people are not having sex as a sort of Russian roulette, for the thrill of the small chance that the fallopian tube will be loaded with an egg. In the best of circumstances, people have consensual sex to emotionally bond with each other and/or to experience pleasure, and many don't use protection, figuring—usually rightly—that the odds of a pregnancy are small. You may be familiar with this logic if you have ever crossed the street against the light, opted not to put on a seat belt when moving your car a short distance, or followed the "five-second rule" for a cookie that fell on the floor. The problem is not with the risk calculation for any one act of sex. If you have ever had heterosexual intercourse when you weren't trying for a baby and you/your female partner didn't become pregnant, then you are one of the lucky ones; the unlucky ones show up at the abortion clinic.

Reproductive health researchers and practitioners often assume that people take risks around pregnancy only when they lack access to or knowledge about contraception. And yes, these reasons do explain why some people engage in unprotected intercourse. Some people lack accurate information about reproductive physiology, the unlikelihood of infertility, and the true risk of conception. Yet there are also a number of benefits of unprotected intercourse, including relationship and sexual benefits. To many couples, the emotional and sexual benefits of engaging in unprotected sex may be more salient than the goal of using contraception every single time.

Compounding a natural inclination to take risks, a large proportion of women have trouble accessing contraceptives. A separate study I did found that two in five women seeking abortions report some problem accessing contraceptives, including one in five who reported that they ran out of contraceptive supplies before becoming pregnant.[23] That's why at clinical and policy levels, we need to figure out how to make contraceptive methods as easy to procure and use as possible, for everyone. This means streamlining access to short-term methods of contraception by, for instance, making oral contraceptive pills available without a prescription, right next to condoms at drug stores. Long-acting, reversible methods of contraception may address some of the problems couples have in assessing risk and negotiating contraceptive use. Women need a wide array of contraceptive choices, methods that are simple to use and obtain, and importantly, methods that do not undermine sensual experience and partner connection.

Everything I learned conducting previous research on unprotected intercourse highlighted for me just how counterproductive it is to make contraceptives and accurate information about contraceptives difficult to access. We've seen this happen more and more with conservative politicians' and interest groups' successful efforts to weaken a health care regulation made by President Barack Obama that mandated that employers offer no-copay insurance coverage of a wide range of contraceptive methods. We've also seen it with the Trump White House trying to defund many of the family planning clinics that provide contraceptive services to low-income women because they separately provide abortions, and to defund international family planning programs if they provide referrals to women who are seeking abortions. To prevent unintended pregnancies, contraceptives need to be available. And new methods need to be developed that meet women's needs.

Currently available methods of contraception do not meet everyone's needs.[24] I have done a lot of research on what women want in a contraceptive method. Let me tell you, women aren't getting what they want. They want a method that is highly effective but that has few side effects. They want a method that is easy to get and easy to use. Many want control over when and whether to use the method. My previous studies have found that existing methods of contraception have less than two-thirds of the features that women report are very important to them.[25]

In general, women of color have somewhat different preferences than white women, for example preferring to have control over use of the method, privacy, and no changes to menstruation. In a separate study I did with UCSF professor Dr. Andrea Jackson, women of color consider more features of contraceptives extremely important than white women do, like wanting control over stopping and starting use of the method or being able to get it without visiting a health care provider.[26] These differences may be the product of a historically justifiable suspicion of health care institutions and providers, as well as of new methods of contraception. The United States has a long history of denying women of color their full humanity and control over reproduction—everything from forced childbearing in the time of slavery to forced sterilization in recent decades.[27] As a result of their different profile of contraceptive preferences, women of color are even less likely to find methods that have their desired features. Some lucky women find methods that meet their needs. But for many, preventing unintended pregnancy involves putting up with a host of side effects, regularly going to clinics or pharmacies, and sometimes paying a lot of money out of pocket just to keep using a method they don't like in the hopes of lowering an uncertain future risk of pregnancy.

The next story is Jessica's, and there isn't a clearer example of a woman needing better methods of contraception. Jessica has medical conditions that aren't compatible with all methods of contraception, and she experiences negative side effects from the methods she is allowed to take. The result of no good options around contraception? "I got pregnant."

JESSICA

God puts everybody here for a reason.
There was a reason for abortion, and it was
for people in situations like I was.

I grew up in a really, really small town in Louisiana. Everybody knows everybody and knows more about you than you know about you. In my high school I graduated with one hundred people. I played sports up until high school. Then I got boy crazy, I guess you'd say. All I ever did was go to ball games with some sport buddies. My mom died when I was a teenager. I left home and kind of raised myself the rest of the way. I was staying with a girl that I babysat for. I babysat her kids, and she let me live there up until I graduated.

I graduated high school, and then I went to college. It was a local community college. I came home from college for a holiday, and I had a severe car wreck and broke my neck. When I had my wreck, I was not able to do anything. A bone in my neck was broken. It was serious. So I had to drop out of college, and then that's when I met John and had my son, Ethan. Right away John became extremely jealous, jealous of anybody that I talked to on the phone, at the grocery store. There was a woman that I had lived with when I was home. He made me delete her number and refused to let me talk to her. He would leave at night and take the car, take the cell phone, and leave me at home with the baby. I wasn't allowed to talk to anybody. It ended up being that he was cheating on me at the time. He was trying to save his butt.

John had some savings bonds. So we cashed his savings bonds in and bought a trailer for four hundred dollars. We lived in a mobile home park. He paid all of the bills, usually, except for the power bill, which my grandparents paid.

When I got pregnant with our first child, I did leave my hometown, but when I left, I was still just ten minutes down the road. I wasn't, like, way far away. I had Ethan before I was 20. That was the end of my childhood after that. My kids' father is the first guy that I fell in love with out of high school. I thought he did no wrong and that no matter what he did, he was forever in love with me. Then I realized that wasn't completely true. It was an abusive relationship, both mentally and physically. John was in and out of jail from the time our first child was born. Instead of "we were married," I would say I raised my husband. I raised him.

When I was pregnant with my first child I had three episodes where I had what I thought was a seizure during the night.

I had seen a person having a seizure on TV. I didn't really know if that's what was happening. John was never at home at night. He went whoring and being drunk all the time. They did EKGs and all kinds of stuff, and they couldn't find anything. The only way they could prove something was for me to have an episode while I was hooked up to the monitors, or to record it myself. I could feel it coming. But it was done and over with within three minutes. So they never got it. After I had Ethan, I had, like, five more seizures. Now, because I wasn't pregnant anymore, I thought, well, maybe it's sugar problems or something that's just not showing up.

When I got pregnant with Madison, I knew I was pregnant. I started feeling bad, and I told John. I said, "I'm pregnant." He was like, "No way." I took, like, five tests. I even bought the expensive one. It still wasn't showing up that I was pregnant. I went to the health department and did a pee test. I still wasn't pregnant. They drew my blood and I was pregnant. I knew I was. My body was just completely shutting down on me. They thought I had fibromyalgia. I couldn't brush my hair. I couldn't do anything. I was ridiculously sick. But then I'm pregnant, so we're thinking she's just literally taking all I've got. I didn't eat. My grandmother would cook me all my favorite food, and I couldn't eat it. It would make me throw up. So they're thinking it's pregnancy. That's all that's wrong with you. My seizures got worse and worse and worse. Two days after Madison came home, I got ill. They threw me in the hospital for three weeks, running all kinds of tests and eventually diagnosing me with multiple sclerosis and severe hyperemesis. I was an hour away in the hospital, but John came and saw me twice. One of his older relatives kept my kids while I was there, and he went and saw them twice. I look back, and I tell these stories, and I think about this stuff, and I am such a dumbass for keeping him around as long as I did. But I wanted it to work so bad.

When I came home, they wanted to put me on this medication. I was having to take seizure medicine, and birth control could interfere with my seizure medicine. I tried the shot, and it made me—I cried the whole time. I hated how I felt. I was miserable. So I was praying for the health department and my doctors to come up with something birth-control-wise. I had to keep taking my medicine, and I didn't want to die. And I got pregnant. Again, I knew I was pregnant. They did the whole rigmarole with tests and stuff. I went to the health department, drew my blood. Sure enough, I was pregnant.

It was one of those "pick between possibly maybe being okay while pregnant—possibly maybe—or dying." Knowing my husband, if something happened to me, he wouldn't take care of my kids. He doesn't take care of them now. He's in jail again. I just couldn't fathom. I had to be selfish, I guess you'd say.

When I found out I was pregnant, I was scared to death. Because they had told me that they would not tie my tubes because of my age, because of Medicaid laws and everything, but that if I got pregnant again, it would not be in my best interests. I had to take six months of chemo after my last baby to get my body back to where it was supposed to be. I still had one more chemo treatment to go when I got pregnant. I already knew the situation. John was never going to change. I mean, when I was in the hospital for those three weeks, he came and saw me twice. He took the cell phone.

I knew if it was not for my health, I could do it. I'd done it before, raised them by myself without him. But the chances of me getting sick like I was again or not even making it. In my whole life I've been totally anti-abortion. I mean, completely, like, it was wrong, no matter what. But then when that happened, it kind of was like: I had to figure out something because I've got to sacrifice something. Is it going to be me and leave Ethan and Madison stranded, or maybe make it with a baby and now have three kids and be by myself?

Multiple sclerosis is incurable. I knew that. I could have a flare-up tomorrow and not be able to get out of bed. What am I going to do? I started doing some deep soul-searching, and it was my ending thought: God puts everybody here for a reason. There was a reason for abortion, and it was for people in situations like I was. The bad part of it was for people that just got pregnant and thought, "Well, okay. I'll have an abortion so I don't have to deal with it." I had to put my strong faith from my childhood behind me and make a decision for me, not based on anybody else but for me and my kids. If God didn't want it to happen, he wouldn't have let them figure out how to do it.

My ob-gyn, I knew him personally. I am from a small town. I knew him personally, and then he was also my doctor. He did not recommend it to me. But he gave me a pamphlet for a doctor for a second opinion. So he gave me a pamphlet, and he said for me not to tell anybody that he gave it to me. But he just thought that I might like to read it. Again, he's known me since I've been a baby. It was a pamphlet for the place that I went. That's what it was.

I had to have money to be able to pay for it. My husband didn't work. One of my third cousins, her husband is a dentist. Me and her have never been close. I had just gotten the pamphlet and she called me. I knew she had the money. It would not hurt for her to miss it. So that was kind of my sign. She said she had just been thinking about me and called to check on me. I ended up going over to her house and I cried. She said if I decided that that's what I needed to do, then she didn't have any problems with it, and she wasn't going to judge me.

The first time I went to the abortion clinic, they were protesting outside—screaming and hollering at people. The next time I went, they were doing the same thing. So my nerves were beyond it. The first time, I had to go by myself. John had other things to do than to go with me. The second time he had to come for the procedure. I couldn't drive. He was not really happy about it; it was all about him. So if it was not convenient for him, he didn't care.

As for them at the clinic, they were very sweet—but it was not a good experience. As far as them not making me feel any worse, they were great about it. But everything was hard. I mean just everything, the sound effects, and the result. I kept thinking, I'm not listening to this on TV. This is happening to me. This is what I have to deal with right now.

My main goal after the abortion was to get up the courage to realize that my marriage was never going to work and make him leave, somehow to get out of that relationship. I'm thinking the good Lord has a good sense of humor. John ended up not paying his bonds, and he went to prison for six months. So while he was in prison, I filed for divorce through an agency that actually law school students put on. It's for domestic violence, people in domestic violence. And that's how I got out of that relationship and got a divorce. Now, it took him two years to sign the divorce papers, but I got out.

I worried when we were in divorce court or when we got in fights, that the abortion I had would be the first thing that he would blast on Facebook and tag the whole world on about it, just to get back at me. My family knows. My husband knows. My best friend knows. That's it.

I still feel really bad when John is in jail. I really did love that man. I put everything I had into it. I threw away every bit of my friends for him when I got with him. But for some reason, still, it bothers me when he's in jail. We've been divorced for a few years now. In those years he's supposed to pay $333 a month child support for our kids. In all that time, he's paid $300 total. My son cries for him still. He thinks he hung the moon. I don't want to tell him that his daddy is a piece of shit. I want my kids to figure it out for themselves because I don't want it to come back on me.

My now-husband is from a little town down the road. I've known Robert for a really long time, but it was never anything. I just knew who he was, and he knew who I was. I always would embarrass him because I would catch him looking at me, and I would tell him to quit staring at my butt. I know that's not funny, but it's funny now. Then he had a little boy. Robert had posted pictures on Facebook, I hadn't seen Robert in a long time, and I sent a message telling him that his child was cute.

So one thing led to another, and we talked for, like, a week. Robert would always hint around about going out somewhere, like, taking me out, but he would never actually ask me.

So I asked him to take me out. We went on a date, and that weekend he came over and he never left. Before we got married, I moved in. His family had left him a house, which is where we still live now. I moved in with him and put my son in school here. Robert's a construction worker. He's only home on the weekends. For the most part, I'm a single mom during the week. I've not had any big flare-ups. I have to fight through it still because I still have two kids and a house to run. The bills still have to go and get paid.

I've been through so much. There is always somebody out there that may not have been through as much as I have, but their kids could be sick or they could not ever get out of bed or something. Something is always worse, so be thankful for what you've got. I've gone this far. I'm not giving up now.

My husband only has the son biologically. I know he wants a baby, but he's very supportive. He doesn't say anything about it. He said, "I'd rather have you, because what would I do without you?" That's how he is. I've even talked to my doctor about it so that maybe one day. But it's just one of those things. You want to go to Hawaii one day. No one can tell you that you can't go to Hawaii. You can still go. Somehow or another, you can still figure it out. Or you want to build a house one day. You may not be able to do it right now, but somehow or another, one day you can. But I can't give him a baby.

Well, this house that my husband's family gave us is just a two-bedroom. We have two kids and then three kids on the weekends every other weekend. My son is nine. My daughter is six, and they're at that age where they don't like each other. So that's our next—that's what we're working on is to get us a house, a bigger house. So, my family has some land. We picked the best spot, and that's what we're going to start saving up for. We got me a car. This time next year I'll have it paid off, and then we're going to start saving for our house. That's on the books right now. I just have to be patient. It'll come when it comes.

Oh, it changed my perspective on abortion. Again, God made them. There's a reason that God let them figure that out for a purpose. There are just people that abuse it like there are people that abuse everything. There is a good purpose usually in everything, some way or another. I don't talk to anybody about it. It still is referred to as the A-word if it's spoken about at all. You've got to make sacrifices sometimes no matter how bad it hurts. Sometimes that's just life. What I did, did possibly save me and let me be here to raise my kids and to marry Robert and to take care of my grandmother when nobody else would, and take care of my pop like I do now.

The only complete meltdown I've had about it was when my kids went to, like, a festival with their aunt and uncle for, like, face-painting. There was carnival rides and stuff. They came home with balloons, and they were anti-abortion balloons. I talked to them when they came in the door and I seen what they said. My kids cried, and my oldest one told me he hated me. I couldn't tell him why, and he didn't understand. Mama just popped my balloon, that's all he knew. My friend lives across the road, and I told her I wasn't feeling good. Could the kids come play? When they went to her house, I just cried.

It was just a sacrifice I had to do. If that wouldn't have happened, I might not be here today. Or my kids might be in foster care. I try to think of the positives. There was a reason. Everything happens for a reason. You might not understand that reason, but one day you will.

Jessica, a white woman from Louisiana, was 23 years old and eight weeks pregnant when she had an abortion.

CHAPTER 3

Access to Abortion
in the United States

J essica, whose story you just read, made up her mind quickly.
She wanted an abortion—for the good of her kids and herself—
and she wanted it soon. Jessica was one of the luckier women in
our study in that she discovered her pregnancy as early as it is
possible to—one month after her last menstrual period. But even
though the 23-year-old mother of two wanted to stop being pregnant immediately, it took an entire month before Jessica was finally
sitting in an abortion clinic, waiting for a nurse to call her name.

Access to abortion depends on when you discover you are pregnant, how much money you have, and, critically, where you live. To
see what I mean, let's imagine how Jessica's story might have gone
differently had she lived in, say, California instead of Louisiana.

For starters, in California her ob-gyn would probably have been
able to discuss the option of abortion openly with Jessica. He might
have helped her weigh the health implications of both abortion and
birth. Then he could have given her an informed referral—telling
her what clinic he recommended and why, rather than surrepti-
tiously slipping her a pamphlet and asking her not to tell anyone
where she got it. Let's take a moment to note, Jessica's Louisiana
doctor did have those pamphlets in his office. She is likely not the
first patient to ever need such a referral. Seeing patients who experience an unwanted pregnancy is a routine part of being a gynecolo-
gist.[1] Jessica's doctor did offer a pamphlet, but it is unfortunate that

he did not feel comfortable making a direct referral, as he would for any other medical care he does not provide, for fear that providing such a referral would tarnish his reputation.

In Louisiana, Jessica had to drive more than 60 miles, over an hour each way, to get to the clinic. In California, the average distance to an abortion facility is seven miles.[2] Jessica had to make *two* trips, the first visit to listen to information mandated by the state designed to discourage her from having an abortion. Then she had to wait at least 24 hours before returning to get the abortion itself—a rule required by law in Louisiana (and several other states) that serves no medical purpose but delays the procedure.[3] Mandatory waiting periods are supposedly intended to ensure that women are completely confident in their decision before having an abortion. However, the backers of such laws likely realize that the result is to make getting the procedure more difficult and expensive. In California, where the law treats abortion like other medical care, Jessica would not have had that two-trip-plus-mandated-waiting-period delay.

At the time she found out she was pregnant, Jessica was supporting a family of four—which included an out-of-work husband, a toddler, and an infant—on $11,000 a year. She had no health insurance. And here is the biggest difference between Louisiana and California when it comes to abortion: California covers the cost of abortion for poor women, just as it covers other pregnancy-related health care. California's Medicaid health care program, Medi-Cal, would have paid for Jessica's abortion (provided the practice she chose accepted Medi-Cal). Louisiana's state Medicaid program does not cover abortions unless the woman is dying or she can prove she became pregnant from rape or incest. So Jessica spent that extra month between deciding to have and receiving an abortion trying to raise the roughly $500 for a first-trimester abortion. In that time, she had to disclose her unwanted pregnancy to someone she wasn't close to in order to ask for money. In the end, an abortion hotline fund paid for part of her procedure, and her distant cousin paid the remaining $160. So in California, not only would Medi-Cal coverage have helped Jessica terminate at an earlier point in pregnancy, it would have preserved her medical and personal privacy.

Jessica's issues with access were, frankly, a best-case scenario, considering she's from a state with few abortion providers and many abortion restrictions. For all the handwringing about women using abortion like birth control, abortion is very difficult to access in most states. Restrictions on abortion, supposedly intended to make abortion safer or reduce the chance of abortion regret, instead put abortion out of reach for some and vastly disproportionately affect the already disadvantaged—low-income women, women of color, women with chronic health conditions, women with very young children, and teenagers.

Financial Barriers to Abortion

Among the primary obstacles people seeking abortions face—the cost of the procedure, the difficulty of getting to the nearest provider, the prospect of onerous abortion restrictions, the fear of stigma in their community, and the presence of protesters at the site itself—the most substantial is financial. As we learned in the last chapter, the most common reason women seek abortion in America is because they can't afford to raise a child or, more often, *another* child. So it shouldn't come as much of a surprise that many women who seek abortion for economic reasons struggle to afford the abortion itself. Needing time to raise money to cover travel and procedure costs was the most common reason for delay among our study participants, with nearly two-thirds of women who showed up close to the clinic's gestational limit reporting such costs as a reason for delay.[4]

All medical procedures in the United States are expensive, and abortion is no exception. The average price of a first-trimester abortion in our study was about $500.[5] Between 14 and 20 weeks, the average price was about $750, and after 20 weeks, it was $1,750.

And these estimates do not include transportation, lodging, and childcare costs, not to mention lost wages from time off work. But public and even private insurance is less likely to cover the cost of an abortion than most other medical procedures. This is no coincidence. It is the result of anti-abortion laws. As of 2019, 11 states prohibit private insurance plans from covering abortions. Twenty-six states restrict abortion coverage in insurance exchange plans. Twenty-two states restrict abortion coverage for public employees.[6] Thirty-four states don't cover abortion for women on Medicaid except in cases of life endangerment, rape, or incest.[7]

These laws have nothing to do with health or medicine. If it was only about taxpayers not wanting to foot the bill for a procedure they object to on moral or religious grounds, there wouldn't be bans on private insurance. Instead, these laws seem to be about making sure women literally pay the price for having had sex and becoming pregnant when they weren't willing to give birth to a child. As with many abortion restrictions, these insurance policies have unintended consequences. Consider Jessica. Louisiana voters may not want their state Medicaid dollars funding abortion because they think women should have to feel the financial pain themselves. But the end result is that Jessica still didn't have to pay anything out of her own pocket—after all, she had no money with which to pay—and her pregnancy was a whole month farther along by the time she got her abortion.

Half of all women seeking abortion in the U.S. live below the federal poverty level, which is about $12,000 a year for a woman living alone and $25,000 for a family of four. For such households, raising hundreds or thousands of dollars in a few days may be impossible. The time women and families take trying to raise that cash delays the abortion to a point where they need a more expensive procedure and have to travel to a clinic that's farther away to get the procedure done. As one 28-year-old woman from Kentucky who finally received an abortion at 21 weeks explained, "I couldn't afford it. They told me it was going to be $650. By the time I was able to raise the $650, they had to do a different procedure, and so the price went up. The price jumped to $1,850 . . . and they don't take insurance." Even though she had a full-time job, the pregnancy jeopardized her employment and her ability to care for her family. She told us, "I knew my boss and coworkers wouldn't have as much faith in me to do my job [if I continued the pregnancy]. I'm the main provider in my family, so if I lost my job we wouldn't be able to provide for the children we have, which is my main priority."

The vast majority of women who do obtain later abortions receive some financial assistance—85% of those after 20 weeks, compared to 44% of those having an early medication abortion. Even with assistance, most women pay a lot for abortions out of their own pockets. For just over a third of women in the first tri-mester and over half of women in the second trimester, the out-of-pocket expenses swallowed more than a third of their monthly income. In other words, if you're poor, you're not getting an abor-tion, unless you have insurance or unless a family member, part-ner, friend, or abortion fund helps you out. If and when they do help, you'll get an abortion at a later gestational age and stay preg-nant longer than a woman who is more financially stable.

Public and Private Insurance

As I noted earlier, nearly a dozen states have banned private insur-ance companies from funding abortion. In states without such laws, many insurance companies do cover abortion. That said, a full three-quarters of the women in our study who had insurance did not receive any assistance in paying for the abortion from their insurance company. We don't know whether this is because they didn't realize their policy would cover abortion, their policy did not cover abortion, the abortion clinic wouldn't accept private insurance, the cost of the abortion was less than their deductible, or they had privacy concerns that kept them from using their insur-ance.[8] This latter scenario spells problems for teenagers on their parents' insurance, like 19-year-old Jada, whom you'll hear more from after chapter 8. Jada was on her father's insurance and worried he might find out about her abortion. Feeling desperate, she took the risk and, living in Illinois, got help directly from the insurance company. But even having insurance that covers abortion may not solve the problem if the woman has to front the money at the clinic and be reimbursed by her insurance later, since that means that she will still need to come up with money she doesn't have.

Public insurance does not, in the case of abortion, cover many women who don't have private insurance. In 1976, just one year into his three-decade congressional career, Henry Hyde, the late Republican U.S. House representative from Illinois, introduced an amendment to a federal annual health-spending bill restricting any federal funds from paying for an abortion, including federal Medicaid. Congress has reaffirmed this policy—known as the Hyde Amendment—year after year.[9] Though initially attached to a health bill, the principle was expanded to banning all federal funding for abortion (excepting life endangerment), including for women in federal prison. In the 1990s, Congress added exceptions for cases of rape, incest, and severe maternal health issues.

So what is Hyde's legacy? My best estimate, based on studies that have been done, is that a quarter of all low-income pregnant people who would prefer to have an abortion instead give birth because public funding is not available.[10] So next time someone says, "Banning abortion doesn't stop abortion," you can say, "Actually, just making abortions unaffordable stops a significant fraction of people from having them."

Fifteen states reimburse clinics for providing abortions to low-income people using state funds rather than federally funded Medicaid.[11] But even when state-funded Medicaid does cover abortion, there can still be problems. We heard reports from women in states where Medicaid covers abortion that they got the runaround when they tried to sign up for Medicaid. We find that women seeking later abortions were twice as likely as women seeking first-trimester abortions to report delays because of difficulties securing public or private insurance coverage for the abortion (41% vs. 20%).[12] More than a third of women who should have qualified for a Medicaid-funded abortion—because they were in a Medicaid-coverage state and met the income criteria—did not receive any state funding for their abortion.[13] Medicaid is also supposed to pay for abortion in other states in cases of rape. Of the 11 women who reported that their pregnancy was a result of rape and could have qualified for Medicaid, only two reported that Medicaid covered it. Another problem with Medicaid coverage for abortion is that the reimbursement rates are terrible, far below the cost of providing the care.[14] Why would any provider agree to provide services when their practice loses money by doing so? Many doctors don't. The motivation of those who provide abortions despite losing money on each procedure is believing that their mission is to serve all women. Staying afloat, however, is a challenge.

It may sound reasonable that if you don't like abortion, you should not have your tax dollars paying for it. Here are the problems with that argument. First, abortion is health care—it's a legal medical procedure or the delivery of prescription medications by licensed medical professionals. A ban on federal public funding affects everyone whose health insurance comes from the federal government: poor women with children, women with disabilities, women in the Peace Corps and military, women in federal prisons, and women who work for the federal government.[15] In all, that's about 7.5 million American women, 3.5 million of whom are low-income.[16] Why are they subject to the moral judgments of a minority of the taxpayers in saying whether this health care is covered? Second, refusing to cover abortion may result in as many as a quarter of women who wanted an abortion carrying an unwanted pregnancy to term. The rest of this book will describe the consequences of that outcome. And if that sounds like a victory to those who oppose abortion, consider this: for the three-quarters who do get an abortion anyway, the result of not covering it via public or private insurance is that abortion is delayed to a point where the fetus is more developed and the procedure is more difficult.

Private Abortion Funds

More than a quarter of women in the Turnaway Study got help covering the cost of the abortion from a private abortion fund.[17] Abortion funds are nonprofit organizations that help poor women pay for an abortion, help them arrange rides to the clinic, and sometimes even put them up in volunteers' homes so they can stay overnight nearby. Examples include the National Network of Abortion Funds, which includes more than 70 local and regional abortion funds; the Dr. Tiller Patient Assistance Fund, named in honor of the doctor assassinated in 2009; the National Abortion Federation (NAF) Hotline Fund; and the NAF Rachel Falls Patient Assistance Fund, named in honor of a hotline director. Some funds are specifically set up to cover abortions in states where Medicaid won't pay, inadvertently complicating social scientists' attempts to assess the impact of Medicaid coverage on abortion rates. These funds, though they currently provide some support for one in seven abortions in the United States, are not a panacea.[18] They are underfunded and understaffed. I was curious about how long it might take to get through to a hotline, so I asked a summer intern to call one of the biggest funds. This dedicated but very bored intern spent three hours with her phone on autodial before the call picked up and another three hours before an operator came on the line, at which point she hung up. (Don't say summer internships with me aren't gratifying.) Can you imagine juggling a job, children, and other responsibilities and spending six hours straight on the phone to try to get help paying for an abortion?

Another kind of cost borne by women who cannot afford an abortion is having to disclose the fact of their pregnancy and their desired abortion to people they were not planning to tell. It can be difficult to protect your privacy when you have to beg for money. Feeling desperate, 20-year-old Nicole, whom you'll hear from after chapter 4, was almost ten weeks into an unwanted pregnancy when she called her ex-boyfriend. She needed the money, and she couldn't get help from her mom. "He wired me money, and if I didn't get that, I don't really know how things would have turned out." Nicole told us, of her ex, "He had told me that if I need anything at all to just ask. When I realized that I needed a few hundred dollars to be able to get rid of it, I knew that he would be a safe option to ask without my parents freaking out. Because my mom wouldn't have been able to even get me that money without my stepdad noticing it, and being like, 'Why did you give her four hundred dollars?' It would have been tricky to ask anybody else." Recall that Jessica decided to tell a distant relative, not because she was particularly close to her but because she knew this relative had the money and she did not know where else to turn. So even though they were not close and Jessica did not know how her cousin felt about abortion, she took that leap and asked.

Travel

Second only to the difficulty of paying for an abortion is the difficulty of getting to a provider. Anti-abortion lawmakers know this. A common type of abortion restriction imposes requirements on the physician or on the facility—for example, requiring that the physician have admitting privileges in a nearby hospital or that the building meet the requirements of an ambulatory surgical center, including hallways of a certain width and procedure rooms. There is no evidence that these laws make abortion any safer. But they do require costly investments into the building that few clinics can afford. As a result, clinics close, as happened when Texas enacted House Bill 2 in 2013, shuttering 17 of 41 clinics in the state, increasing the distance women had to travel, and reducing the abortion rate by 14%.[19] Passing laws that shutter clinics is like a ban on abortion for people who cannot easily travel to a more distant facility.

In the Turnaway Study, one-quarter of women (23%) having

a first-trimester abortion traveled more than 100 miles. For later abortions (after 20 weeks), 30% traveled more than 100 miles.[20] Longer travel distances to an abortion facility added even more costs. Women seeking a later abortion spent an average of $100 (up to $2,200) on transportation to the facility. Women seeking a first-trimester abortion spent an average of $23 for travel costs.[21] Women seeking later abortions were also more than twice as likely as first-trimester patients to report that difficulty getting to the abortion facility slowed them down (27% vs. 12%). For example, a 35-year-old black woman who was raising two children in the Central Valley of California had to travel 90 miles to get to an abortion facility that could perform her abortion. As she describes her reason for delay, "I didn't trust my car on the freeway and had to get it fixed before I could get to the clinic."

In 2014, Dr. Rachel Jones, a sociologist from the Guttmacher Institute, found that across the country nearly all abortion providers offered the procedure up to eight weeks from the last menstrual period. Seventy-two percent of clinics offered abortions up to 12 weeks. But after the first trimester, the availability of abortion care sharply declines. Only one-quarter of abortion clinics go up to 20 weeks, and one in ten clinics goes to 24 weeks.[22] So a woman might have to make a lot of calls to find the right place. In our study, women seeking later abortions called an average of 2.2 abortion facilities. But sometimes the gestational limit isn't given on the phone or the woman doesn't know how far along she is, and so she goes to multiple places, each time being referred on to yet another provider who goes a bit later in pregnancy. Michelle, the 18-year-old Latina from California, had visited three clinics and was nearly five months pregnant when she finally gave up and accepted that she was going to carry the pregnancy to term. Michelle had finished high school a year before and believed that having a baby now was going to hamper her future. She was also struggling with the boyfriend whom she became pregnant with, a man she described to us as "[not] a healthy functioning person." Her search for an abortion did not work out the way she hoped.

"My first choice was abortion because I was in no financial state to really take that on at that time," she said. "Just to be sent to, like, a different clinic because I didn't know when I had become pregnant, and each time they were like, 'Oh, we think you're too far along.' So I was sent to another place, and then they would say, 'Oh, you're too far along, but this person can do it.' 'You're too far along, but this person . . .' So, finally I was sent to San Francisco, where I got connected with this study."

In all, 58% of later abortion patients visited more than one facility, and 12% visited three or more facilities. In contrast, only a third of women seeking a first-trimester abortion visited more than one clinic. Note that these numbers represent the experiences of women who successfully found a place to perform their abortion. Because we are studying women who did make it to an abortion clinic, we cannot know how many more women never got that next referral or gave up because they didn't get the information they needed.

Having the money to pay for the abortion and being able to get to a clinic are just the logistical obstacles. Now let's turn to all the restrictions that state governments have placed on abortion provision and how they affect women's access to care. These include laws requiring women to be offered a view of the ultrasound image; mandatory waiting periods; parental-involvement requirements; rules about abortion counseling; laws that make it easier for anti-abortion protesters to picket clinics; and bans on abortion after some number of weeks of pregnancy. As part of the Turnaway Study, we studied how some of these policies affect women seeking abortion.[23]

Ultrasound Viewing

Anti-abortion advocates hope that seeing an ultrasound image will reveal to the woman that her embryo or fetus is a person and will change her mind about having an abortion.[24] There is no proof this happens, but the imagined power of viewing an ultrasound has inspired laws requiring abortion providers to offer a view of the ultrasound and, in some states, to verbally describe the image, whether or not the woman chooses to view it herself. Interestingly, some facilities offer patients a view of the ultrasound without being legally required to do so; this varies either by facility policy or the practice of the individual ultrasound technician on duty. In the Turnaway Study, almost three-quarters of the women (72%) had their abortion at a facility that had no official policy on whether to offer a view, one in five (21%) were in a facility where they were required to be offered a view by state law, and the remaining 7% went to facilities where it was the voluntary policy of that practice to offer all women a view. About half of the women in the study (48%) were offered the opportunity to view their ultrasound image, and of those, almost two-thirds (65%) chose to view it. Women who had never had a baby were somewhat more likely than women with children to choose to view (68% vs. 60% among those who were offered). Women who were in states where an offer to view was mandated were much less likely to choose to view than women in states with no policy (48% vs. 82% among those offered a view). What I learned from this is that some women want to view, perhaps out of curiosity about their pregnancy (which would explain the higher rates among women who haven't yet had children) and that when ultrasound technicians have the freedom to decide whom to offer a viewing to, they offer it to women who they believe will want to view the image.

To find out the effect of ultrasound viewing on women's feelings about the pregnancy, we asked women who had seen the image, "How did you feel about the ultrasound, either during the ultrasound or afterwards?" We asked this open-ended question to allow women to express whatever they felt without being influenced by any list of preconceived answers. And it is a good thing we did because I don't think any of us expected the results we got. My colleague Dr. Katrina Kimport, a sociologist, led this analysis.[25] She went through all 212 open responses to this question and coded them into groups of different types of emotions. The most common emotions, expressed by a third of women, were neutral—neither positive nor negative. These include a 30-year-old woman at five weeks' gestation, who said she felt, "Fine. I just wanted to see what it looked like out of curiosity—no attachment," and a 24-year-old woman at 24 weeks' gestation, who reported that she "didn't have much feeling" about it. The next most common emotions were negative, like sadness, guilt, or feeling upset. A 23-year-old woman at six weeks reported she felt "sad—I wanted to cry." A 24-year-old woman at 20 weeks' gestation said of viewing her ultrasound, "It upset me at first, but I knew I couldn't afford another child, and I knew the decision that I had already made." And, surprisingly, a significant fraction of women felt positive emotions. An 18-year-old at nine weeks' gestation said that viewing her ultrasound made her "kinda happy. I can't explain it—I just was." And a 19-year-old at 23 weeks' gestation reported, "It made me happy because it was nice to see it alive and see it moving." Some women may have been responding positively to the option to view in addition to the image itself. One 28-year-old woman, at 10 weeks' gestation, said she was "glad to see it, wanted to, and glad to have that choice."

What interests us about these findings is that some women choose to view the image; for some it is a way of coming to terms with the fact of the pregnancy. And even though some women feel bad about seeing the image, they may still choose to view it as part of their experience of the pregnancy and abortion. Another striking finding is that there is no relationship between what they view—at six weeks an embryo is less than an eighth of an inch and has no recognizable body parts, while at 23 weeks, a fetus is typically about 11 inches long and looks fully formed—and their emotional response to seeing the image. What women seem to be responding to is not the level of fetal development but their own emotions about having become pregnant and deciding on abortion. We'll discuss the findings about emotions and mental health more in chapter 4, but for now, in this chapter on access to care, we can conclude that merely offering women the chance to view their ultrasound image does not create much of a barrier to accessing abortion care so long as women are allowed to opt in to viewing and not made to feel that the experience is a state-imposed punishment. In contrast, laws that require multiple visits to view an ultrasound and then impose a mandated period of deliberation may do a lot of harm, not by the ultrasound viewing but by causing delay and increasing women's costs and travel time.

State Counseling

Some states have passed anti-abortion laws that require physicians to tell people seeking abortion specific information, including patently false statements. In the booklet that Pennsylvania law required abortion providers to give to Nicole, nearly a quarter of the statements about fetal development were found to be false by Callie Beusman in an investigation for *Vice News*.[26] The booklet that Texas required Amy and Camila to receive claimed, "Some women have reported serious psychological effects after their abortion, including depression, grief, anxiety, lowered self-esteem, regret, suicidal thoughts and behavior, sexual dysfunction, avoidance of emotional attachment, flashbacks, and substance abuse." All of which is highly misleading—some women may report this, but there is no solid scientific evidence that these poor outcomes are caused by abortion. In addition, the booklet implies that women who have abortions may have trouble conceiving in the future and may be at higher risk of breast cancer, even though neither infertility nor breast cancer is linked to abortion.[27] Over a third of the statements in Texas's booklet about fetal development were inaccurate, according to Beusman.[28]

The stated purpose of these laws is to ensure that women understand the risks of and alternatives to abortion, but they are not required to discuss the risks of carrying a pregnancy to term and giving birth, so clearly this isn't a question of ensuring there be informed medical decision-making around the pregnancy for the woman. These laws may be motivated in part by a lack of trust that an abortion provider would give an unbiased account of the risks of abortion or by the suspicion that providers may try to push women into having the procedure. In addition to inserting the non–medically informed opinion of politicians into the counseling at a clinic, these laws (in 14 states) actually increase the cost and travel burden by requiring that women have two visits and wait for a specified period of time between receiving counseling and having an abortion procedure.[29]

The Turnaway Study allowed us to look at the effect of such laws. Do women feel they are being pushed into an abortion decision at the clinic? Do these state-mandated counseling scripts improve patients' experiences? My colleagues Heather Gould and Sarah Roberts analyzed the data on women's experiences in the clinic—whether they received counseling about the abortion decision, and if they did receive counseling, whether the counselor encouraged them to have an abortion, discouraged them from having the abortion, or supported whatever they decided to do.[30] Gould's paper on counseling showed that two-thirds of the women reported having received counseling about the abortion decision. All the facilities report that they ask women about their decision to be sure the decision is their own. The difference between two-thirds of the women reporting that they were counseled about the decision and all the facilities covering the topic may be a result of what women consider "counseling" to be. Of those reporting having received counseling, 99% reported that the counselor let them know that she or he would support whatever decision they made, 3% reported that the counselor encouraged them to have an abortion, and less than 1% reported that the counselor discouraged them from having an abortion. Forty percent reported that the counseling they received was extremely helpful, 28% quite, 17% moderately, 10% a little, and only 4% reported it was not at all helpful. Women who received counseling at a clinic where a standardized counseling script was mandated by the state were significantly less likely to report finding counseling extremely or quite helpful (60%) compared to 75% of women who went to a clinic without state-mandated counseling. We conclude from the Turnaway Study that state-mandated information laws do not improve women's abortion experiences.

Women in the Turnaway Study report having to overcome extensive hurdles required by state laws in order to get their abortion. For example, after chapter 4 you'll hear Nicole's story about trying get through to a state hotline for state-mandated information, as part of Pennsylvania's informed consent law. She felt like she was dialing a radio call-in line. "If they didn't answer, you had to keep calling back," Nicole told us. "I felt like I was trying to get, like, tickets to a concert from a radio show. You keep calling, and you're like, 'Am I caller number nine? Am I getting it?' " Like several of the other women profiled in this book, Jessica lived in a state that required her to have two separate appointments at the abortion clinic and wait at least 24 hours in between, which was a big challenge considering she had two small children at home and very limited funds for things like gas money for long drives.

In the next chapter, we'll get to the issue of whether there is a need for the state to intervene to make sure that women feel confident in their decision.

Protesters

At many abortion clinics, the final hurdle before women can get inside is to pass a throng of protesters. Protesters may actually discourage some people from getting an abortion, but we cannot know that from the Turnaway Study because we only recruited women who made it inside the clinic. It seems unlikely that protesters would continue to protest without ever dissuading a woman from entering. However, sociologist Dr. Ziad Munson argues that the anti-abortion movement grew by giving supporters a way to become involved, that many people participate in pro-life activism first and then become ideologically committed to the pro-life cause.[31] And so even if protesters are not effective in stopping a significant number of people from getting abortions, they may have an important anti-abortion movement-building purpose.

At the time we collected data from Turnaway recruitment sites in 2011, most of the facilities in our study reported regular protesters. Just under half of the women reported seeing protesters. Of those who saw protesters, a third merely saw them, a third reported being spoken to, and another third reported that a protester tried to stop them from entering the clinic. Among those who did have contact (seeing, hearing, or being stopped), half of them didn't find the protesters upsetting at all. A quarter found them only a little upsetting. And 16% found them quite a bit or extremely upsetting.

Sue, a 25-year-old white woman from Missouri, was denied an abortion after having recently had a baby. For her, just going to the abortion clinic was an unpleasant experience, and the protesters outside made it far worse. Sue told us, "I remember the people standing in front of the clinic that day, and the names they called me and things when I walked in there, and I was in tears already when I got there, besides the fact that I was an emotional basket case. I don't think I'll ever forget that day."

For the anti-abortion activists protesting outside one Chicago clinic, Adrienne, a 34-year-old black woman, might have seemed like one of their victories. She was not expecting the protesters when she made her appointment, and their presence made her so upset, she ended up leaving. "I remember [the protesters] on the day of the clinic, and they were saying all these harsh things," Adrienne recalled. "They had pictures, like, this poster. And it was saying, you're going to kill a life, you're going to take a life. . . . I went into the clinic and I sat for a minute, and I was waiting on the nurse or waiting on them to call my name. And I just got up and left because I really wasn't sure at the time." But despite how these protesters and their words might have unsettled Adrienne on her first visit to the abortion clinic, it did not change her decision to have the abortion. "I came back the next day, and then I was ready." Adrienne's reaction to the protesters is consistent with our findings from survey responses where women who had difficulty deciding whether to have an abortion were more likely to report that the protesters were upsetting.

We also find that the more contact the protesters had with women (stopping vs. only hearing vs. only seeing), the more upset the women were. Two-thirds of women whom protesters tried to stop from entering the clinic reported that the protesters were upsetting, compared to the 36% of those who only saw the protesters but didn't hear them. One week after the abortion, whether there were protesters at the facility or whether the women had more or less contact with them, there were no differences in the emotions women felt about their abortion. It would be easy to take from this that protesters have no effect on women's emotions about their abortion. But we must note that clinics with active protesters report spending a lot of time trying to mitigate the harm and calm their patients down. So rather than saying that the protesters are completely ineffective in making women feel bad about their abortion, it may be more accurate to say that clinics are able to provide the support that women need if they are upset by run-ins with clinic protesters. Of course, in that case, the cost of protesters is borne in part by the clinics, which must invest in extra staff time for that purpose.

Gestational Limits

Since the 1973 decision *Roe v. Wade*, the Supreme Court has allowed states to ban abortion around viability (with exceptions for women's health and life). Some argue that a compromise between women's rights and fetal rights is to ban abortions earlier in pregnancy than viability. Even some pro-choice advocates and politicians recommend that pro-choice movement leaders should come to a sort of compromise and agree not to support abortion rights beyond some point in pregnancy.[32]

Once, after I had given a talk at the University of California, Berkeley, about the Turnaway Study, a visiting scholar from Denmark approached me and shared what he thought was a clear solution to the mess that is abortion-rights politics in the United States. The Danes had already figured this all out, he informed me, his tone growing exasperated. Why were Americans so backward? If people stopped advocating for access to later abortions and just agreed to set a nice low limit like Denmark's 12-week limit, which currently the vast majority of U.S. women seeking abortions would be able to meet, the controversy around abortion would evaporate.

An evaporation of controversy would suit me just fine. Wouldn't it be nice if we could just agree to set a limit and stop arguing about this? Anti-abortion advocates could stop protesting outside clinics, and lawmakers could stop writing sham restrictions in the name of safety whose real purpose is to close clinics. We could even maybe regulate abortion according to the actual small risk it entails instead of the political imperative to make it more difficult to access. If politics were no longer an issue, a woman who did not want to be pregnant and was early in pregnancy could just pick up her medication abortion pills from the drugstore, without a prescription. And if she didn't want to use pills or she wanted to talk to a clinician, she could go to a clinic.

Why might a first-trimester gestational limit work in Denmark? Because Denmark has the United Kingdom and the Netherlands nearby, where women can go when they are beyond 12 weeks. So Denmark gets its feel-good, we-have-it-all-figured-out solution, while the presence of English and Dutch services provides an escape valve that allows people seeking abortions beyond that limit to be served without upsetting the social contract. Two other differences separate the U.S. and Denmark. First, we have a very powerful religious influence in our politics. I do not think that setting a 12-week limit would satisfy those who believe that life starts at conception. Second, it is a very different thing to force a woman to carry a pregnancy to term and give birth in a country with a year of parental leave, government-provided medical care, subsidized child care, and a strong social support system, like Denmark has.

Who gets later abortions?

If supporters of legal abortion in the United States were to agree to a Faustian bargain where they abandon the principle of women's bodily autonomy for the promise of easy access to early abortion, social order, and peace, let's consider who actually would be making the sacrifice.

Dr. Katrina Kimport and I wrote a paper describing women who have later abortions. In this paper, we compared women having abortions in the first trimester to women having abortions at or beyond 20 weeks. Our findings surprised me—it turns out that women who have later abortions are similar to women obtaining earlier abortions. We found no differences between the women having early versus later abortions by race, ethnicity, number of children or past abortions, mental or physical health history, or substance use. The common differences we did find relate to a woman's age, her economic resources, and when in pregnancy she discovered she was pregnant. Young women, for example, are particularly at risk for late discovery of pregnancy—and thus more likely to have later abortions than women over 25—because young women are more likely to have irregular periods, a sense of invulnerability, and unfamiliarity with the risk and symptoms of pregnancy. Fifty-nine percent of women having later abortions were younger than 25, compared with 41% of women having first-trimester abortions.

Just knowing that young women, low-income women, or women without pregnancy symptoms are at particular risk doesn't really tell us who the women having later abortion are. So we decided to look at the data another way, this time sorting by characteristics like demographics, life circumstances, health, and feelings about pregnancy, to see if we could sketch out the characteristics of people more likely to have later abortions for reasons other than maternal or fetal health. We came up with five profiles that describe 80% of the women having abortions at or after 20 weeks: women raising children alone; women who are depressed or using illicit substances; women who have conflict with a male partner; women who had trouble deciding what to do with their pregnancies followed by difficulty accessing care; and finally, teenagers who had never had a child.

It is easy to condemn later abortions in the abstract. It's harder when you realize that real women sometimes find themselves in a circumstance where they need one. So here are five profiles of women who have later abortions, each illustrated by one woman from the Turnaway Study who fit that profile.

Almost half of women seeking later abortion (47%) are women already raising children on their own. Angel, a 24-year-old white woman from Maryland, was raising a ten-month-old daughter while she looked for a job. Her husband had recently been put in prison, leaving her with no household income. As Angel explained, her daughter was her top priority. She first realized she was pregnant at 22 weeks, because her periods were still irregular from having given birth to her daughter. She said, "I knew I couldn't continue with [the pregnancy]. My daughter isn't even a year." She was able to quickly decide on having the abortion, but finding a clinic was much more difficult. The closest one that could help her at her point in pregnancy was three hours away and was charging $2,700. But as Angel said, "I was determined." She paid $300 herself, borrowed $400 from her mom, and received aid from three abortion funds. She had her abortion at 24 weeks.

About a third of women having later abortions (30%) have mental health or substance-use problems. For example, Rose, a 25-year-old American Indian woman from Texas, was living with her boyfriend and was financially stable when she had her abortion. She had a full-time job and good physical health. However, she also had a history of major depression and bipolar disorder, for which she was receiving medication and cognitive behavioral therapy. She had been physically assaulted at ages 12 and 22, traumatic experiences that had a long-lasting negative impact on her life. Rose used Xanax recreationally about once a week as well as sometimes using amphetamines and binge drinking. Rose did not want any kids. She found out she was pregnant while she was still on the pill, at 19 weeks, and was "shocked and not happy about it." Deciding to have an abortion was easy, but just like for Angel, finding a clinic was much more difficult. Rose called four clinics and visited another one before finding a clinic four and a half hours from her home that could perform her abortion at 20 weeks at a cost of $1,750.

Almost a quarter of women having later abortions (24%) experienced conflict with their male partner or domestic violence. Lesley, a 34-year-old white woman from Tennessee who worked as a medical professional, lived with her eight-year-old daughter. For the whole of her 11 years of marriage, her alcoholic husband physically abused her. This abuse had caused her to experience episodes of depression and symptoms of post-traumatic stress disorder. Although she discovered the pregnancy early, at five weeks' gestation, Lesley was deeply conflicted about whether to carry it to term in an abusive relationship and whether to stay in the marriage. While she was trying to decide what to do with the pregnancy, Lesley left her husband. After counseling from a private therapist and with the support of two friends, Lesley got an abortion at 20 weeks. The procedure cost her $1,700. Although she felt guilty about the abortion, she said it was the right decision for her, and hoped that in a year her divorce would be final and she would be raising her daughter as a single mother.

One in five women having later abortions (22%) experience trouble deciding, followed by difficulty accessing care. Amber, a 24-year-old black woman from Mississippi, had two young children. Amber worked part-time, and because the father of her children failed to provide child support, she rarely had enough money. She received food stamps for her family and was insured through the state Medicaid program. Amber discovered she was pregnant at five weeks and eventually decided at 14 weeks to have an abortion because, as she said, "I couldn't afford another child. The dad didn't want to be with me. Me and him weren't going to be together, and he told me that I was going to have to raise the baby myself." But accessing abortion care was difficult, especially since Medicaid would not cover the procedure. Amber called two clinics and visited a third before finding a clinic three hours from her home that could perform her abortion. Getting there was a challenge, and by the time she got a ride, she was 20 weeks along and required a different and more costly procedure, which she struggled to afford. In the end, she received nearly $600 from an abortion fund, her ex-boyfriend paid $600, and she paid $300 for the abortion. She also paid $150 in transportation costs. Although Amber "tries not to think about" the abortion, she said it was the right decision for her.

The final category of women who have later abortions is teenagers who have never had a child (12% of those having a later abortion). Lana, a 15-year-old Latina from California, did not learn she was pregnant until 21 weeks into her pregnancy. She was a full-time high school student living with an aunt and brother. Lana became pregnant with her boyfriend, despite their condom use. Although her boyfriend wanted her to continue the pregnancy, Lana knew she wanted an abortion immediately because of her age. She explained, "I was too young, and I barely started going back to school and getting my life back on track. I wouldn't have enough things to support a baby." Lana had her abortion two weeks after learning she was pregnant, at 23 weeks' gestation. She had to travel four hours to reach a facility that could perform the procedure, the cost of which was covered by public insurance. After the abortion, Lana said she felt relief.

In addition to these five profiles of women seeking later abortion, I want to call attention to two characteristics that make abortion access more difficult—young age and obesity.

In the Turnaway Study, we find that teenagers discover pregnancy later for physical reasons—because their periods are already irregular, because their abdominal muscles are tighter and so they pop out later—and for cognitive reasons, such as their being less familiar with the symptoms of pregnancy. They also have less independence and therefore less access to money and transportation. On top of being a vulnerable group by virtue of all these factors, teenagers under 18 years are then subject to extra state restrictions. Almost three-quarters of U.S. states require parents to be involved in a minor's decision to have an abortion. Three states require that *both* parents consent, yet almost a third of young people don't even live with two parents, as a result of many factors, including separation, divorce, incarceration, death of a parent, deportation, and homelessness.[33] Some states mandate that minors have to have notarized signatures from parents or their birth certificate as proof of age.[34] As my colleague epidemiologist Dr. Lauren Ralph points out, the goal of parental involvement requirements is not to promote the health and well-being of young people, it is to put insurmountable obstacles in their way. As a mother of teenagers myself, I have to say that parental involvement might sound like a good idea at first—a parent should know what is going on with their child. But in the case of abortion, where failure to access a wanted abortion results in the child herself becoming a parent, the data have convinced me that it's the right moment to ensure she is making decisions for herself. Two-thirds of teenagers tell a parent without state mandates.[35] And for the other third, data suggest they may have good reasons not to tell, including concern about being forced to continue the pregnancy, getting kicked out of the house, and, in rare cases, being subjected to violence.

One group, in addition to teenagers, that has particular difficulties with abortion access is obese women. You'll meet Sofia after chapter 10. Her body weight falls just over the threshold for obesity and she experiences many of the extra challenges associated with higher weight. Obesity is associated with irregular periods, which makes an unexpected pregnancy trickier to detect. And greater girth might reduce the chance that pregnancy is suspected when a woman's abdomen becomes hard. To add to these difficulties, providers are sometimes unwilling to treat an obese patient because they don't have an exam table, blood-pressure cuff, or other supplies in the right size, or because they find the procedure to be more challenging.[36] One 27-year-old black woman from California, who sought an abortion at 21 weeks, said, "The first clinic that I went to [turned me away because of my weight and] didn't tell me that there was another option." The problem of denial of care for obese women is not infrequent. One hospital-based abortion provider told me that a full quarter of the patients they see were previously turned away by other providers because of obesity.

The Turnaway Study gives us some understanding of the circumstances of women seeking later abortions. We have a system that places greater burdens on women who are more disadvantaged—because they have fewer resources, discovered their pregnancy later, or have less support from family and partners. The more time you need to raise money, find a provider, or find a way to get to a clinic, the more likely it is that you will be denied care. Addressing the social bias against women seeking later abortions becomes more important as more states consider legislative bans on abortion at or after 20 weeks (or even earlier). In some tiny percentage of cases, this deadline for abortion may speed up women's decision-making. However, our findings suggest that several of the reasons women delay seeking abortion (e.g., late discovery of pregnancy, conflict with the man involved) cannot be reduced by shortening the window for abortion care.

It is easy to demonize women who have later abortions. The assumption is that they failed to prevent pregnancy and then they took too long to get an abortion. When there is public testimony from women having abortions after the twentieth week of pregnancy, we almost always hear from a woman with a wanted pregnancy who had a fetal anomaly or whose own newly emerged health condition threatened both her life and her fetus. But the quiet truth about abortion between 20 and 24 weeks is that it is often a problem of late recognition of pregnancy followed by real obstacles—financial, travel-related, and legal—to getting an abortion. Making abortion more difficult to access does not mean that only the morally deserving get their abortions. It means that only adult women who don't have any physical or mental health issues and who have money and social support get their abortions.

MARTINA

*It was definitely the hardest decision
I ever had to make in my entire life.*

My father is a contractor, and so we moved around for my father's work. I had a pretty idyllic childhood. I grew up mostly in a small town where everybody kind of knows everybody else. They have, like, two high schools, one Walmart, barely a shopping mall. We grew up lower-middle class. Our vacation was going to the national park to go camping; our vacation wasn't going to Disneyland. But I got to spend a lot of time outdoors fishing, camping, hiking. My dad was a hunter, and he taught my younger brother and me hunting skills. When I was older, my parents started the divorce process. It didn't necessarily impact my life. You know how some children grow up with separate homes, I didn't have that until later in life. These days I don't have my father in my life anymore, which is unfortunate. That was the result of the divorce. I think he didn't have any responsibilities to a grown-up child. Now my mother works in the public school system as a teacher's aide.

My mother is from Central America. She moved here to go to Bible college to become a missionary. That's where she met my father. They ended up getting married and started having kids. Until I was three, we mostly spoke Spanish in our home. My mom used to make a lot more ethnic foods like tamales and beans and rice. I would have to say that we are definitely Americanized.

She definitely wholeheartedly embraced American traditions like Christmas. They had a lot of the same traditions where she grew up; it's not that different. They had the same ideals, my parents, and are really old-fashioned.

I was going to college. And I think I had been there for two years at that point. I was working as a server. Just living that college-kid life—get up, go to class, get out of class, go to work, hang out all night with friends, and then get up and do it all again the next day. I worked, like, 40 hours a week on top of going to school full-time. Any extra time was spent hanging out with friends. I was partying Thursday, Friday, Saturday night. It's not like I was going to school completely wasted or hungover or anything like that. I had a small group of girlfriends. It was a lot of getting dressed up, going out. I can't even imagine the hundreds of dollars I spent, just on drinks and random outfits that I don't even have anymore.

My goal was to finish college. At that point I probably had a good two, two and a half years left of college. I had already missed a semester because I had gotten mono. I was out of school for three weeks and ended up withdrawing from all of my classes. After a certain point they don't refund your tuition, and it's pretty much like you failed a course. Then I got kicked out the next semester because my grades were not good enough. I took about a year off, so I was still halfway through my college career at that time. So my main focus was to finish school.

I had met this guy on the internet. He didn't live in the same town as me, but he traveled for work and would come on his way to his job to see me. We hung out a couple times, and then, you know, decided to try having a relationship. We were both young, and in hindsight it was not the right choice. But when you're young, and you're just like, "Oh, this guy is so cute, and he's into me," you throw caution to the wind.

We dated for almost a year. He already had a kid with another woman, which probably should have been a red flag. We mostly used condoms. But I was on birth control pills, so I thought we'd be fine. Which turns out was not the case. Of course, I'm sure that I wasn't as religious as I thought I was with taking my birth control at the time. I might have taken it every day, but I've done more research now, and there's definitely a science behind taking it at the same time every day and not wavering from that, especially when you're on extended cycle. Knowing what I know now, I would have been much more religious about it—or changed to another type of birth control a long time ago.

He was a couple years younger than me, and I found myself trying to take the role of parent for his toddler, even though I was like—I don't even want to have a kid right now. When we would spend time, as a "family," the three of us, the dad did not have a good handle on how to be a parent. I babysat and I have dealt with small children a lot. I thought, how am I being a better parent than you are right now by telling this child that "It's nine o'clock, you need to go to bed now," as opposed to letting the kid run around until she falls asleep?

It was a difficult relationship, where I felt like I was trying to be a parent to his kid and allow this child to come into my home. We even moved in together to a two-bedroom apartment to accommodate this.

When I found out I was pregnant, it was one of those shifts. Like, I'm so screwed right now. It was "I"—it was not "we, we as a couple," are so screwed right now. It was me, I am screwed. That was probably one of the moments when I should have realized, this is a bad relationship, just leave. But I didn't. I told him about it, and he was like, "Well, I have to go to work tomorrow. Do you want me to stay?" And I was like, "Well, no. I'll just deal with it myself." The fact that you're even asking me if you need to stay tells me that I'm going to do this by myself, because you don't care. There should have been no question of, do you need to be here?

He was an over-the-road trucker. I think it was a Saturday or a Sunday when we found out and took the pregnancy test. The next day he had to leave.

My parents are super old-fashioned. I knew that if they found out about it, I would be in so much trouble. I didn't—I honestly didn't know what they would do; I just knew I would be in trouble. It turns out that probably wasn't the case. I think it definitely stemmed from, as a child my parents spanked, which is fine. I agree with it. But any time I get in trouble with my parents I still—it's just, like, oh my God, this is the worst. So how I reacted to it was a very—a very childlike reaction—oh my God, I can't tell my mom. She will kill me, literally. I did not tell anybody, to be honest with you. He knew, and that was pretty much it for the longest time.

And ironically enough, my best girlfriend at the time, the one that we went out Thursday, Friday, Saturday night every week, she had just had a late-term abortion. I couldn't even tell her. I couldn't even tell my friends that I knew had been in the same situation as me. I told her probably a good month, two months, three months after it happened.

It's like, I did this. I have to be the one responsible enough to take care of it. I don't have any other option. Knowing that I couldn't—or my brain telling me that I couldn't—tell my parents. It was, like, I couldn't carry a baby to term—I'd have to tell my mother that I was pregnant. I can't tell my friends this because they won't understand. I can't talk to my friends who can't have kids, because why would I just get rid of the one I could have? I had a friend who gave up a baby, and now she has two other children of her own. She's a single parent. How can I tell her that doing that is not right for me? So I felt very alone.

I did think about adoption, but at the same time, carrying the baby to term would have meant having to tell my parents that I was pregnant. So that wasn't an option for me. I never thought I would get myself in a situation where I would have to have an abortion. I grew up in a super-religious household, where my parents taught no sex before marriage—they wouldn't even let me hold hands with my high school boyfriend in the house. But my whole life I have been more liberal than my parents. It's kind of hard to keep your kids on the straight and narrow when they have access to all this technology. I had always known about abortions.

I had always felt it's a woman's choice. But I never thought I would have to make that choice.

My experience at the clinic, honestly, was as good as it could have been. Everybody at the clinic was really nice and polite. The way that the clinic is set up, it's downtown on a one-way street. The parking lot is across the street, and they do have picketers. They have volunteers out front. They realize that they're in a tough spot because there's really only one way to get there, and that you have to cross the street. So that was hard. Just walking in the door was hard. But once I was inside, the volunteers were all really nice. They actually started a group session—there were a couple of us there that day. I was the only person who was by themselves. Everybody else had one other person with them.

Then it was waiting time until it was my turn to see the doctor. I was fine until I actually got into the procedure room with the doctor. She was so nice, but when she started getting everything ready, I started crying, and I couldn't stop crying. She was like, "Are you okay?" And I was like, "Yes. I'm okay. I'm just going to cry. You know, just let me cry. It'll be fine." She was super nice about everything. Once I was done, they took me into a recovery room with nice, comfortable chairs. Something they had that I thought was amazing, they had therapy journals to write in. And they didn't take out the entries from the people that had been there before. They left those entries in.

I was reading a couple journals, and I got to page through and read other people's stories. And it was actually really helpful to be able to read other people's stories about why they had had their abortion. And you know what? Everybody's situation is unique. A lot of the reasons behind getting an abortion are not what people think. One story I read, a woman's husband wouldn't let her get birth control, and she kept getting pregnant. Since she was able to pay for abortions with cash, he didn't know that she was continually getting abortions because she continued to get pregnant. And they already had, like, three or four kids. He basically thought that he was right, she didn't need to have birth control, they just won't get pregnant again, you know? But no, she had three additional abortions because he wouldn't let her get birth control. There were some other stories from kids my age. There was even a story from a mom who had to bring her daughter in. So that was really, really nice to read those. I might not know them, but there are quite a lot of other people out there.

A day or two later I was pretty much fine, back to normal as far as my physical body. But emotionally I would say I was pretty numb. I can't talk to anybody about this, so I'll just keep going back to business as usual. I was thankful that I had school to go to. My parents were not contributing to my college education at all. So it's like, I am paying for this. I have to go. Having class to go to every day was actually kind of good.

I was still with the father of the baby. This all happened in April. Only in December were we done with the relationship. I finished taking classes in May, and we moved into that two-bedroom apartment right around Thanksgiving time. And then we had Christmas together. He ended up cheating on me right before the relationship ended. It was just a mess of a relationship. The abortion happened, like, within the first three months of us seeing each other, which was also pretty crazy.

It was definitely probably the hardest decision I ever had to make in my entire life. I have to live with it. The first couple years I did not accept it. I blacked it out in my mind even though I had the interviews every few months that would bring it up again. Probably for the first two to three years after it happened, my life was just kind of blank.

And so now as I get older and learn more about myself and my personality and the things that I care about and the things I believe in, I definitely wish I would have been able to be more open about it when it happened because I have found that I have a great support group. My friends and family love me no matter what. So I am super lucky on that front. I feel empathy for the people that don't have a support group and still have to go through this.

I've always felt like it is a woman's choice. I do realize that there are some dads out there who take their responsibility seriously, but because it's not the dad's body, it is kind of hard to say this woman should have that kid for you. It's the woman's body. It's her right to choose whether or not she goes through with it. But it is hard now to look at a man and say, "I'm sorry. I can't have this for you."

I don't regret the abortion at all. I'm where I am supposed to be in my life. So I know that I made the right decision for myself. But I definitely feel like I should have been more open and honest with my friends and my family at the time. It would have helped me process it a lot quicker. Instead it has taken me, like, five or six years to really feel confident about my decision. When I think about it now, I don't look down into that deep, dark spiral of, oh my God, I can't believe that that happened. Now it's like, that was a part of my life. It happened. I learned from it. I've grown from it.

The people in my life are still going to love me. So that has definitely helped me be able to talk, especially with my mom, about some other difficult things that have come up, be it financially, emotionally, or other relationship stuff. And even my brother—I have actually told him, too. And he was definitely accepting. He's in a relationship with a girl, and I think that my experience has probably helped him be like, "Girl, we've got to be honest, if we're going to be sexually active, you know? I don't want what happened to my sister to happen to you." I definitely feel like he is careful about stuff like that. And I think it has helped him to be even more respectful towards women and their choices, which I really like.

Ironically, now everybody is like, "You're so tough for having gone through that," and "I don't know if I could have done it." And I go, "Well, you probably could if you had to." Some of the friends that I had back during that time have been like, "Why didn't you tell me when this happened? I would have been there for you even though you may not think I would have been there for you." Even when I meet new people, if that topic of conversation comes up, I don't feel shame. I actually feel empowered to say, "This is what happened to me, and this is how I dealt with it. This is where I am now; if you can't accept that that's part of my life, we are not going to be good friends." But I'm not hiding in pain anymore, which I think is really good.

I graduated from college two years after I had the abortion, which was great. I needed to get out. I moved to Minneapolis to look for a more professional career. I didn't find it. I ended up continuing to bartend. I worked in the Mall of America, which was a blast in and of itself. And I met my current partner. We've been together for two and a half years now. He introduced me to mountain biking, and I love it. We went on a couple of trips and went biking in the Rocky Mountains. We went to California and I just loved it—loved it, loved it. So we decided to move. After our trip, we saved money for six months. We decided, on top of moving, we're going to take a three-month bike trip. So we saved and saved and saved. We biked near Zion National Park, and outside Arches National Park. And then we went to Wyoming and to South Dakota. And we biked for three months straight. And then we went back to Minneapolis, rounded up our stuff, and moved out to California. I love it here.

I am absolutely where I am supposed to be. I finally have a professional position. I'm the assistant manager of a store here. It may have taken me a couple, three years to get my life to where I want it to be. I feel that my relationship with my family, my mom and my brother, is stronger than ever. There's parts of my life that just suck—I've been fired. I've lived from paycheck to paycheck. I lost my job, and it definitely was a huge frustration. But it was like, opportunities are still coming.

Hopefully we can agree that it's difficult no matter what you choose, and people just need to be supportive. Women don't need to be told this isn't the right choice. They just need support. So hopefully, if we can all come to that, it would just make it better, where people aren't afraid to talk about it or to get help or to have that conversation. If anything, having an abortion definitely made me even more accepting of it. Being able to see there are other reasons why other women have had abortions. And, like, it's not about whether it's right or wrong, period. It's about whether or not it's right or wrong for you. I am even more pro-choice now because everybody has different circumstances, and it's unfair, I think, for any one person to be able to tell any other person what they can or cannot do.

If I had had the baby, I would have slowly tried to finish school because I had committed so much time. But I probably wouldn't be living in California. I definitely wouldn't be in the relationship that I'm in. I probably wouldn't have left my hometown, just because of the financial cost of raising a child. I might've even had to move back home.

And now I don't want children. I think I've always kind of leaned that way, but now it's definitely cemented that I don't want children. It's not necessarily because of the abortion; it's more because of the lifestyle choices that I've been making. For so long our society has said, you graduate high school, you get a job—or you go to college, you get a job, you have kids, dog, picket fence, blah, blah, blah. I'm realizing that that model is not going to work for me. I want to use all of my time and resources to explore versus finding that nuclear family. I find myself having to talk to people who are like, "Oh, you'll change your mind eventually." And I'm like, "No, I'm sure—99.9% sure—that I am not going to have to make that decision again." I wanted to get an IUD for the longest time, but it wasn't covered under my health care. And then when they passed the Affordable Care Act, it was. As soon as I found that out, I went ahead and got an IUD so I won't have that issue again. By getting an IUD, I am cementing my lifestyle choice—I want to explore versus create that family.

We want to take another monthlong trip this year. And maybe even do a couple extreme sports because, as a woman in the mountain-biking world, I am definitely in the minority. This year the chance of being at the top of an event is very high, and it's definitely on my list of goals to do some of those really intense events. We've also decided that we might want to move to South America.

I definitely want to visit Southeast Asia, and also take my mom back to Central America to visit her hometown.

I don't think that abortion needs to spell the end of a woman's life. I feel like right now maybe our society puts it that way, like if you have an abortion, you're damaged goods. I don't think that's true at all. I'm proof of it. I'm proof that having that abortion did not end my quest to take over the world. I hope that dialogue can be created that encourages, not encourages abortion, but encourages life after. It's not something that defines my life. It's just something that happened.

Martina, a Latina from Arizona, was 22 years old and nine weeks pregnant when she had an abortion.

CHAPTER 4

Mental Health

Martina's story presents a perfect opportunity to raise the question of whether abortion causes psychological or emotional harm. No doubt about it, Martina was extremely upset around the time of her pregnancy and abortion. She was concerned that her parents, who opposed premarital sex, would disapprove of the pregnancy and the abortion. She didn't think her friends would sympathize with her choice—not her friends who were trying to become pregnant, not a friend who had placed a baby for adoption, and not even a close friend who had recently had an abortion. And her boyfriend's response to the news about the pregnancy revealed how little he seemed to care about her. For years after her abortion, Martina had difficulty coping and said her mind was blank. She reported more symptoms of depression one week following her abortion than most of the women interviewed (she reported five symptoms, including feeling hopeless, lonely, and worthless, while other women in the first-trimester sample reported an average of two). It was unclear whether her distress was due to the abortion itself, to the circumstances that led to her wanting an abortion, to other people's reaction to her pregnancy, or to her feelings of social isolation and lack of social support. Would Martina's mental health have been better if she had not received the abortion and had carried the pregnancy to term?

None of us know, as we move through our lives, what would have been at the end of the roads not taken. I suspect that whichever path we take, when we look back, we want to feel like we

99

made the best decisions possible—that everything worked out for the best. So Martina's statement that "I don't regret the abortion at all. I'm where I am supposed to be in my life" could be an after-the-fact rationalization of her experience. But the strength of the Turnaway Study design is that by looking at women who are in similar positions but, through no choice of their own, are routed a different way, we can explore the effect of taking alternate paths. When we compare the outcomes of women whose pregnancies were just above and just below the gestational limit, we can get an idea of what might have been—as well as how women's mental health is affected by receiving or being denied an abortion. This unique study design allows us to explore whether the abortion or other factors were the cause of the distress experienced by women like Martina.

The initial motivation for the entire Turnaway Study, after all, was to answer the question *Does abortion hurt women?* For decades and in the absence of reliable data, anti-abortion advocates have asserted that abortion causes mental health problems. They have even created a new mental health condition, *post-abortion syndrome*, although it has not been accepted by any leading medical or mental health organization. More than 2,000 crisis pregnancy centers across the United States, mostly run by evangelical groups, attempt to discourage women with unwanted pregnancies from aborting by telling them about the supposed psychological and physical harms of abortion.[1] Even in the liberal San Francisco Bay Area, anti-abortion activists put up billboards proclaiming "Abortion Hurts Women" to protest the anniversary of the January 1973 *Roe v. Wade* Supreme Court ruling that a woman's right to choose to have an abortion is protected by the Constitution.

This notion that abortion has long-term consequences to women's emotional and psychological health has permeated our society and inspired policies that restrict people's access to abortion. In the introduction, I told you about Justice Anthony Kennedy's majority opinion in the 2007 *Gonzales v. Carhart* Supreme Court case, in which he wrote, "It seems unexceptionable to conclude some women come to regret their choice to abort the infant life they once created and sustained. Severe depression and loss of esteem can follow."

The assumption that the decision to have an abortion is inherently difficult and painful leads people to assume that the aftermath of an abortion must also be pain and difficulty. I witnessed firsthand the pervasiveness of this view when I first requested that my university's institutional review board (IRB) review and approve the Turnaway Study. One of the most important steps to launching a study involving human subjects is to get ethical approval. UCSF has a large medical school and many of the studies at my university are clinical trials — testing whether a medical intervention improves the course of a disease. The IRB has to decide for each study whether the potential benefits outweigh the risks of the intervention, whether all risks have been minimized, and whether study subjects are well informed of the risks and benefits before they agree to participate. In the Turnaway Study, we researchers did not have a say in whether or not a woman received an abortion — the gestational limits already in place at the clinics determined who would get an abortion and who would be turned away. Thus any hardship from receiving or being denied an abortion would not be caused by our study. But we were going to ask the study participants a lot of questions, some of them potentially distressing. So it was our responsibility to make sure women were answering voluntarily and knew that they could skip any questions they didn't want to answer. And we also needed a plan for what we would do if someone expressed imminent intent to harm themselves or others. In that case, we clearly needed to intervene, even if it wasn't our questions that upset them or motivated their desire for self-harm.

There was one psychologist on the IRB committee who believed that abortion causes mental health harm and increases people's risk of suicidal ideation and behaviors. He was concerned that study participants, particularly teenagers, might be suicidal due to the abortion. Specifically, he declared that "teenagers might want to be reunited with their dead fetuses." (I am not sure where he got that idea from. He certainly didn't get it from the existing scientific literature on the topic.) But it was true that by following so many women and checking in with them every six months, our researchers would potentially encounter some women with severe psychological distress, for myriad reasons. We wanted to be prepared to do what we could to ensure that our participants were supported in the event that they experienced severe psychological distress. So we consulted with a licensed clinical psychiatrist and decided to use a standardized assessment for suicide risk, provide referrals to the National Suicide Prevention Lifeline if anyone reported suicidal ideation, and intervene if women were assessed to be at imminent risk of hurting themselves. In such a case, our protocol demanded that we speak to a mental health provider with whom the participant had a relationship or an adult in the home who could take responsibility for the woman seeking care. Our last resort, if no other adults were present, would be to call the police. It seemed like the right thing to do, but in retrospect, I don't think we did anyone any favors, for reasons I will explain below.

Why might abortion harm women's mental health?

Before we look at the data, let's take a moment to consider the ways that abortion might possibly harm women's mental health. First, if a woman considers abortion akin to killing a baby, the feelings of guilt and remorse might cause serious distress. Most abortion patients don't believe that abortion is the same as killing a baby, but a small percentage do. In a separate study I led in one midwestern clinic among women in the waiting room before they had spoken to counselors, 4% agreed with the statement "At my stage of pregnancy, I think abortion is the same as killing a baby that's already born."[2] The vast majority of these same women also agreed that "Abortion is a better choice for me at this time than having a baby." Some women with strong anti-abortion sentiments still choose to have abortions. Approximately one in five women seeking abortion in the Turnaway Study thought abortion was morally wrong or should be illegal.[3]

Some women reconcile their anti-abortion views by characterizing their own abortions as moral given their particular circumstances. Jessica, whom you heard from earlier, identified as "totally anti-abortion" before she was faced with an unwanted pregnancy. She concluded that God created abortions to be used for certain purposes. Kamali, a recent African immigrant to the U.S. and a newlywed, had sought and obtained an abortion because she and her husband were working a lot and didn't feel like it was the right time for a baby. She ultimately felt relieved to have the abortion, but she said that, given her Christian faith, she believes abortion is morally wrong. "Well, for me I did have the abortion, but I still feel even though I did it, I still feel it's not something right unless you have a good reason to do it, because that's just how I grew up, and that's just the kind of teaching I've always known." Many clinics screen women for anti-abortion sentiment and if they find any, urge them to postpone or forgo the abortion.[4] However, it's fair to hypothesize that women who do have abortions and who truly feel the abortion is morally wrong even in their particular circumstances may experience mental health harm due to the abortion.

Second, even if women themselves do not feel that abortion is morally wrong, they may experience negative reactions from others and feel judged by their community or people close to them. One week after obtaining or being denied an abortion, more than half of the women in the Turnaway Study described feeling that they would be looked down upon at least "a little bit" by people close to them (60%) or by people in their community (56%) if others knew they had sought an abortion.[5] Olivia, a 23-year-old white woman living in Minnesota, kept her abortion secret for this very reason. "I was always taught that [abortion] was wrong," Olivia told us. "I guess there are so many people that don't know about [my abortion] because that was always the way it was projected to us, that it was wrong. So, I kind of had to just keep it to myself and numb it to myself because you couldn't really talk to anybody about it. You know, it was always one of those things, you just don't do it. My sisters would have been like, 'I would have taken [the baby].' Or, even my dad or boyfriend's parents would have said the same thing. For so long, it was just so hard because you had to figure out how to keep it to yourself. And knowing that you had this human being inside of you, the hardest part was, I need to talk to somebody about the fact that we could have gone with other options, but this was what best suited us."

Third, physiologically, women's mental health could potentially be affected by the sudden change in hormones that comes from not being pregnant anymore, the same changes that are thought to partially explain the experience of postpartum depression (although the latest scientific review casts some doubt on the role of hormone changes in predicting postpartum depression).[6] Some women experience depression symptoms in response to the normal hormonal changes in the menstrual cycle, so it is possible that some women would have reactions to the sharp drop in estradiol and progesterone that accompanies the end of pregnancy.

Fourth, getting an abortion can be isolating. Like Martina (whom you just met) and Camila (whom you'll meet after chapter 7), some women don't share their experience with their family and friends, or when they do, some receive a negative stigmatizing reaction. In our study, nearly one-third of women told no one other than the man involved that they were seeking an abortion.[7] Give birth and you may make friends with women in the waiting room of your doctor's office, with parents in the park, with strangers in the supermarket. Really any mom within a mile radius of your home whose kid is the same age as your kid, whether you have anything else in common or not, is a potential new friend. The same is definitely not true of abortion. As far as I know, there are not special friend groups who all got their abortions at the same time.[8] Now, it could be that people don't need support for getting over the emotions of an abortion like they need support for the continued demands of raising a child. But a total lack of support may cause distress and isolation.

Fifth, the procedure itself can be unpleasant and painful, even emotionally traumatic. A friend of my mother's had an abortion in the 1970s and reported that the doctor performing it said he was making sure it hurt so she wouldn't get herself into that situation again. I know another woman who, in the middle of a two-day abortion procedure (the purpose of the first day is to begin gently opening the cervix), started to experience cramps and raced back to the clinic. Unfortunately, the clinic wasn't open yet. Her fetus and the placenta fell out into her underwear in the parking lot of a locked clinic with nobody to help her. She stood there thinking her uterus had just fallen out of her body and that she was about to bleed to death. The vast majority of abortions are not like these two cases, but it is possible to have a terrible experience.

And finally, the explanation that I think is most likely for why an unintended pregnancy might bring up negative emotions and cause depression or anxiety: An unintended pregnancy is a moment when your life feels like it is out of your control. Your body is creating another life against your will. You may feel it is your fault, that you have made a mistake or put yourself in a bad position, adding guilt to the feeling of helplessness. Realizing that your life isn't stable enough, your partner or family isn't support- ive enough, and your bank account isn't big enough can come as quite a reckoning. You'll see in the stories woven throughout this book that the reaction of the man involved to hearing about the pregnancy is often a low point emotionally of the woman's story. It can come as an unpleasant discovery to find that your partner doesn't have the same vision for the future as you do.

Why might abortion not adversely affect women's mental health?

So with all these arguments for how abortion might harm women's mental health, what are some reasons why abortion *wouldn't* harm women's mental health? First, having an abortion is something that women choose to do. If they thought they could not deal with the consequences, they might not choose it. They have weighed their options and decided that they would be better off terminating the pregnancy than having a baby. So even if they think it may be difficult to cope with the abortion, they anticipate it being better than coping with a birth.[9] Such was the case for Sydney, a 30-year-old black woman from Illinois, who definitely did not want to be forever tethered to the "verbally abusive boyfriend" whom she was with when she became pregnant. Sydney's abortion experience was unpleasant. She was in her second trimester, and she did not like that it was a multiple-day procedure; it disturbed her to think about the fetus inside of her. This was her second abortion, and she remembers her first, at age 21, as "excruciatingly" painful. But even that first experience did not dissuade her from having another abortion because she knew she still was not ready to be a parent. And she says she felt neither regretful nor depressed after either abortion. "Having a child is a beautiful, wonderful thing. But for me at the time, it just wasn't a good thing. I don't regret it, but sometimes I'm wondering, am I going to be able to [have a child] when the time comes?"

The second reason that abortion might not hurt women's mental health is that many women have much bigger things going on in their lives besides the abortion. You will get a sense of that in the section on post-traumatic stress. There are events that are strongly associated with lifetime mental health harm: childhood abuse, childhood sexual abuse, and violence. In a long, complicated life, abortion may not be a big enough event to disrupt a woman's psychological well-being. That definitely was the case for Melissa, whom you will hear from later in this book. The mother of four was experiencing poverty, depression, and anxiety at the time she became pregnant with a relative of her incarcerated husband. She did not have enough money to feed all her kids and had to take them to various soup kitchens. She was desperate for an abortion and greatly relieved when she got one. And for some women, an abortion seems to have no emotional impact at all, as you'll see in Nicole's story, which follows this chapter.

Mental Health History
of Women in the Turnaway Study

The whole premise of the Turnaway Study is that what separates the women who received an abortion from those who were denied is a few weeks of pregnancy, and that they are otherwise similar. If that is so, whatever differences emerge over the five years after seeking an abortion would likely be due to whether they got an abortion or were turned away. So here is the first test of the study design. Did the women who received an abortion and those who were denied differ on baseline mental health? In terms of history of mental health disorders, there is no difference between women who were just over and just under the gestational limits: one-quarter of women had at some point been diagnosed with anxiety or depression (5% with only anxiety, 10% with only depression, and 10% with both anxiety and depression).[10] In terms of experiences of violence and trauma, other known risk factors for future mental health problems, there is no difference between women just over and just under the gestational limits: 14% had experienced violence or the threat of violence from an intimate partner in the past year, more than one in five had a history of sexual assault or rape, and 26% had a history of child abuse or neglect. And for what may be either a symptom or a cause of mental health problems, there were no differences in reporting of any illicit drug use (14%), binge alcohol use (24%), or problem alcohol use (6%)—for example, drinking first thing in the morning or experiencing blackouts. Both Brenda and Margot had many of these difficulties. Both experienced troubling teenage years and were sent to traumatizing lockdown facilities. Both later dealt with drinking problems and forged romantic relationships with abusive men. But Margot received her abortion, and Brenda did not.

You may be surprised by how high these numbers are, in part because these are topics we rarely discuss in a data-driven way. Actually, women seeking abortions are no different from women in general. The proportion of women in our study who have used drugs, who have a history of heavy alcohol use, and who experienced a history of depression are all similar to national estimates.[11]

The Mental Health Consequences of Abortion versus Birth after Unwanted Pregnancy

Social psychologist Dr. Antonia Biggs, my colleague who wrote the paper about why women have abortions, also analyzed most of the mental health data in the Turnaway Study. The paper she led about the five-year trends in women's depression and anxiety is, deservedly, one of the most heavily cited from Turnaway.[12] It was the second-most-viewed article in *JAMA Psychiatry* in 2016 and 2017 and was featured in more than 68 news outlets, including the *New York Times* and Fox News. This is the paper that Justice Kennedy was looking for when he bemoaned the lack of reliable data a decade before, and the paper that Surgeon General Koop had requested decades earlier.

It thoroughly quashes any idea that abortion causes depression or anxiety. Starting one week after they had first sought an abortion, we asked women every six months about their symptoms of depression, anxiety, and post-traumatic stress using validated measures—survey questions that have been tested in other studies and have been shown to accurately identify respondents who have a certain condition or characteristic. We asked about suicidal thoughts, alcohol and drug use, self-esteem, and life satisfaction. By the time of our first interview, eight days after the women received or were denied an abortion, women in both groups were equally likely to report symptoms of depression, post-traumatic stress, or suicidality. But there were short-term differences on other mental health and well-being outcomes. Shortly after being denied an abortion, women had more symptoms of anxiety and stress and lower levels of self-esteem and life satisfaction than women who received an abortion. Over time, women's mental health and well-being generally improved, so that by six months to one year, there were no differences between groups across outcomes. To the extent that abortion causes mental health harm, the harm comes from the denial of services, not the provision.

The higher initial distress observed at baseline may be because the experience of an unwanted pregnancy is upsetting. Such distress may include the anticipation of all the extra social, emotional, and financial costs, and future health risks associated with birth and parenting, as well as the search, travel, and other hurdles experienced trying to obtain an abortion. So some of the worse mental health outcomes among those denied abortions may be due to the stress of still seeking but not finding abortion services.

Yet once the pregnancy was announced, the baby born, and the unknown fears and expectations realized or overcome, the trajectory of mental health symptoms seems to return to what it would have been if the woman had received an abortion. I admit I was surprised about this finding. I expected that raising a child one wasn't planning to have might be associated with depression or anxiety. But this is not what we found over the long run. Carrying an unwanted pregnancy to term was not associated with mental health harm. Women are resilient to the experience of giving birth following an unwanted pregnancy, at least in terms of their mental health. This doesn't mean that there aren't cases of perinatal depression, as Camila describes experiencing just before her baby was born. In general, women's symptoms of depression and anxiety are slowly relieved following an unwanted pregnancy, regardless of how that pregnancy ends.

We also find no evidence that having a later abortion is associated with greater risk of mental health harm compared to an earlier abortion. Women having later abortions reported elevated stress and depression at the first interview (one week after seeking an abortion) compared to first-trimester patients, but after that first interview, there were no differences over the remaining five years. That is, women who received later abortions had the same frequency of depression, anxiety symptoms and cases, self-esteem, and life satisfaction as women in the first-trimester group. Next time you hear that women are particularly troubled by having a later abortion compared to an early one, know that the science doesn't bear that assertion out.

You might think that the similarity between women who received and women who were denied is because both groups are doing miserably—one group is depressed because they had an abortion and the other because they are raising a child that they didn't want. But you would be wrong. Look at Figure 2, which shows the actual trajectory in depression over time. Mental health outcomes improved among all groups of women over time.

Figure 2

Trends in Symptoms of Depression

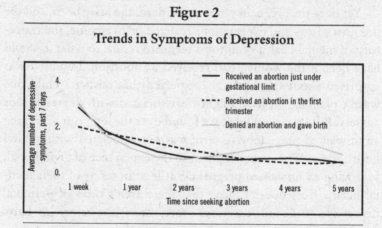

Adapted from Biggs MA, Upadhyay UD, McCulloch CE, et al. Women's mental health and well-being 5 years after receiving or being denied an abortion: a prospective, longitudinal cohort study. *JAMA Psychiatry.* February 2017;74(2):169–178.

Suicidal Ideation

As I described earlier, we did collect data on the incidence of suicidal ideation. As part of one set of validated survey questions about mental health, we asked women whether they had thoughts of ending their life and, on another, whether they had thoughts that they would be better off dead or thoughts of hurting themselves in some way. If a woman answered yes to either of these, we stopped the interview and started a separate set of questions that looked at whether she was imminently suicidal: whether she was planning to kill herself or hurt herself so we would know whether to intervene.

Dr. Biggs found very low incidence of suicidal thoughts among women in the study.[13] Over 7,851 interviews, there were 109 times when study participants reported any suicidal thoughts. In only four interviews did the woman express that she had an actual plan to harm herself. We called the police to the trailer of a Spanish-speaking woman in Texas. She was alone with three children when she reported to us that she had a plan to kill herself. That call to the police could have made things much worse for the woman if police intervention had jeopardized her custody of her children, by casting doubt on her ability to raise them. Fortunately, she participated in subsequent interviews, her mental health improved, and she still had her children at the end of the study.

One other episode occurred the day before Christmas Eve, early in the study. A young woman with a history of depression and sexual abuse reported to our interviewers that she had been cutting herself. She was alone at the time of our interview, so we put her on hold and tried to reach her father to come be with her. I stepped in for the interviewer and called the participant's father to tell him that his daughter was hurting herself. I told him that his daughter was in a health study in which we ask about mental health. And he immediately said, "Oh, is this the study we signed up for at the abortion clinic?" It turns out he had accompanied her to the clinic and knew all about it. She was already receiving treatment for suicidal ideation so I don't think that getting a call from us changed her course.

The third woman had been in a serious car accident and was experiencing post-traumatic stress disorder symptoms stemming from the accident and the death of her mother and son. And the fourth had off-the-charts symptoms of anxiety and depression as she fought for custody of her two children during an acrimonious divorce. All four of these women reporting suicidal ideation had personal histories of abuse or neglect. All four had received their wanted abortions (two in the first trimester and two in the second) and all felt that the abortion was the right decision for themselves.

We told all women in the study that they were free not to answer any questions that made them uncomfortable. We also told them we might intervene if they mentioned any plans to harm themselves or others. To test the possibility that women who were suicidal might have simply skipped these questions, we looked at who refused to answer these questions. Only seven women skipped a suicidal ideation question at any of their interviews, a lower fraction of missing responses than most questions. All these women were just under the gestational limit or in the first trimester. Dr. Biggs conducted a separate analysis where we assumed that five of the seven, those with any symptoms of depression, may have had unreported suicidal thoughts. Even including these five, there was no difference between women who received and women who were denied abortion in the probability of having suicidal thoughts over the next five years.

And finally, to make sure that we had a complete measure of suicidal ideation, we needed to make sure that nobody who was lost to follow-up actually died by suicide. So after we completed all the interviews, we searched for death records of any women in the study who did not do all five years of surveys. Eight women who enrolled in the study died over the next five years. Four women received abortions just under the gestational limit and four were denied the abortion and gave birth. None were in the first-trimester group. None had a history of depression or suicidal thoughts. Two died in car accidents, one who received and one who was denied an abortion. One woman who received an abortion died from a heart attack, and three women died from unknown causes (one who was denied and two who received abortions). If you're doing the math, you'll notice that still leaves two deaths to be explained. I'll tell you more about those in the next chapter, the saddest results from this whole study, in the section about women who die after giving birth.

The Turnaway Study data are clear. There is no evidence that receiving an abortion increases the chance of suicidal ideation. In our study, what predicts suicidal thoughts is a history of depression or anxiety and prior problem levels of alcohol use.

Drugs, Alcohol, and Tobacco

My colleague Dr. Sarah Roberts, whose paper on substance use as a reason for abortion I mentioned in chapter 2, is an expert on the topic of substance use in pregnancy and so she was aware of the well-documented reductions in drinking, smoking, and drug use that often accompany pregnancy. In the Turnaway Study, she was interested in whether women who carry unwanted pregnancies to term experience these same reductions. I was interested in what happens to women who get their abortions—whether these women might increase alcohol or drug use as a response to abortion, as suggested by anti-abortion advocates.

Dr. Roberts found no differences between women who received and women who were denied an abortion in alcohol use, binge drinking, smoking, or drug use in the month before they realized they were pregnant; the two groups started out the same. But over time, their substance use differed substantially.[14] Even one week after seeking an abortion, women who were denied the abortion were less likely to be drinking alcohol and less likely to be binge drinking than women who received one, not because the women who received an abortion were drinking more but because those who were still pregnant were drinking less. See Figure 3. Unfortunately, we did not see the same reductions in smoking or drug use during pregnancy among those who were denied the abortion and carried the pregnancy to term. Among those with symptoms of an alcohol disorder (like blacking out or drinking first thing in the morning), we also didn't find reductions in alcohol use among women continuing their pregnancies. Neither women who received nor those who were denied an abortion showed an increase in alcohol problem symptoms, tobacco use, or drug use over the five years: these were level over time. That means that women are not turning to these substances to cope with having an abortion. But it also means that women who are carrying unwanted pregnancies to term who smoke, use drugs, or have problem alcohol use may need help to reduce substance use and the resulting chance of adverse outcomes for the baby.[15]

Figure 3

Trends in Alcohol Use in the Past Month

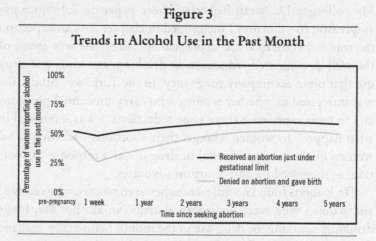

Adapted from Roberts SCM, Foster DG, Gould H, Biggs MA. Changes in alcohol, tobacco, and other drug use over five years after receiving versus being denied a pregnancy termination. *J Stud Alcohol Drugs*. Mar; 79(2):293–301.

Self-Esteem and Life Satisfaction

There are some areas for which we thought that women who have babies would be better off than women having abortions. We anticipated that women who had babies might have higher life satisfaction, even though they originally wanted an abortion. Raising a child might be a challenge, but it can also bring joy, a sense of accomplishment, and recognition from one's community: people throw baby showers but almost nobody throws an abortion shower.[16]

However, Dr. Biggs did not find higher life satisfaction among those forced to carry the pregnancy to term than those able to get their wanted abortions.[17] Women denied an abortion initially reported lower self-esteem and life satisfaction than women who sought and obtained an abortion. These were measured on a five-point scale: 1—not at all, 2—a little bit, 3—moderately, 4—quite a bit, and 5—extremely. For the question "In the past week how much have you felt high self-esteem?," the averages are 2.6 (among women denied) versus 2.9 (among women who received). For life satisfaction, "In the past week how much have you felt satisfied with your life?," the difference is 3.1 versus 3.3. These are small but statistically significant differences. For both women above and those below the gestational limit, self-esteem and life satisfaction improve over the next few years, but with women who were denied abortions and carried the pregnancy to term improving more rapidly, so that by six months to a year, they were similar to women who received their abortion just under the limit. Women having babies caught up to women having abortions in life satisfaction and self-esteem, but the joys of motherhood that I anticipated finding did not lift women denied abortion above those who received one. We also measured the woman's emotional bond with the child born after the denial of abortion and compared it to bonding with the next child born among women who received an abortion. I'll share those results in more detail in chapter 7. Suffice it to say here that women report poorer bonding with the child born from an unwanted pregnancy than the child born from a subsequent pregnancy, one they chose to carry to term.

Stress and Social Support

Perceived stress is an individual's self-reported appraisal of the degree to which situations in her life are overwhelming. Stress in pregnancy is associated with poor outcomes for the woman and baby. One could easily imagine that becoming pregnant when you don't want to be would be highly stressful. We measured stress through the Perceived Stress Scale: four questions asking study participants about how often they felt overwhelmed or unable to cope, such as "How often have you felt difficulties were piling up so high that you could not overcome them?" and "How often have you felt that you were unable to control the important things in your life?"[18]

Dr. Laura Harris, at the time a medical student at UCSF and now a physician in Contra Costa County, California, led this analysis focusing on the first 2.5 years.[19] She found that, at the baseline interview, women who were denied abortions reported higher stress in the previous week than women who received an abortion (5.7 vs. 4.7 on a 16-point scale where higher indicates higher stress). However, we were fascinated to learn that by six months the two groups had converged and stress levels were similar between women who received and women who were denied abortions for the next two years.[20] Women in the first-trimester group were less stressed than women in the group that received an abortion just under the clinic gestational limit—further evidence of the trials associated with the hunt for a clinic that can perform their abortion, and the economic stress of paying for the procedure and handling the costs and logistics of getting there.

We measured social support through 12 questions about the availability of emotional support from friends, family, and others (how much the women agree with statements like "I can talk about problems with my friends"). We were surprised to find no differences in emotional support between women who received abortions and those who were denied and delivered babies—not at one week and not over the next five years. Women scored 3.2 on a scale where 4 represents the highest level of emotional support, with no differences between women who received and women who were denied an abortion.

In retrospect, I wish we had measured financial and logistical support, rather than just emotional support. I suspect that the amount of partner and family practical support is critical to women being able to take care of their children. Such was the case for some of the women recounting their experiences in this book, including Brenda (whose mom helps her take care of her baby before eventually adopting the child), Camila (whose husband supports her financially and whose aunt gives her a flexible job), Melissa (whose family helps out immensely with her fifth child, allowing her to go back to school), and Sofia (whose mom doesn't know about her first pregnancy but really helps out with the second). As we noted earlier, women experiencing unwanted pregnancy and seeking abortion are disproportionately low-income (half have incomes below the poverty level). And you'll see in chapter 6 that denial of abortion exacerbates these financial difficulties. Where one might hope that a woman having a baby after an unwanted pregnancy would be supported by family, we do not see evidence of that in terms of an increased chance of living with adult family members in the long term.

Post-traumatic Stress Disorder

The Turnaway Study presents an opportunity to see whether women who have abortions experience more symptoms of post-traumatic stress disorder (PTSD) than women who carry an unwanted pregnancy to term. Any medical procedure could be a traumatic experience, and abortion is no exception. We heard many reports of women who felt that the care they received was gentle or kind, as well as a few who felt it was not. It is also possible that the experience of becoming pregnant when one does not want to be, not to mention the 11 pregnancies caused by rape, would be traumatic in and of itself. For a woman who wanted a child but did not have the social support or resources to raise a child, there could be a feeling of abandonment by her lover, friends, and family.

There are screening tests for PTSD used in medical clinics to identify patients who need help. We used the Primary Care PTSD Screen. The question starts, "In your life, have you ever had any experience that was so frightening, horrible, or upsetting that, in the past month you . . ." and then lists four symptoms of post-traumatic stress (PTS): "had nightmares or thought about it when you didn't want to; tried hard not to think about it or went out of your way to avoid situations that reminded you of it; were constantly on guard, watchful, or easily startled; or felt numb and detached from others." If a woman said yes, we asked her what event was so upsetting and the date or age at which the event occurred. My colleagues Antonia Biggs and Brenly Rowland (then an interviewer for the Turnaway Study and now a medical student at UCSF) independently coded the events into broad themes including pregnancy, experiences of violence, relationship issues, and other factors. They determined who had any symptoms (yes to any of the four), who was at risk of a clinically significant case of PTSD (yes to three or four of the items) and who identified the pregnancy, abortion, or birth as the source of their symptoms.

Dr. Biggs found that almost two in five women (39%) in this study reported any PTS symptoms and 16% were at risk of PTSD.[21] In the baseline interview one week after the abortion was sought, there were no differences in symptoms by whether the woman received or was denied an abortion. It doesn't seem like abortion can be a major cause of PTSD when women are just as likely to have PTS symptoms whether they got their abortion or not. So what did the women in our study report was the cause of their PTS symptoms? Really awful events. Among the 139 women at risk of PTSD (exhibiting three or more symptoms), 44% reported violence, abuse, or unlawful activity, like the woman whose abusive partner strangled her and put her in a coma for two weeks. Or the woman who, as a teenager, was, for three days, locked in a room, raped, and beaten. One in six (17%) reported nonviolent relationship issues like their mother's drug use or their husband going to jail. Another one in six (16%) reported nonviolent death or illness of a loved one with, for example, HIV or cancer. Seven percent mentioned health-related reasons including mental health issues and substance use, like the woman who said, "I have allergies so I almost died. I didn't know if the people around me were going to save me," and the woman who reported, "I almost died from being on drugs." Finally, 5% of women at risk of PTSD reported issues around their custody or with caring for their existing children, like the woman who said, "My kids are in foster care; my visits with my kids are very hurtful." Or the one who reported: "I was molested when I was younger, so I'm afraid for my daughter."

Many people in our study have very difficult lives with traumatic events and challenging circumstances that could easily overshadow the experience of an unwanted pregnancy or abortion. Yet 19% of those who reported any symptoms of PTS reported that the index pregnancy (for which we recruited them into this study) was the source of their stress. We found no difference in whether the woman received or was denied the abortion in reporting the index pregnancy as a cause of her symptoms. Overall, of all the women in the study, 14% of those at risk of PTSD at baseline reported the index pregnancy or abortion as the source. What did women mean when they reported the index pregnancy as a cause of PTS symptoms? Some (19) women simply said "the abortion"—without describing whether it was needing an abortion, the procedure, the decision, or some other reason that was the cause of their stress. A few women (3) specified that arriving at the decision to have an abortion was the source of their symptoms; as one woman put it: "The actual decision to have the abortion. To know the baby's not going to be here and there was a baby." Some (20) women attributed PTS symptoms to the pregnancy experience; for example, "Finding out I was pregnant because I was nervous and had all the sickness." For four women, it was other people's response to the abortion, such as the woman who observed, "My cousin was against it because she couldn't have a baby. My cousin said horrible stuff about it to me," and for three participants in the study, it was being reminded about the pregnancy, for example, "Seeing small children makes me feel guilty that I did something wrong." Five women reported that the rape that caused the index pregnancy was the source of their symptoms and one reported that her distress was from being denied the abortion. Over time we found that the index pregnancy as a source of trauma declines for all groups of women in the study. The finding that PTS symptoms were similar regardless of whether women got the abortion or not suggests that it is the circumstances around the pregnancy rather than the abortion procedure or internalized stigma/guilt about abortion that causes PTS symptoms. But abortion is a personal event and women vary in their responses. The abortion experience may cause PTS symptoms in rare circumstances, even if, as is the case in this study, the vast majority (92%) of women who had an abortion and report PTS symptoms still indicate that abortion was the right decision for them.

Emotional Response to Abortion and Abortion Denial

Even if women don't experience a deterioration in their mental health, as measured in clinical diagnoses or symptoms of depression or anxiety, we anticipated that they still may have emotional responses to having had an unwanted pregnancy and to having an abortion. And so we asked women about six emotions: four negative (regret, anger, sadness, and guilt) and two positive (relief and happiness). At their very first interview, we compared the emotions of women one week after they either received or were denied a wanted abortion. Before the Turnaway Study, no reliable data existed as to whether women's emotional responses vary based on how far along they are when they seek an abortion—do women feel worse about a later abortion than an earlier abortion? And we had very little idea what it would be like, emotionally, to be denied a wanted abortion because nobody had studied people in that situation.

We came up with a few improvements over how abortion emotions have been studied in the past. First, we wanted to know how women felt about the pregnancy separately from the abortion. If you ask someone, "How was it to have an abortion?" they could say, "It was terrible" and mean, *It was terrible to be in the situation where I needed an abortion but given that I was in such a situation, the abortion wasn't too bad.* Or they could mean, *The situation was difficult, and getting an abortion made me feel much worse.* So we asked women what emotions they'd had about the pregnancy in the past seven days and, separately, what emotions they had about the abortion. Second, we asked about the six emotions independently. So one could report being both happy and sad, both regretful and relieved. Finally, we were also able to ask those who were unable to get their abortion how they felt about being turned away. My colleague, epidemiologist Dr. Corinne Rocca, analyzed these data.[22]

How did women feel *about their pregnancy* a week after seeking the abortion?—at least "a little bit" of sadness (74% of women), regret (66%), and guilt (62%), and just under half reported feeling anger (43%). There was no difference between women who received versus were denied an abortion in how they felt *about their pregnancies*, with one exception. We were asking about emotions one week after women either received or were denied the abortion and, at that point, women who were denied were more likely to feel happiness about the pregnancy than women who received an abortion (60% vs. 27% for those just under the limit who received). However, the fact that women denied abortions were still less likely to report happiness about the pregnancy than regret and sadness tells me that we can't say that those who report happiness were entirely glad they became pregnant.

In contrast to emotions about the pregnancy, emotions around the abortion—or the denial of the abortion—differed significantly one week later between the women who received and those who were denied. Overwhelmingly, the most common emotion felt after having an abortion was relief (90%); meanwhile, the most common emotion a week later about having been denied an abortion was sadness (60%), followed by regret (50%), relief (49%), happiness (43%), and anger (42%).

Perhaps not surprisingly, some women were more likely to feel negative emotions about having had an abortion than others. In general, we found few differences in emotional response by age, race, ethnicity, and education. Over the five years, women who reported having more difficulty deciding to seek an abortion also felt more negative emotions, as did women who perceived that abortion was looked down upon in their communities and women with less social support.

Dr. Rocca, who led this analysis of women's emotions after abortion, is also an expert in measuring how women feel about pregnancy, both before and after it occurs. She doesn't view pregnancies as either entirely intended or entirely unintended. Instead, she believes women can have a range of nuanced or complex feelings about pregnancy that fall on a spectrum of intendedness. One measure of how "intended" pregnancies are is called the London Measure of Unplanned Pregnancy; you'll see more about it in chapter 7 on children's outcomes.[23] As for women's emotions, we found that the more planned in advance a pregnancy was (based on this London Measure), the more likely women are to have negative emotions after the abortion. So a woman who perhaps wanted another child but couldn't afford to raise one might have experienced more sadness and guilt after her abortion than a woman who definitely didn't want to get pregnant at all.

Contrary to many people's assumptions about how difficult it must be to have an abortion later in pregnancy, as stated earlier, we don't find differences in the emotions women have about the abortion by whether it happened in the first trimester or later in pregnancy. I think most people would find this very surprising, but remember that most women who have later abortions haven't been agonizing about it for months. Instead, many have only recently discovered they're pregnant. (Of course, this doesn't apply to women carrying wanted pregnancies who later find out about serious fetal anomalies or dangerous health risks and are suddenly faced with a tragic decision. But again, we did not study women seeking abortions for these reasons.)

Some abortion opponents argue that abortion probably causes emotionally damaging effects that might not exist right after the abortion, but might emerge later, after some time has passed. Our study was able to look at how the emotions expressed a week after seeking the abortion changed over five years. Overwhelmingly, women who had abortions expressed declining intensity of all emotions—both negative and positive—over time, with the biggest declines happening in the first year. By five years, only 14% of women felt any sadness, 17% any guilt, and 27% any relief, with relief remaining by far the most commonly felt emotion five years after.[24]

The most common emotional response to having had an abortion is none. Over time, two-thirds of women say that they experience no or very few emotions about the abortion anymore. Using a scale where 0 means "never" and 4 means "all the time," the answers to the question "How often do you think about the abortion?" show a decrease over time. At six months, the average was equivalent to thinking about the abortion "sometimes" (1.8). By three years, the average was "rarely" (1.2). Women in the Turnaway Study may think about their abortions more than women who were not in the study since we reminded them about their abortion every six months as part of the interviews. As Amy said, she thought about her abortion "only when you call me."[25]

We were not surprised that some women in our study expressed some negative emotions about having had an abortion. Feeling bad does not indicate a clinical pathology. Negative emotions can be a normal response to a life event or difficult decision. If we found increases in negative emotions over time, that would be concerning—an indication that women were having difficulty coping with their abortion or having a change of heart. But instead we found decreasing negative emotions and, in fact, a decrease in intensity of all emotions and less frequent thoughts of the abortion over time.

Reporting That Abortion Was the Right Decision among Those Who Had One

And finally, here is the most famous statistic from the Turnaway Study. The idea that women regret their abortions has had powerful sway in legislation and policy. Justice Kennedy upheld a law banning a later abortion procedure with the justification that "some women come to regret their choice to abort." As we've seen, the idea that women are likely to regret ending their pregnancy is part of the justification for various restrictions: mandated waiting periods between seeking an abortion and receiving one, patient information scripts, ultrasound viewing, and parental consent. Before Turnaway, we didn't really know how often women actually regret their abortions. Clearly some do, like Kaya, a participant who completed an in-depth interview five years after signing up for our study. Kaya grew up on a Native American reservation and later moved to Oklahoma. She told our team that she thinks having an abortion in 2008 allowed her to have a third baby at a better time in her life. But she also reports feeling a lot of regret and doesn't recommend it to other women. "I felt really regretful afterwards," Kaya said. "I called my cousin right away and I cried to her over the phone. I told her this was awful and I will never do it again." There are websites and social organizations for women who feel that they suffered for having had an abortion. Testimonials from women who regretted their abortions submitted as an amicus brief to the Supreme Court were likely where Kennedy got the idea that women feel regret.[26] At least he was wise enough to say that the data are not necessarily representative of all women seeking abortion.

Dr. Rocca found that, at every interview over the five years after their abortion, 95% of women reported that having the abortion was the right decision for them.[27] In a statistical analysis that adjusts for baseline characteristics of the women and the gradual loss to follow-up of some participants, we found that the chance of saying that abortion was the right decision increased gradually over the five years.

You might wonder who the women were who, over time, felt like having had an abortion was not the right decision. One group of women more likely to report that abortion was *not* the right decision over time was women who reported high community stigma about abortion; that is, they felt that people in their community would look down on them if people knew they had sought an abortion. The other group less likely to feel that they had made the right decision was, not surprisingly, women who said in our first interview that the decision to have an abortion was "very difficult." But over time, even women who reported that the decision was very difficult were increasingly likely to say that the abortion was the right decision for them, nearly approaching the level of decision rightness among women for whom the decision was not difficult. See Figure 4.

Figure 4

Percentage of Women Who Received an Abortion Who Report It Was the Right Decision, by How Difficult It Was to Decide to Have the Abortion

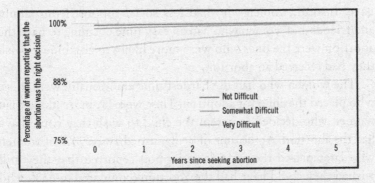

Adapted from Rocca CH, Samari G, Foster DG, Gould H, Kimport K. Emotions and decision rightness over five yers after abortion: an examination of decision difficulty and abortion stigma. *Soc Sci Med.* 2020 Jan 2:112704.

The Turnaway Study provides strong evidence that the vast majority of women do not experience difficulty coping with their abortion and that, consistently over time, they believe that the choice to end their pregnancy was the right one for them.

Reporting That They Wished They Could Have an Abortion among Those Who Were Denied

How do women feel about having been denied an abortion? Initially, bad. But over time, most of the women who ended up carrying the unwanted pregnancy to term reconciled themselves to their new reality, especially after their babies were born. One week after abortion denial, 65% of participants reported still wishing they could have had the abortion; after the birth, only 12% of women reported that they still wished that they could have had the abortion. At the time of the child's first birthday, 7% still wished they could have had an abortion. By five years, this went down to 4%.[28] Who are the small percentage of women who have a baby but still wish they could have received an abortion? Dr. Rocca found no differences by age, race, ethnicity, or the number of children they have. Instead, women who had less social support from family and friends and women who had an easy time deciding to have the abortion were the ones who were more likely to continue to wish they had received an abortion.

The women who had the hardest time emotionally were those who placed the child for adoption. They were far more likely than women who decided to parent the child to wish they could have had the abortion. At the time of being turned away, 90% of women who later placed the child for adoption reported that they still wished they could have had the abortion (compared to 63% who later chose to parent the child). At five years, 15% of women who placed for adoption, compared to 2% of women who parented, reported that they still wished they could have had the abortion. I'll discuss more findings about adoption decision-making in chapter 7. But I think it is fair to say that women who chose to place the child for adoption may have had different circumstances—ones that did not offer the option to parent. Not raising a child means the woman does not have to reconcile what might be a jarring disconnect between her current love for a child and her previous desire for an abortion. She may feel more free to continue to wish she could have had the abortion.

Some women view the experience of having the child as a total positive—like Camila, whom you'll meet after chapter 7, who says about having been turned away from an abortion, "I could not imagine my life not choosing to keep my baby—to keep the decision that the clinic gave me." And then there are women like Brenda, whom you'll meet after chapter 9, who might have rather had the abortion but were eventually able to find some silver linings from having been turned away.

Conclusions about Mental Health after Abortion and Abortion Denial

The Turnaway Study documented the trajectories in symptoms and diagnoses of depression, anxiety, PTSD, suicidality, and alcohol and drug abuse for women five years after they received or were denied an abortion. We found that, in the short run, women *denied* abortions have worse mental health—higher anxiety and lower self-esteem—than women who receive an abortion. The longer-term results are surprising, no matter what side of the abortion debate you are on. There are no long-term differences between women who receive and women who are denied an abortion in depression, anxiety, PTSD, self-esteem, life satisfaction, drug abuse, or alcohol abuse. This is *not* because both groups are miserable. In fact, mental health steadily improves for both groups of women. This improvement over time tells us that the experience of becoming pregnant and discovering that one lacks the social and material support to support a baby can be deeply distressing. Whether one has an abortion or even carries an unwanted pregnancy to term, mental health improves. Women are resilient. Women don't often say they want an abortion for fear of what an unwanted pregnancy would do to their mental health. And mental health rarely seems to suffer, even when abortion is denied.

Some events do cause lifetime damage, but abortion is not common among these. What is linked to higher likelihood of mental health problems over the long term? The biggest predictors are a history of mental health problems and a history of traumatic life events such as childhood abuse and neglect.

Women experience a range of emotional responses to having had an abortion, including a small subset of women who report regretting their decision. The concern that women might experience negative emotions or regret does not suggest to me that the government should step in and try to make decisions for them. I do not think it is the government's role to mandate extra time to think about the decision, especially since mandated waiting periods make the experience more expensive and difficult for women and providers. Women should have a right to make their own personal decisions, even decisions that they might regret. The idea that denying someone the autonomy to make decisions is worse than the possibility that they might feel regret is what Katie Watson, a bioethicist at Northwestern University, has called the "dignity of risk," as she wrote in an essay in *JAMA: The Journal of the American Medical Association*.[29]

> The dignity of risk is a concept articulated in the 1970s to challenge clinicians' impulse to withhold options from people with disabilities unless good outcomes were guaranteed, and it's shorthand for the fact there is no opportunity for success without a right to failure. The dignity of risk reminds us that overprotection is harmful too. American patients' modern status as autonomous decision makers is grounded in the foundational premise of bioethics: that competent adults must be allowed to take chances and risk pain in pursuit of a better life. The unstated premise of the abortion regret claim

is that regret is bad—regret harms patients in some way, and patients should be protected from harm—but we can't have it both ways. To the degree decisional regret is harmful, the regressive remedy of eliminating or reducing competent adults' decision-making authority is worse.

The next woman whose story you'll read breaks every taboo about abortion emotions and regret. She does not conform to any expected narrative about the contrition women are supposed to feel about having become pregnant. Nicole expresses no feelings for her embryo. This clearly surprised the staff at the abortion clinic, who made her speak to three counselors before proceeding to give her an abortion. I don't think her attitude is typical; instead her story helps illustrate the range of emotional responses that women have when they experience an unwanted pregnancy.

NICOLE

*I'm glad that I did it. I just wish that I didn't have
to be in that situation where I needed to do it.*

I grew up in a college town in Ohio. So I was exposed to a heavy
party/drinking type of an atmosphere and all the stupid that
came with it. When I actually got to that age, I didn't not drink,
but I didn't get stupid with it because I'd seen all the crazy things
that the college students do.

I grew up in this historical reenactment group. There were
weekends where we would go to an event with a whole bunch
of other people. It was kind of cool because the historical group
always had the best Halloween costumes. It really separated all of
us from the other kids. We were creating things with our hands
and doing all sorts of work and being self-reliant. My mom's side
of the family thought it was pretty cool. My mom's side is filled
with academics. There's a ridiculous amount of hard scientists that
are in historical reenactment. There's not as many historians as one
would think because we aren't super into making it completely
accurate. We like comforts like propane cooking and sneakers.
Historical shoes really hurt.

When I was really little, my dad left. And there are different reasons why, but I'm not entirely sure what all it was. But for the most
part, it was my mom who raised me, and then during the summer
I would go up to my grandparents'. My dad I would see generally
on weekends and in the summer, but there were a lot of times that

I don't really remember where he was. Whenever he got back into the town, he would try and have me with him for a while.

My mom had me in a Catholic school, and because of the science that was in my life, I asked a lot of questions that they didn't like me asking. Up at Grandma's I knew not to even bother trying to ask some of those questions because I knew it would just not end well.

I was in college, and I was in a relationship that really wasn't healthy at all. I just wanted a guy. I started seeing this kid, Charles. One of my friends said that he was kind of crazy, but I blew it off. On the phone after a while he did start to get kind of crazy, but by that point I had already signed a cell phone contract with him. I felt like I was stuck to him for the next two years; I was thinking I'd just deal with it. It was a long-distance relationship at first. We were on other sides of the state. He would get crazy protective and super jealous and freak out. For a month we broke up and I started seeing somebody else, and then we got back together. He thought that I had been cheating on him, even though we were broken up. And then a few months later I moved in with him. That summer I got pregnant. For a while I was just hoping that I was just really late because I was stressed and that maybe it would kind of come back and my flow would be there, and everything would be fine.

I really didn't want to believe that I was pregnant. And then I started feeling really unwell in the morning. And I accepted my fate. What really pushed me into accepting it was that I had gone home for the weekend, and my mom took one look at me and was like, "Are you pregnant?" "No." She kept bugging me all weekend about it until I finally caved in and told her that I hadn't had my period in a while. She said that she wasn't going to tell my dad or my stepdad because they were likely to kick my boyfriend's ass.

I'm really bad at making doctor's appointments. I don't even know why. It would have been a lot cheaper if I had called and gotten it taken care of earlier because they would have just been able to give me a pill. I was trying to pretend that it wasn't there, but once Mom got involved that wasn't an option, because she actually

Nicole

kept up on me to make sure that I got rid of it before it became a permanent issue. Because, like, my parents didn't like him. I knew I wanted to get rid of it. I just didn't really know the process, and I was really scared. I wanted so much for it to go away on its own because I knew it was going to be expensive.

Luckily I had health insurance at the time through my mother, and I went to the gyno. They did a test, and they said, "Yeah, it's there." She told me what I need to do to be able to get rid of it. I knew at that point I didn't want to spend the rest of my life tethered to this guy because of a kid. I was still in college. I didn't see any reason at all to keep it. Charles tried to talk me out of it a few times. He knew that I was not one for children. But he thought, now that we're pregnant, maybe this will change your mind. It's like, no, this is just bad; this needs to stop.

I was only even able to afford to do it because I had called my ex-boyfriend. The ex I would talk to every now and then. He really didn't like Charles, either. He wired me money, and if I didn't get that, I don't really know how things would have turned out. He had told me that if I need anything at all to just ask. When I realized that I needed a few hundred dollars to be able to get rid of it, I knew that he would be a safe option to ask without my parents freaking out. Because my mom wouldn't have been able to even get me that money without my stepdad noticing it, and being like, "Why did you give her four hundred dollars?" It would have been tricky to ask anybody else.

I definitely didn't want to do adoption because there are already enough kids in the foster programs. There doesn't need to be another one. That, and because of my asthma and everything. I can hardly breathe inside or outside; I don't want to pass on all my medical stuff. I think that's kind of cruel, especially when there are so many kids that need a home. If I consent to taking care of a child, I'm going to pick up a kid that needs a home, not create one.

My mom was upset that it happened, especially since I had been on her insurance—I could have had birth control. I had just not made it to the doctor to actually get it. So she was a little upset.

133

When I finally got myself to go to my doctor, she gave me piles of information. She told me that there was a place in Pittsburgh that would do it. The only hoop that I had to jump through was that in Pennsylvania you have to make this phone call, and you have to do it between these certain hours in the day where the doctor can give you a disclaimer about how you don't have to have an abortion. If they didn't answer, you had to keep calling back. I felt like I was trying to get tickets to a concert from a radio show. You keep calling, and you're like, "Am I caller number nine? Am I getting it?" That was the most annoying part of getting everything set up to go there.

It was during summer. I was working at a rest stop. When I had to take off to go and get it taken care of, I talked to my one manager that I felt comfortable with. I told her, "Hey, this is happening, and I have to go get rid of it." And she's like, "Okay. Take as much time as you need. I'll get it covered. And just get them to write you a generic doctor's note." She was the only one there that knew about it, but she said that she was going to take care of everything on the managers' side so that the other managers didn't get weird or question me about why I suddenly needed several days off. She was really helpful with that.

At the clinic they were really nice. They seemed a little shocked that I wasn't stressed, or as stressed as they expected me to be. I guess for the most part they deal with women who are getting an abortion because they have to, not because that was their first decision. They also spoke to the guy that I was seeing, and he needed the support from them more than I did. I understood why I had to go and I had to talk to all these people, and I had to do all this stuff before they would finally suck it out. They were really nice about it. It was just annoying to me—just get it out of me. Like, shove a vacuum up me and rip that thing out and let me go home.

There was a lot of talking about my feelings and going over the different things, like, that could happen psychologically. There was one discussion that I felt was relevant was the medical side effects and how my hormones would be reacting the days after that. And how to take care of myself for the next few days. I had to see three different psychologists before they would finally let me get it done. I don't know if everyone had to see all three or if it was just because I was like, yeah, no, I'm just getting this abortion, and they thought I was trying to hide how I was feeling. A lot of the other girls that were there, some of them were definitely really stressed out by the entire situation.

I'm a wimp, so I made them knock me out. And the last thing I remember is I was talking to the anesthesiologist. I told her that I have asthma. And she said, "That's fine. I have an inhaler right here next to me." And she put me under—she set everything up so I'd go under. I saw on the monitor where it was attached; it kind of looked like a peanut. I remember being a little surprised by the doctor because he just shoved that thing right up there. Didn't give me any warning. I was just like, "Whoa, Doc, got to ask a lady out to dinner first." And we kind of joked around a little bit. They were really funny up until I passed out. And then I woke up in a chair, and I was wearing a diaper because I guess a lot of stuff comes out afterwards.

Because of everything involved in that and the crazy hormone spikes, I grew really attached to Charles again afterwards, and I stuck around, even though he was verbally and even physically abusive at that point. He had quit his job just after I had the abortion because he wanted to be home for me, and then he never, never got a job after that.

I was also taking one summer class, and it was really stressful. It was also really stressful because Charles kept thinking that I was seeing somebody else when I was on campus studying. I couldn't study in the apartment because he would smoke, and my asthma was really bad. There was, like, no circulation in the place, so the smoke just stayed in the air. I was having a whole lot of trouble breathing all the time. And if I was trying to study in the apartment, he was always wanting to be having sex, or if he was watching something on TV, he would call out for me to come and see whatever it was that was on TV, and by the time I got there, of course, it wasn't there anymore. So I didn't get any studying done.

Then the semester after the pregnancy it was really annoying because I had to work until ten o'clock at night, and I'd have to be at class at eight o'clock in the morning, and I just wanted to study and go to bed. He would just come in randomly, and if I didn't give in to him, we'd end up fighting. I would fight until I was tired. I was uncertain that he would let go of me and he'd pull my head out of the pillow. After a while it started to get really bad whenever I wouldn't sleep with him. Charles would say all of the regular things that abusive guys say, like, "Oh, you know, nobody is going to love you like I do. You're just trash."

My parents didn't really know what was going on, and they still don't know everything that he did to me, so it also put a big strain on my relationship with my parents. My mom would call, but she would hardly ever come down to visit. My stepdad and I really didn't talk at all. It was really just my dad that stayed active in my life, and I'm really glad that he did. Because towards the end, that really helped when I was like, "No, I'm done with you. I have to leave." That would have been a year after the pregnancy, and two years that we had been together.

My best girlfriend, Hannah, found out that her boyfriend was cheating on her. So I went back home to help her out. While I was home and around my friends again and away from him, I realized how much happier I was. I started trying to figure out how to leave because I felt like I was trapped there. I had felt like everybody abandoned me—that nobody wanted to deal with me and all of the stuff with him. Being home was when I realized—it's like, no, no, I still have a whole lot of people.

Later I drove back down and packed up a whole lot of my stuff in the apartment. I had to work, and I told my manager that I needed to go home and get out of this really bad situation, and he was really good with it and gave me a whole bunch of boxes. While Charles was away, I packed up most of the rest of my stuff and then just left. So I was gone by the time he came back home.

Last I heard, the next girl he started seeing, he pushed her, and she wasn't having any of that shit, and she called the cops. I haven't talked to him in years.

I started seeing all my friends that I didn't get to see because of Charles. One friend died in the Middle East protecting the rest of the people that were with him. He was the only one that even got hurt, let alone killed. I didn't get to go see him while he was back home that summer because if I had said, "Hey, I'm going to go visit my friend on the other side of the state. Oh, by the way, he's a guy," that wouldn't have ended well at all.

At the end of that spring, I moved back home. I decided to take a break from school. It was supposed to be my final year there. But my [grades] started to fall because I was really depressed about my friend. The next semester I tried again to pick everything up, and I couldn't do it.

A couple months later, I started seeing this guy, James, but I wasn't being too serious. I had just gotten out of a relationship. I didn't want anything. I'm still with him. Last fall we moved to Colorado to go to a school for technology. We knew it was a pretty risky thing at that point. We'd been together for three years. We didn't have the money to be able to move in together, so I was still living with my parents. He was still living with his parents. The only personal vacation the two of us took was when we came out to visit the school for a week. So we didn't really know what it was like to live together, and we were moving all the way to the fourth corner of the country. We knew it was dangerous. But we really liked the way the school looked, and when we came to visit, we had a whole lot of fun together. We just hit our four-year mark. It's abso-fucking-lutely amazing.

I can breathe in Colorado. Except for that little dry spot in the back of my throat. I can smell things. I'm a lot healthier. I'm not in better shape, but my lungs are healthier. I don't live on my inhaler anymore.

Because of my transfer credits from the previous university, I'm going to graduate here next year. We just had career fair last week;

I met somebody from really big companies in the tech industry. He gave me a whole lot of pointers. James and I got to go to dinner with him, and he's awesome—really cool. So a lot of cool things have even happened this last week.

I'm kind of getting a little worn out, and the school provides free therapists. At the end of the summer semester I started seeing one, because—it sounds weird to me when I say it—but when Robin Williams died, my world kind of crumbled. They suggested seeing her because, like a lot of the times before, comedy was one of the things that helped me get through stuff, and Robin Williams specifically helped me get through a lot of stuff. Finding out that he wasn't there anymore, it just kind of crashed a little bit. But I'm seeing her, and I'm feeling a lot better. We're actually going to start working on everything with Charles next. I'm a little afraid to do that, but I know that I need to, and while it's free I should.

That entire abortion experience is something that I use to help other girls that I talk to figure out stuff. There's a girl right now who is in an emotionally abusive relationship. He hasn't crossed the threshold to being physically abusive, although he has done some things that I consider to be warning signs. I've told her this guy knocked me up. I'm fine with getting an abortion, but if you're not, that baby is going to tether you to him for the rest of your life.

Some of my friends knew. But my dad still doesn't know that it ever happened. Once he was watching the news, and I looked at him, and I was like, "So, like, if you find out that I had an abortion you'd be pretty furious with me?" And he's like, "Yeah, I would be really mad at you." It's like, "Oh, okay. Not going to tell Dad about that." No one else in the family knows it happened other than Mom.

I'm upset that I was in this situation, but I'm really glad and proud of myself for actually getting the abortion and not caving in to what he wanted. I'm glad that I did it; I just wish that I didn't have to be in that situation where I needed to do it.

It looked like a peanut. In the ethics class, we were talking about when is something considered alive. I've always thought it was when it has a personality of some sort. I'm really not interested in having or even raising children. I've always really wanted to have a farm full of horses, and both of those things are very expensive. I would rather have the horses. James wants kids, and that's the only point in our relationship that I'm a little uneasy about, because I don't. He doesn't want to push me into doing a life commitment that I don't want. And I don't want to keep him from having kids. I don't know if this is just time I get to spend with him until he leaves to go off and have a family. He feels like he can convince me that having kids would be awesome. But right now I work at the local library, in their computer lab, and I do not enjoy those children. I put up with them, but I do not enjoy it.

I want to definitely graduate by the end of May. That's partially because I'm also going to run out of financial aid, so I have to. I guess for life goals, there are a couple of companies that I think would be really amazing to work for, but my ultimate dream has always been a farm with horses. I'm pretty hopeful because everything with the career fair, everyone seemed to really like me. Everyone that my career adviser talked to said that they really enjoyed talking to me. Everything seems to be looking up right now. I feel like—I feel like I got this.

Nicole, a white woman from Ohio, was 20 years old and 10 weeks pregnant when she had an abortion.

CHAPTER 5

Physical Health

State governments have enacted 555 restrictions on abortion since the Turnaway Study began recruiting women in 2008.[1] As we've learned, some of these—mandatory waiting periods, ultrasound-viewing requirements, state-written counseling scripts—may be intended to make sure that women are fully informed when they make the decision to terminate a pregnancy, that they feel confident about this decision. Of course, the need for such decision-making help from the state is not rooted in evidence. What Turnaway data show, as I discussed in the previous chapter, is that very few women regret their decision to have an abortion. Other restrictions claim to be justified on the promise that they will improve the safety of abortion. These abortion-safety laws include those that mandate that a physician have admitting privileges at a nearby hospital, meaning the doctor has to have an agreement with a local hospital that they can admit patients to the hospital and care for them there in the case of an emergency. An agreement like this is difficult to obtain and maintain, since it often requires a certain volume of patients needing admission to the hospital. Another law justified on the grounds of abortion safety demands that outpatient abortion clinics adopt the infrastructure of ambulatory surgical centers, such as wider hallways and specialized recovery rooms.[2] Is there a need for more laws to increase the safety of abortion?

If you've seen movies like 2008's *Revolutionary Road*, where Kate Winslet's character is deeply unhappily pregnant with a third child, you could be forgiven for thinking abortion is dangerous (spoiler: things don't go well for Winslet's character). One in six women die after having an abortion—that is, if the abortion occurs *on television*.[3] But you don't have to be watching fictional movies or TV shows to get this impression; interviews with advocates on both sides of the abortion debate emphasize its dangers. People advocating for legal abortion hark back to the pre-*Roe* era, when there were whole hospital wards treating women for sepsis after they had gone to untrained providers or tried to self-induce an abortion with unsterile instruments, like coat hangers. Those opposed to abortion rights claim that mortality following legal abortion is still high and in need of government regulation.

So let's review the actual facts about abortion risks.

My colleague Dr. Ushma Upadhyay studied complications after abortion in the California state Medicaid program (Medi-Cal). California is one of the 15 states that covers abortion for low-income women regardless of their reason for wanting one.[4] She found that complications occurred after 2% of abortions—lower than the risk of wisdom-tooth extraction (7%), tonsillectomy (8–9%) and childbirth (29%).[5] The risk of a major complication from abortion—needing surgery, a blood transfusion, or hospitalization—is less than one-quarter of 1%. That is, one major complication in 436 abortions. The risk of a minor complication—such as bleeding or a treatable infection—is one in 53. And what about deaths from abortion? Dr. Upadhyay relied on data from 54,911 abortions performed in California between 2009 and 2010. There were no deaths following abortions paid for by Medi-Cal in these years. The death rate from abortion was zero. One state, even a large one, is not a big enough sample to study abortion-related deaths because they are so rare.[6] So let's turn to national data from the Centers for Disease Control and Prevention over eight years (1998–2005). Drs. Elizabeth Raymond and David Grimes found that one woman in 160,000 dies as a consequence of receiving an abortion, while one woman in 11,300 dies from childbirth. A woman in the United States is 14 times more likely to die from carrying a pregnancy to term than from having an abortion.[7]

Pregnancy is not a disease, but it is a major body change that is associated with very serious risks. The pregnant person's entire circulatory system goes into overdrive, producing 50% more blood than normal, with radical changes in hormonal systems and metabolism.[8] Physically, all the abdominal organs and muscles have to move to accommodate a ten-plus-pound uterus. The joints in the pelvis and spine loosen to allow for the pelvis to open enough to let the baby's head pass through. And all of that is just for the pregnancies that go normally. Although efforts are under way to reduce this rate, one-third of deliveries involve major surgery, a Cesarean section.[9] One in four births in the U.S. is associated with some serious complications, including obstetric trauma and laceration (8%), infection (6%), hemorrhage (4%), gestational diabetes (4%), and severe preeclampsia (3.4%) and eclampsia (high blood pressures in pregnancy that can develop into dangerous seizures) (0.1%).[10] For women with chronic health conditions, pregnancy is even more complicated. The list of conditions made worse by pregnancy fills medical textbooks. The fact that women regularly choose to endure this and are often thrilled with the outcome shouldn't blind us to the fact that pregnancy is a risky endeavor.

Synthesizing the scientific literature on abortion safety, the National Academies of Sciences, Engineering, and Medicine issued a report summarizing the data in 2018, its first report on the safety of abortion since 1975.[11] The National Academies report found that "clinical evidence clearly shows that legal abortions in the United States—whether by medication, aspiration, D&E, or induction—are safe and effective. Serious complications are rare."[12] The report did point out that later abortion is associated with greater risks than earlier abortions. They write, "The risk of a serious complication increases with weeks' gestation. As the number of weeks increases, the invasiveness of the required procedure and the need for deeper levels of sedation also increase." So this leaves open the question of how a later abortion compares to giving birth. Since all national statistics comparing birth and abortion include intended pregnancies, it was not known, prior to the Turnaway Study, how the relative risks of birth and abortion compare in the context of an unwanted pregnancy.

Women sometimes have abortions to end wanted pregnancies—these are the tragic stories of women with life-threatening health conditions or fetuses with serious anomalies. Some of these abortions are taking place in circumstances in which the woman's health is already compromised, so physical health outcomes may be worse than for abortions of unwanted pregnancies. We thought the risk from birth might also be different for deliveries following unintended (versus intended) pregnancies for two reasons. First, women who are in good health may be more likely to choose to become pregnant and, once pregnant, may be more likely to choose to give birth than women with serious chronic health conditions. In the Turnaway Study, recall that one in 20 women seeking abortion did so because they did not feel healthy enough to continue the pregnancy and give birth.[13] By limiting the comparison to women with unwanted pregnancies, we can compare the relative risk of birth versus abortion for women who are pregnant and don't want to be. Second, women who don't want to become pregnant aren't taking prenatal vitamins, getting medical care, or abstaining from drugs or alcohol in preparation for pregnancy. About half the women in our study who were denied an abortion didn't realize they were pregnant until the second trimester. If a lack of prenatal care or pregnancy preparation put women at risk of worse outcomes, we would expect that women delivering an unwanted pregnancy might have worse outcomes than those who deliver a wanted pregnancy.

The Turnaway Study gives us the chance to address questions about pregnancy, abortion, birth, and health. The study design—comparing women on either side of the gestational limit—has an additional advantage in that it created a data set of women who were later in pregnancy than most women seeking abortion. So we have a large sample of women having a late second-trimester abortion to look at how the risk of a later abortion compares to an earlier one. As the National Academies report finds, abortion is safer the earlier in pregnancy it occurs. That's because early in pregnancy, a woman has an option to either take pills (known as a medication abortion[14]) or have a simple procedure in which a clinician uses a small tubular vacuum to empty the uterus (called manual vacuum aspiration or MVA). The pills in medication abortion can be used up until 10 weeks of pregnancy and are even safer than commonly used medications such as Tylenol, aspirin, and Viagra.[15] Later abortions, defined as abortions after 20 weeks, make up just over 1% of all abortions.[16] But they require special skill and training to perform and are associated with greater risk due to the increased technical difficulty of the procedure, the need for the cervix to be dilated, and the increased blood flow to the uterus as the pregnancy advances.[17] Many health risks of pregnancy increase as the pregnancy progresses, separate from the risk of the procedure. So if someone is forced to delay getting an abortion, they may, in the meantime, develop dangerous health conditions like preeclampsia.[18]

Before we get to the Turnaway Study results, let's check the study design—that recruiting women just over and just under the gestational limits produced comparable groups of women healthwise. Eighty-one percent of women in the study reported that their health had been good or very good before they became pregnant, with no significant differences between women, regardless of whether they received a first trimester abortion, received a second trimester abortion or were turned away. There were no differences in the experience of life-threatening accidents (17%) or serious illness or injury (14%). Prior to pregnancy, the playing field was level. Differences we see in physical health over time, therefore, are likely due to the experience of pregnancy, abortion, birth, and child-rearing.

Risks of Abortion versus Birth

Ibis Reproductive Health epidemiologist Dr. Caitlin Gerdts led the analysis of Turnaway Study data on the outcomes of pregnancies, both abortion and birth, with nursing doctoral student Loren Dobkin and University of California, Davis, physician and professor Dr. E. Bimla Schwarz.[19] Our interviewers asked each woman whether she experienced any side effects or health problem directly from the pregnancy, abortion, or birth. Interestingly, for all three of our study groups—those who had first-trimester abortions, those who had abortions just under a clinic's gestational limit, and those who were turned away and gave birth—a similar proportion, around 10%, reported side effects and complications.

However, those side effects and complications were not equivalent. Women having abortions reported pain (5%), cramps (3%), bleeding (2%), and nausea/vomiting (2%) after the abortion. For women who gave birth, the complications were much more serious: preeclampsia (2%), anemia, blood loss requiring transfusion, eclampsia, fractured pelvis, infection, postpartum hemorrhage, and retained placenta. When this team of scientists categorized the reported complications by whether they were life-threatening, they found that 6.3% of women who gave birth reported potentially life-threatening conditions, compared to 1.1% of women who were just under the clinic gestational limit and 0.5% of women receiving a first-trimester abortion. We asked women whether there was a period after the abortion or birth when they were physically unable to do daily activities such as walking, climbing steps, or running errands. The days of limited activity also reflect the higher risk of giving birth: women who gave birth reported an average of 10.1 days of limited activities, compared to about three days among both early and later abortion groups.

Longer-Term Risks of Abortion and Birth

One of the most important findings from the Turnaway Study has to do with the long-term health effects of abortion versus birth. Very few studies compare the longer-term health consequences of either of these outcomes for women experiencing an unwanted pregnancy. My colleague Dr. Lauren Ralph analyzed the data on the longer-term health outcomes.[20] For this analysis, Dr. Ralph divided the abortion sample strictly by gestation (first trimester, second trimester) rather than by study group in order to make the most of our data on women having later abortions.[21]

Over the five years, some health outcomes were similar between women who received abortions and those who gave birth. We found no differences in asthma; nongestational hypertension; diabetes; or chronic abdominal, pelvic, and back pain. Also, a bit of bad news for all of us who would like to blame our growing waistline on having had children: we find that the rate of obesity was the same between women who received abortions and those who gave birth. (My mom used to tease my sister and me, "I never had gray hair before I had you." The downside of being a scientist is now I know that blaming my pants size on my kids is equally illogical.)

To the extent that there were differences in health outcomes between women who received and women who were denied an abortion, they were all to the detriment of women who gave birth. Women who were denied abortions and delivered the unwanted pregnancy were more likely to have chronic head pain—23% chronic headaches or migraines among women giving birth, compared to 17–18% of women receiving an abortion. Women denied abortions were also slightly more likely to report joint pain. On the broadest measure of health, asking women to rate their overall physical health on a five-point scale from very poor to very good, women who received an abortion showed slight improvement over the five years, but those who gave birth were increasingly likely to report poor health. After five years, 20% of women who had a first-trimester abortion and 21% of women having a second-trimester abortion reported poor or fair health. Among women denied an abortion, 27% said their health was fair or poor. See Figure 5. This difference may seem modest, but it is extremely important. This one question about self-rated overall health has been shown to be a strong predictor of a person's future health and mortality.[22]

Figure 5

Trends in Self-Reported Fair, Poor, or Very Poor Physical Health

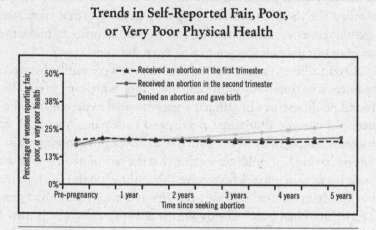

Adapted from Ralph LI, Schwarz EB, Grossman D, Foster DG. Self-reported physical health of women who did and did not terminate pregnancy after seeking abortion services: a cohort study. *Ann Intern Med*. 2019;171(4):238–247.

One of the risks of continuing a pregnancy is the risk of gestational hypertension—increasing blood pressure that can lead to preeclampsia and even death. Gestational hypertension and preeclampsia also increase the risk of developing cardiovascular disease later in life.[23] Women denied an abortion were more likely to experience gestational hypertension over the five years—9.4% of those who gave birth, compared to 4.2% of those who had a second-trimester abortion and 1.9% of women in the first trimester. At first glance, this finding is not surprising since women denied abortions remained pregnant for many more months after they were denied the abortion. But, as you'll see in chapter 7, many women have pregnancies in the following five years, so this index pregnancy wasn't the only opportunity to develop gestational hypertension. Having gestational hypertension in one pregnancy puts women at increased risk for having it in subsequent pregnancies. So denial of abortion may put subsequent pregnancies at higher risk.[24]

Interestingly, over the five years, we found no differences in chronic conditions, chronic pain, and overall self-rated health between women having a first-trimester abortion and those receiving a second-trimester abortion. Considering that later abortion procedures are more difficult to perform and are associated with a greater risk of complications than an early aspiration abortion or use of medication abortion, we were pleasantly surprised to have found no residual long-term health consequences.

Deaths

The serious risks of continuing a pregnancy were clearly demonstrated by the women in our study. One day, we received an awful call from a woman asking us to withdraw her daughter from our study. Her daughter had died in her mid-twenties, days after giving birth, from an infection that is rarely fatal outside of the context of pregnancy. Her mother called us after she discovered the Turnaway informed consent form while she was sorting through her daughter's affairs. Shockingly, her daughter wasn't the only woman in our study who died after giving birth from a pregnancy she had preferred to terminate.

After we completed data collection for the whole study, we reviewed public records, looking for any additional deaths among women who did not finish the five years of interviews. We wanted to document whether any of these deaths might have resulted from physical health complications or mental health problems stemming from the pregnancy. In our search, we found another tragic maternal death—a woman who died of eclampsia soon after childbirth, just three months after being denied the abortion. Had she arrived at the abortion clinic five days earlier, she would have been able to end her pregnancy and might have had a long life ahead of her. The baby survived and is now, along with the woman's previous children, orphaned.

This level of maternal mortality is shocking. These two deaths translate to a maternal death rate of about one per 100 women delivering in the Turnaway Study. For comparison, the U.S. rate of maternal deaths per live birth is 17 per 100,000 (0.017%).[25] So 1%, the rate in our study, is astronomical, 100 times higher than national maternal death rates. Clearly, there is a large margin of uncertainty around this figure of a 1% death rate because death is such a rare event. To come up with a definitive death rate, one would want to study hundreds of thousands of deliveries. But it does highlight the fact that carrying a pregnancy to term and childbirth are risky, much riskier than abortion. All the stresses of carrying an unwanted pregnancy to term and perhaps the lack of social support that made that pregnancy unwanted in the first place may substantially increase the risk of death for women who prefer an abortion.

We find no deaths stemming from abortion in our study. Four deaths occurred to women who received an abortion just under the clinic gestational limit. These deaths were not related to any physical risk from the pregnancy or abortion; they occurred at seven months, one and a half years, three years, and five years after the woman received an abortion. For the half for whom we know the causes of death, they were due to freak events like car accidents and heart attacks that are very unlikely to be consequences of abortion. All these deaths, of young women who should have had their whole lives ahead of them, are tragedies. Because of that, I feel even more strongly that it is important to let people live the life they want to live and not insist that women defer their dreams to an uncertain future.

Conclusions about Physical Health

The greatest irony about the ever-more-restrictive nature of abortion in America lies in the reasoning often given to defend such laws: they are supposed to protect women. Politicians and religious-right interest groups tell us that abortion is dangerous. They claim it can kill you, instantly or more slowly in the form of breast cancer or suicidal ideation.[26] That is the stated premise behind literally hundreds of abortion restrictions passed all over the country in just the last decade. The evidence shows that the opposite is true. Not only is abortion a safe medical procedure; its alternative—continuing pregnancy and giving birth—is far riskier.

The United States is currently facing a crisis in maternal mortality—deaths related to pregnancy and birth. Trends are going the wrong direction compared to nearly every other country, and it is even worse for women of color. Maternal mortality is now twice as high as it was in 1987, with 17 deaths for every 100,000 live births in the United States.[27] Black and Native American women have an over three times greater chance of dying from pregnancy and childbirth than white women. Why? Largely because of systemic, institutional racism and discrimination, which can take the form of doctors and health providers ignoring their patients' serious symptoms and complaints of pain.[28] Of course, it's not just pregnant women of color whose symptoms often go ignored. Jessica is white, yet we see that she also experiences disregard for her symptoms in her previous pregnancies.

Kiara, whom you'll meet next, has a story that leads perfectly into the next chapter, which shows how the ability to access abortion services can shape a life trajectory—the way in which future relationships, children, and careers all hinge on having control over which pregnancies to carry to term and which ones to abort. As Kiara says, "If I hadn't had the abortion, the calmness and the strength and everything that I feel now, I don't think that any of that would have been here. I feel like my life would still be as chaotic and kind of crazy. Even, I think, meeting and marrying my husband I don't think would have been possible had I had the second child."

KIARA

*This termination showed me
the inner strength that I have.*

I have lived just about everywhere. I lived in New York twice. I've lived in—oh, I'm trying to go through all of the states that I've lived in. Let's see. Kentucky, Oregon, California, New Jersey, Florida, Hawaii, North Dakota, Colorado. Virginia. My father was in the military. And then my mom remarried and my stepfather was in the military. So we got to travel quite a bit.

When I was younger, it was always fun for me in the summer. It was like okay, we're getting ready to move and start in a new place. Then towards the end of middle school going into high school, I was like, okay, I'm over moving everywhere and I would like to settle down. It got to be more of a headache and a hassle than an adventure. I told myself I'm not going to move as an adult. I'm going to settle down somewhere and be in one place. And that has yet to happen. I tend to get bored and start looking for somewhere new.

I'm the oldest of three. I'm pretty close to all of my siblings. Because there's such a wide age gap, I tend to be sister-mom, where they come to me asking for advice, or how should I approach Mom and Dad about this. But my mom was always there.

My dad and my mom split up, and then my mom remarried. Then the rest of my siblings came along. My stepdad was in the military. So there's always been structure involved. My mom and

I were just talking about this the other day, and it's always been exciting and loud coming from a big family. We had lots of good, funny memories. We always made dinner together, especially on Sundays. I had an absolutely good childhood.

We come from a Christian background, so we did Christmas and Thanksgiving and all of those things, but it wasn't super strict.

When I got pregnant with my daughter, I decided to move from Kentucky back to New York to be close to my mom. I stayed with my mom throughout the whole pregnancy and for the first 18 months of my daughter's life. Then when my daughter was 18 months, I walked into the kitchen and told my mom, I'm moving back to Kentucky to try to work things out with my daughter's father and I'm leaving in 30 days.

It didn't work, and I decided to stay in Kentucky and continue to go to school and work just because I was comfortable there and the cost of living is fairly low. So I was able to go to school and still provide for my daughter and not feel like I was going to struggle like I would have if I had gone back to New York.

When my daughter was almost three, I was dating this guy who was a horrible guy in every sense of the word. The relationship was physically abusive, mentally abusive. He stalked me. I was already in the process of breaking up with this boyfriend, and then I found out that I was pregnant. I was absolutely devastated. I remember sitting on my couch with my roommate and just crying and sobbing. I just remember us both looking at each other and going, well, what are we going to do? I was like, I will figure it out. But there is just no way that I can keep this baby.

My two options were either I was going to keep the baby or I wasn't going to keep the baby. But it was going to be an immediate decision. I was always one of those people who goes with my gut and my first instinct. My first instinct was to terminate the pregnancy, and I just kept going. I knew that making the decision would be my way out of this relationship and I could close that chapter and go forward and not have to look back or have any strings holding me back. The situation was just a very bad situation. I was continuing to try to be a good mother for my daughter and realizing that I was in no way or shape or form wanting to be connected to this person for the next umpteen years of my life. I was barely making it as a single mother with just one child, let alone two of them.

The clinic was about an hour and 15 minutes away from where I was living. I realized that that was where I needed to go. With what was going on with school and work I knew that I could not go through an entire pregnancy and then give it up for adoption. There was just too much riding on my shoulders for me to have to have any physical downtime.

I had a roommate. Our agreement was I would pay the rent and she was kind of my in-house daycare for when I was at school and at work. I was going to school full-time. I was enrolled in culinary school, almost done, and I was working at that time as a bartender. I was probably working 60-plus hours a week on top of going to school full-time to make ends meet. My roommate basically said, whatever it is that I felt that I needed to do, she would be there for me and that she was there to support me. She didn't really give me any of her own opinions. She just let me know that she'd support me in my decision.

I called the clinic, and they asked me how far along I was. We scheduled an appointment, and they told me what the fee would be and what I needed to bring with me. Since it was so far away from my house, they wanted me to make sure that I had everything with me, because I obviously wouldn't be able to go and then come back. I think the initial phone call was tough, just because I knew that I was going to follow through with it.

Based on my religious upbringing, I did have a little bit of mixed emotions about terminating a pregnancy. I had a little bit of turmoil. I remember when I was pregnant with my daughter, I had told myself that the next time that I got pregnant would be under the right circumstances, where I would be married and be ready to have a second child. Calling to make that appointment and realizing that it didn't happen that way made me pretty sad and disappointed in myself because of what I was trying to accomplish. Having everything just kind of go astray because of an impromptu decision.

I had lapsed in my birth control by, like, two days. My refill was late, and so I had to go back and get it. It was just a lapse in judgment. I was like, oh, it will be okay. And then it wasn't.

The staff at the clinic was very helpful; everyone that I came into contact with was very warm and very nice. I don't remember having any bad feelings about anyone at the clinic or even about the clinic itself. The procedure itself was a little painful. I ended up having to go to the procedure by myself; I drove myself and was there alone. I remember feeling very lonely. Then, I think after the actual procedure itself, sitting in recovery, I was feeling kind of numb. It was towards the very end of the hour and a half drive back to my house that it hit me all at once, and I had to pull over and cry and get myself together.

The emotions that hit me on my way home—those feelings were a little bit of everything: relief that the situation was over and knowing what I would have to do to get away from the situation that I was in; sadness because of terminating the pregnancy; and a little bit of anger, because I was all by myself, because my ex-boyfriend had let me down. But also a little bit of—I don't know if relief is the right word—an acknowledgment that although this was tough and although the situation was really hard, going through it by myself, him having disappointed me again, it solidified that I was making the right decision.

From the very beginning, even though I knew what I was going to do, I did let him know. "Hey, I'm letting you know I'm pregnant; this is what I'm going to do." He let me take the reins on it: "Whatever it is that you want to do." Then, two weeks before my actual appointment, I called him, and I said, "Hey, this is the situation. This is what I'm going to do. I've got the money for this. I'm going to take care of this. The only thing that I need you to do is to ride with me down there and then ride with me back. You don't even have to pay for gas. I will drive. I just would like you there." I remember him saying, "Okay okay okay." Then, two days before my appointment, I sent him a text to remind him, "Hey, the appointment is in two days; I just want to make sure you're going to be there, or do you need me to come pick you up or meet me at my house?"

I didn't get any response for the two days, no response the day before. Even the morning of, in the back of my mind I thought, this is something serious and big. He's not going to just not show up. But he didn't. I literally waited until the very last minute, knowing when I needed to be there for my appointment to give him that time. He didn't call, didn't text. I didn't hear anything from him.

My roommate had offered to go with me, but she also had to stay with my daughter, so there was no choice. I was like, well, I have to go. I have to go. I don't have anyone else to go with me, so I have to go and do this. I was so angry driving to my appointment. It was the sign that I made the right decision. He couldn't be there.

He didn't have any decency to even text and say, "Hey, I'm not going to come," or "Hey, you need to find somebody else." He just left me standing there holding the bag. At that point I was like, this is the best decision because if he can't even be there and ride along with me to my appointment, if I kept the baby, where would we be?

I still feel that it was the best decision. I have never had any second thoughts or second guesses about the decision to terminate. If I were to go back and do it over again, I would still make the same decision.

I moved from Kentucky to New Mexico. I rekindled with an old friend and we got married. We just had a baby. I'm looking at him right now. He's three months old. I am now a stay-at-home mom, which I enjoy very much, because a lot of that time with my daughter was missed because I was working and going to school. So now I get to enjoy taking her to school and picking her up and being a class mom and spending time with my son. That's the last five years in a nutshell, really.

Certainly life itself has become more calm. I have learned a lot about myself—how strong I can be and things that I can overcome. This termination being the thing that showed me the inner strength that I have. Dealing with the abortion, getting out of the abusive relationship and coming out of that intact and whole and still being the person that I am was the biggest thing. Then, obviously getting married and having another child after all of that, it showed me what a strong person I am. My life has come full circle.

My daughter is getting bigger, losing teeth and all of those things. Having the ability to be a stay-at-home mom is a great feeling. I have been going, going, going, so I think the biggest thing for me is being okay with not getting up and working. I worked very hard up until two days before I gave birth. I worked full-time, 45-plus hours a week. I've always worked, worked, worked.

Realizing that yes, I'm a stay-at-home, this is my job, and it's okay to just do it. We're going to sit and relax today and that's okay. That takes a little bit of adjusting for me. I feel like I'm constantly like, oh, I've got to do laundry. I've got to wash dishes. I've got to *do*. My husband's like, you can relax. Take it easy. You give everything 110%, but it's okay. It's been almost four months, and I'm kind of like, okay, I can take it easy, but I don't want to be lackadaisical and feel lazy. So I feel like, what can I fix here, what can we do here?

My daughter has helped me. Especially when it was just the two of us, I always wanted to be able to look her in the eye and have her be proud of me, whether it was with situations that she knew about or didn't know about. Getting up every day and forcing myself to get going and pushing and going harder. She was always my motivating factor.

She was three at the time [of my abortion], and she has very little recollection of anything back then, which is fantastic. She was always the voice in the back of my head that was, you've got to get up. You've got to put one foot in front of the other. You've got to pick up that extra shift. You've got to keep going. That was for her and that always has been.

I am a firm believer that everything happens for a reason. I feel like I needed to know, in order to go forward and be married and bring anything to the table in a new relationship, how I can stand on my own and what I'm made of. So, although yes, it probably would have been easier had I reached out to family members or different friends and overcame it differently. But hindsight's 20/20. Like I said, I still would do the same thing. I would probably do everything the exact same way.

With this newest baby, my husband and I weren't actively trying, but we weren't not trying. It actually happened fairly quickly, so I was like, it was meant to be. I don't think you're ever ready fully. You always go, "It's a good time; let's have a baby." Then, you get pregnant and you're like, "All right, wow. Here we are." So I feel like the timing was as good as it could be.

My life is much more calm and more ready. I was able to enjoy this pregnancy. Not that I didn't enjoy my daughter's pregnancy. But the one that was terminated, there was just no way that I was going to be able to enjoy it. It would have been more of a burden than a blessing. The abortion was a very small piece of my life, but it was also a big factor. After the abortion I really made sure that I was up on my birth control. I didn't want to make any more mistakes. I didn't want to have to put myself back in that situation or have to even entertain that avenue again. Even with my religious upbringing, I feel like my stance on abortion is that it's there in cases of making a mistake. In cases of a rape or something along those lines and a mistake.

A mistake in my mind is you do it once and you don't ever do it again because it's a mistake. A mistake also becomes a learning lesson. If you continue to do the same mistake over and over again, it's no longer a mistake. It's a habit, and I just wanted to make sure that it wasn't a habit.

It was a turning point for me. I became more selective of who I dated, who I let into my circle, who I let affect me, all because of that relationship and that abortion. So it was a very defining moment for me.

I still have some turmoil as far as religious values go. It's something that I will have to deal with in the life after, come Judgment Day. But, because of all the good that's come from it and because of everything, I do feel that it's something that—and this is just my belief—but I feel like it's something that I will be forgiven for and that I have been forgiven for. I did ask for forgiveness.

I thought about it a lot immediately after. Then, moving forward after I made my peace with it, and I've gone forward from there. I don't think about it as much. If the topic comes up or people ask my opinion, I generalize the statement without being personal. It does cause me to pause and reflect about it but it doesn't weigh heavily on my mind all of the time.

If I hadn't had the abortion, the calmness and the strength and everything that I feel now, I don't think that any of that would have been here. I feel like my life would still be as chaotic and kind of crazy. Even, I think, meeting and marrying my husband I don't think would have been possible had I had the second child.

I get a little sad sometimes because I think of the person that I was at that point with everything that was going on. It was a very rough and lonely time, not just with the actual abortion itself, being by myself, but just that time in particular. I still get a little bit angry sometimes at myself for having to allow myself to have gone through that. And I still have the feelings of relief of knowing that I made the right decision and that I was able to make that decision, that it was something that was available to me. I've always felt that life was precious. I've always felt that it was a gift. I don't think [the abortion] changed my perspective. It just made me appreciate others who have gone through that situation, whereas before I was like, "What? How can you do that?" Then, when you're in that situation yourself, it's a little bit different. But, it just kind of opened my mind to people and their situations but did not necessarily change my outlook on life itself.

I'd like to have possibly one more child in the future. If it happens, that's great. If it doesn't happen, that's great, too. Personally, right now my goal is making sure that my daughter gets through school, and she's well-adjusted, and making sure this little guy gets to sleep through the night.

If we don't have another child, then once my son is in pre-school, I'd probably like to go back to school to finish my bachelor's degree. Even if we have another child, it would be something that I would still pursue. It's something that I want to do and I will do, but it's so far in the future that I'm like, we'll cross that bridge when we come to it.

I want to bring that same joy and laughter and silliness that I had growing up to my family now so that they experience it. It does resonate with you. It stays with you as you get older and continues to propel you for your life. I had a great childhood and upbringing and I want to pass that on to my children, so that they can pass that on to their children and keep it going. It all starts from there.

Kiara, a black woman from Kentucky, was 26 years old and 13 weeks pregnant when she received an abortion.

CHAPTER 6

Women's Lives

In 1973 the U.S. Supreme Court established that abortion is a constitutional right, on the basis of privacy. I'm a scientist, not a lawyer, and for the longest time I thought "privacy" in this context meant a teenager could hide her pregnancy from nosy neighbors. Or that a woman didn't have to tell her in-laws that she and her husband did not consistently use condoms. Turns out, that's not what privacy means in the legal world. The U.S. Constitution sets limits on which decisions may be made by government and which are reserved for private citizens. In *Roe v. Wade*, the majority of the Supreme Court justices determined that reproduction is a *private* matter, to be decided by the nation's citizens, not its government. It's a fundamental right. Privacy in this context means the freedom from government intrusion.

Privacy is, to date, the most successful legal argument for reproductive rights. But legal minds have proposed other very powerful arguments, such as equal protection, the idea that everyone should be treated equally under the law. The 1992 Supreme Court decision *Planned Parenthood v. Casey* did not cite the equal protection clause, but the majority opinion asserted, "The ability of women to participate equally in the economic and social life of the Nation has been facilitated by their ability to control their reproductive lives."[1]

Supreme Court Justice Ruth Bader Ginsburg is a longtime critic of *Roe v. Wade*, which was decided 20 years before she joined the Court in 1993. It's not that she opposes the legalization of abortion. Instead she takes issue with what she once called the Court's "incomplete justification" of the decision. Back in 1984, while a judge on the United States Court of Appeals for the District of Columbia Circuit, Ginsburg gave a lecture to law students during which she contended that when it came to *Roe*, the Court should have focused on constitutional arguments centered on equality and sex discrimination.[2] Ginsburg wrote in the lecture, published by the *North Carolina Law Review*, "The conflict, however, is not simply one between a fetus' interests and a woman's interests, narrowly conceived, nor is the overriding issue state versus private control of a woman's body for a span of nine months. Also in the balance is a woman's autonomous charge of her full life's course."

This brings us to the central findings of the Turnaway Study, which allowed us to examine how abortion access affects the course of a woman's life. There's good reason to think that having a baby when one is not ready — or is in an abusive relationship or is already struggling to provide for existing children, say — might make a big difference in one's life's trajectory. Most women (70%) seeking abortion fall between the ages of 15 and 30. These are the years when we decide who we are. The decisions we make — to go to school, to learn a trade, to pursue a career, to settle down with a romantic partner, to have children, to form a new life dream — reverberate for the rest of our lives.

Even without an unwanted pregnancy, the years of early adulthood bring substantial challenges, as can be seen among the women whose life stories intersperse the chapters in this book. Some are in tough situations, raising young children while their husbands are in jail (Jessica and Melissa) or feeling trapped in abusive relationships even as a brighter, more independent future beckons (Brenda, Kiara, and Nicole). For others, the barriers to getting through college were significant, including a car accident (Jessica), mononucleosis (Martina), severe asthma (Nicole), and boyfriends who seem to be actively thwarting their studies (Nicole and Sofia). Some are just beginning their adult lives, unsure about what opportunities might lie ahead (Jada and Sofia).

This chapter is about how receiving or being denied a wanted abortion affects women's employment, education, life aspirations, accomplishments, and even their attitudes toward abortion legality. Remember that the leading reasons women give for wanting an abortion relate to their life circumstances (whether they have the resources, living situation, and social support to have a baby), as well as their life course (whether their hopes and dreams for the future would be thwarted if they had to carry an unwanted pregnancy to term).

Some of the largest differences in the Turnaway Study between women who received and women who were denied abortions are found in this chapter—an increase in poverty; a decrease in employment that lasts for years; a scaling back of aspirational plans; and years spent trying to raise a child without enough money to pay for food, housing, and transportation instead of pursuing other life goals.

We find that women who receive an abortion stay on a steady course, continuing work and school, planning for the future, like Ariela. At age 19, Ariela, a Latina who was among the 31 women who participated in in-depth interviews, had a second-trimester abortion in San Francisco. She'd been pregnant with twins, and it had been a painful decision. But it had also been the right one for her. Ariela had big plans that would have been stalled by having children at that precise time. But more importantly, she felt unequipped to raise a baby, let alone two. "I gave up two lives for myself," Ariela would later tell our research team. "I knew I couldn't support them and I was uneducated, and that always keeps me motivated. Like, I gave them up so I could have a better job, which I do, and so I could go to school, which I'm halfway there, and to have a better life, which I think I'm doing okay." Indeed, following her abortion, Ariela finished college, had a baby when she felt ready, and five years later had plans to go to law school.

It is the women denied an abortion whose life trajectory often took a detour. Amina, another woman who did an in-depth interview, immigrated to the U.S. from Africa by herself when she was

16. Her foster parents were "just okay," she told our team, and she had no network of family support when she became pregnant a few years later and was too far along to get the abortion she wanted. At the time, Amina was already raising a child, and they were barely scraping by. She had chosen abortion to improve life for herself and her existing child, but the clinic turned her away. Two years later, the father of this new baby left, and Amina was alone with the two young children, working hard, living on food stamps, and barely making ends meet, and still without the higher education she'd wanted to pursue when she'd gone to the abortion clinic. "I was trying to go to school to become someone, but I couldn't go because of the pregnancy," Amina told us. Being denied the abortion "does affect my life because I couldn't finish the education that I wanted to."

One-Year Plans

Once every six months, Turnaway Study interviewers called our study participants to ask more than a hundred questions. A few questions were about the abortion participants had, or tried to have, when they first signed up for the study. But most questions were about how their lives were unfolding. These comprehensive surveys might last anywhere from 30 minutes to over an hour. The very last questions were open-ended, and always the same: "How do you think your life will be different a year from now?" Followed by: "How do you think your life will be different five years from now?"

Previous studies have gauged the impact of abortion on women's lives by measuring all women against the same preset goal, like graduation from high school. There's a famous study from the late 1980s led by Dr. Laurie Zabin of Johns Hopkins University, who tracked nearly 400 African American teenage women in Baltimore to learn whether abortion versus birth affected young women's ability to graduate from high school. Back then, it did. Two years after the pregnancy, 90% of the teenagers who chose to have abortions either had graduated or were still in school, while 69% of the teens who chose to give birth either had graduated or were still in school.[3] In the Turnaway Study, we did something different. Instead of measuring everyone's success by the same goal, we let the women tell us their plans, then asked whether they'd achieved what they had set out to do.

Recall that one of the leading reasons for wanting an abortion, reported by one in five women, is that carrying the pregnancy to term would interfere with future opportunities. Many of the other reasons that women reported—not having enough money, not having the right partner, not being ready for a baby—also suggest that having a baby would make it more difficult to pursue one's dreams.

My colleague Dr. Ushma Upadhyay led an analysis of how having an abortion affects one's ability to realize a one-year life plan.[4] The team looked at 1,304 one-year plans reported by study participants a week after seeking the abortion. We categorized all the answers by outlook, determining whether stated plans were aspirational ("Have a better job"), neutral ("Kids will be older"), or negative ("I will probably have less money"). Then we compared their data after one year to see if their lives had changed in the ways they had anticipated.

Women seeking abortions have a lot of plans for the coming year, an average of almost two plans per woman. Most of the plans (80%) were aspirational. This is clear among the ten women we've profiled in this book. The year Amy terminated her pregnancy in Texas, she was 28. She and her husband had just bought a house, and they were planning to soon send their daughter to a private middle school. That same year, over in Arizona, mono got the better of 22-year-old Martina, forcing her to repeat a semester of college. She was determined to complete her degree in the next two years. "My goal was to finish college," Martina said. In Louisiana, 23-year-old Jessica, having gotten the abortion she desperately wanted, was planning to file for divorce from her abusive husband.

About 17% of plans were neutral. In West Texas, abortion-clinic staff informed 22-year-old Camila that she was too far along to have an abortion. They told her she could try Albuquerque, but she opted to have the baby, communicating to our research team a plan that was matter-of-fact, devoid of positive or negative sentiment: "This is your new life, and this is just what's going to happen."

Only 2% of the one-year plans were negative. These were somewhat more common among study participants who had been denied an abortion (8% vs. 1% among those who received the abortion). Twenty-four-year-old Brenda, for example, was too far along when she tried to get an abortion in California and suddenly found herself indefinitely tethered to her violent partner. "I mean, I had no money, no employment prospects," Brenda said. "Because you're not going to hire someone who is fucking four months pregnant, five months pregnant. People just don't do that. So that left me entirely dependent on him for my income. And that was a very bad thing."

Women who were denied abortions were also much less likely to have an aspirational plan for the coming year (56%) than women who received an abortion (86%). In other words, denying women wanted abortions causes them to scale back their plans for the coming year, while allowing women to have a wanted abortion enables them to set more aspirational plans for the coming year. The Turnaway Study also found that the nature of a woman's plan varied according to whether or not she was going to carry an unwanted pregnancy to term. Women who were denied abortions were more likely than women who received them to give child-related one-year plans, like "give a good life to my kids," and less likely to mention employment plans, like "find a new job," or relationship plans, like "I'll be married." Women are changing their plans and dramatically scaling back their non-child-related plan in response to being denied a wanted abortion. Figure 6 shows the types of plans and aspirations among women seeking abortion in the Turnaway Study.

Figure 6

One-Year Plans at the Time of Seeking an Abortion

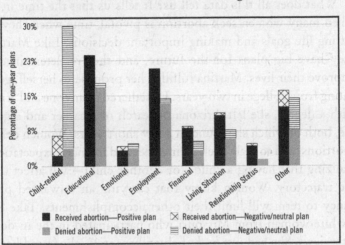

Adapted from Upadhyay UD, Biggs MA, Foster DG. The effect of abortion on having and achieving aspirational one-year plans. *BMC Womens Health*. 2015;11(1):102.

Who achieved their aspirational plans one year later? Among the more than 1,000 aspirational plans we learned about, 87% could be measured with the data we collected in the study. These were specific, concrete plans like earning more money, staying in school, having a full-time job, moving, or having one's own place to live. Among the plans that were both aspirational and measurable, women achieved almost half (47%) of their one-year goals. Women were most likely to achieve child-related plans (89%) and financial plans (73%), and least likely to achieve educational plans (31%) and relationship plans (18%). We did not find any difference in achievement in aspirational plans among those who set one by whether they received or were denied an abortion. However, since women denied were less likely to have an aspirational plan, they are also less likely to achieve one. Women who received an abortion were much more likely (48%) than women who were denied an abortion (30%) to both set and achieve an aspirational plan.

What does all this data tell us? It tells us that the time in life when many women seek abortion is pivotal, time when they are setting life goals and making important decisions. Like Martina, they have big plans for the future, and they're determined to improve their lives. Martina fulfilled her promise to herself, graduating from college in two years. Untethered to anyone and armed with a degree, she left Arizona in search of a career and a good life, both of which she found in a few short years. Women denied abortions tend to scale back their career and financial expectations, realizing that having a child—or another child—will affect their life trajectory. Women know that carrying an unwanted pregnancy to term will limit their other accomplishments. Take Sue, a white woman from Missouri who participated in the in-depth interviews. She had *just had* a baby when, at 25, she found herself pregnant again, and panicking. She and her partner had opted for abortion, because they didn't think they could financially support two babies at the same time. And Sue had had plans. Her first child had interrupted her college education, but she'd been planning to go back and pursue that degree. When Sue discovered she was too far along to get an abortion in Illinois and later discovered that both of her young children have autism, she changed course, eventually finding a job where she could be with her kids and not have to worry about daycare. She put her dreams on hold. "I'd like to go back to school, but I just don't know what hour of the day I would study," she told our team. "So that'll probably be something that I'll have to do either later on, or just a class at a time or something. But eventually I would like to go back and get my degree, but . . . that may or may not happen."

Attitudes toward Abortion Morality and Legality

Before we examine how women's life outcomes vary by whether they received or were denied an abortion, let's examine whether the experience changed their view of whether other women in similar situations should be able to access abortion services. In the Turnaway Study, we found that participants' attitudes toward abortion legality are more favorable than those of the general public. In our interviews, we asked, "Do you believe that abortion is morally wrong?" and "How would you describe your political view of abortion: in favor of women having the legal right to have an abortion, in favor of women having the legal right to have an abortion but only in special situations like rape or incest, or against women having the legal right to have an abortion in any situation?" Only 3% of the women in our sample opposed the legal right to an abortion in any situation; this is much lower than the 15–20% of the general public who report this view.[5] However, it was fascinating to see that there is still a lot of reported ambivalence about the morality of abortion. My colleague Dr. Katie Woodruff found that six months after seeking the abortion, nearly all the women supported abortion legality in all (80%) or some (18%) situations, but 20% also believed abortion is morally wrong.[6] This is still notably less than the 47% of Americans who said abortion is morally wrong in the most recent polls.[7]

Women who had been denied an abortion were more likely than those who had received one to say they had become less supportive of abortion rights (21% vs. 9%), while women who received an abortion were more likely than those turned away to say they had become more supportive of abortion rights (33% vs. 6%). Yet when we asked the same question four and a half years later, about 95% of women who were denied an abortion supported women's legal right to end their pregnancies. Many women, both those who received and those who were denied, reported that the experience made them more sympathetic toward others in the same situation. As Kiara, whom you heard from earlier, reflected five years after her second-trimester abortion: "I've always felt that life was precious. I've always felt that it was a gift. I don't think [the abortion] changed my perspective. It just made me appreciate others who have gone through that situation." Ariela expresses similar thoughts five years after her experience: "It's changed my view of abortions. At first I thought that no one should be allowed to have an abortion with the exception of women who were raped. . . . Then, when I was there with a bunch of girls who were also having an abortion the same day, I kind of understood why women would have an abortion. It's not because they want to, it's because sometimes they have to. Sometimes they would have a better life for themselves because they wouldn't be able to survive their life with a child."

Interestingly, attitudes toward abortion morality are among the few outcomes where race and ethnicity seemed to make a difference. Latinas who'd had abortions were less likely to express that the abortion was the right decision than non-Latinas, both a few days after and years later.[8] Similarly, Latinas who'd had abortions were somewhat more likely to experience negative emotions, including regret, and also more likely to be opposed to abortion rights. African American women were less likely to perceive community stigma around abortion than white women, but also more likely to think that abortion is wrong and be opposed to abortion rights.[9] However, in both abortion emotions and stigma, the broad differences by race or ethnicity explain very little of any individual woman's experience of abortion.

Self-Reported Economic Well-Being

You'll meet Melissa after this chapter, but what's worth noting here is that when the 26-year-old Georgian became pregnant in 2010, she was unemployed, depressed, and desperately trying to feed and raise four children on her own. Her husband was in jail, and Melissa never filed for public assistance because she did not want him to be on the hook for child support when he got out of jail. So she spent her time traveling from one soup kitchen to the next. She felt relief after she received her abortion. She couldn't have imagined supporting a fifth child at that time, under those circumstances.

Not having enough money to provide for a child, or for another child, is the most commonly reported reason women want to terminate a pregnancy. Limited finances might be women's primary reason for abortion, or one reason among many. Either way, not having enough money is understandable, given the high cost of raising a child in the United States. Most women seeking abortions are already experiencing financial hardship. Just over half of the women seeking abortion in our study were, like Melissa, living below the poverty level at the time they sought abortion, consistent with national figures on poverty among people having abortions in the United States.[10] Three-quarters reported that they didn't have enough money to pay for basic living expenses like food, housing, and transportation. We found that women who sought earlier abortions, like Amy, whose story followed chapter 1, were less likely to be poor—likely because having money makes the search for a provider, paying for the procedure, and traveling all so much easier to cover and cover quickly. Not having enough money to raise a child often means you don't have the cash on hand to pay for the abortion, either. Melissa certainly didn't. "It was panic at first, and then it was depression because I thought there was no way I can pay for an abortion, so I'm screwed." In the end a friend helped Melissa, but many women in desperate circumstances are not so lucky. And as we saw in chapter 2, a leading cause of delay in seeking abortion is trying to raise the money to pay for it. It becomes a vicious cycle where delay makes the procedure cost more, and then one needs more time to raise more money. Eventually one may be turned away for exceeding the gestational limits of the abortion clinic.

Whenever we started a new analysis for the Turnaway Study,

like physical health, mental health, and, in this case, economic well-being, we began by checking that those women who were denied an abortion because they were just over an abortion clinic's gestational limit are similar at baseline to those who were just below a clinic's gestational limit and received the abortion. I led the analysis of the economic outcomes, and I found, right off the bat, that these two groups were actually different at the start. Women who were turned away were more likely to report being unemployed at our first interview, one week after seeking an abortion: 60% among women denied an abortion compared to 45% among those who received one. They were also more likely to live with adult family members, such as their own parents (49% vs. 36%).[11] Some of these differences could be because we measured baseline values one week after they were denied the abortion, so they may have moved in with their parents and stopped working in preparation for having a baby. However, because the two groups did appear to differ at our baseline measure, I couldn't just look at whether they differed over time. I needed to determine whether the differences over time between those who received and those who were denied an abortion were more than we expected given the differences at baseline. With the expert help of Maria Glymour, a professor of biostatistics at UCSF, we examined changes in household composition, employment, income, public assistance, and income adequacy.[12]

When women are denied an abortion, their household grows by one person at the time of birth because, as I reported in chapter 4, few women choose to place the child for adoption. Contrary to expectations, carrying the pregnancy to term does not significantly increase the likelihood of living with the man involved, as you'll see in chapter 8. In the short term, women denied abortions are more likely to live with other adult family members. Over time, women denied abortions gradually dissolve their relationships with men and move away from other family members, so that by the end of the five years they are more likely to be raising children alone than women who receive an abortion (47% vs.

39%). What we see in these data is that the burden of raising a child often falls to women alone rather than being shared with a partner or supported by a whole extended family.

Among the women who received abortions, the rate of full-time employment slowly increased from 40% at the time of the abortion to 50% five years later. Among women who were denied abortions, only 30% were working full-time at six months. If this seems low, it really isn't. Remember, they had recently given birth. Some of the women who stopped working around the time of the birth did so involuntarily. Sue, the 25-year-old Missouri woman, was denied an abortion and reported, "A week before I was supposed to go on maternity leave, I got let go, so that was kind of traumatic, because I was eight months pregnant, and now I'm jobless. So, that was very hard, and I don't think that I actually went back to work until my baby was about six months."

It took four years for women who were turned away and gave birth to catch up to the level of employment experienced by women just under the limit who received their abortion. Those years of either steady or unstable employment can have significant impact on women's and their families' economic well-being. It certainly did for Olivia, a 23-year-old white woman in Minnesota who had dropped out of college so she could work and raise her eight-month-old child. When she became pregnant again, she was working as a manager for a retail business and didn't think she could achieve her professional goals at that time with a brand-new baby. So she ended the pregnancy. "Well, I stayed with that employer . . . for ten years, to be successful with what I was doing," Olivia explained. "I was able to travel for them, you know, on a consistent basis, because I had a flexibility with just one kid. I was able to go off and become very successful and teach people things in different states." Both Olivia and her partner felt ready — financially and emotionally — to have a second child a few years after Olivia's abortion. They were planning to buy a house and had enough money to put down a good down payment and hopefully avoid a giant mortgage. "The timing was perfect," Olivia said of this second child. "The only reason I felt that was, we had money—backup, too, if there was an emergency. Whereas before, I didn't have a penny to my name."

To compensate for the loss of employment income, some women who are denied abortions receive public assistance. One in six women (15%) denied an abortion compared to one in twelve women (8%) who received one were receiving welfare benefits at six months, a difference that was significant up until the five-year interview. Food stamp use is higher (44% vs. 33%) among women who are denied abortions. Half of women who are denied compared to only 8% of women who received an abortion participated in the Special Supplemental Nutrition Program for Women, Infants, and Children (WIC)—a nutrition program for new mothers. That was the case for Sue, the woman from Missouri who was denied an abortion; she accessed WIC while she was pregnant and said the program helped her immensely with doctor recommendations and spotting autism early in her children. By one year, there was no longer a difference in WIC use between women who received and those who were denied a wanted abortion, likely reflecting the short duration of WIC eligibility after a birth.

There is little difference in total household or personal income both before and after pregnancy between women who received and women who were denied an abortion. This must mean that gains in public assistance offset losses in employment income, but the comparison is misleading because the same income has to cover more people in the household for the women denied abortion. Imagine trying to raise a baby given all the associated new costs—diapers, childcare, clothes, furniture, toys, formula and/or breast-milk-pumping supplies (especially if you have to go back to work soon)—on the same income that was previously insufficient for just yourself. As a result of being denied a wanted abortion, women are more likely to live in poverty. Six months after our study participants either terminated their pregnancies or gave birth, 61% of those who were turned away were living below the poverty level, compared to 45% who received the abortion. See

Figure 7. They remain significantly more likely to be poor for the next four years. At every interview from six months to five years after seeking abortion, women who were denied an abortion are more likely than women who received an abortion to report that they didn't have enough money to pay for basic living expenses like food, housing, and transportation.

Figure 7

**Trends in Household Poverty for Five Years
after Receipt or Denial of Abortion**

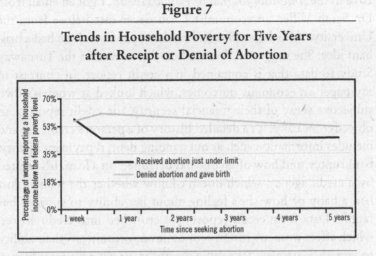

Adapted from Foster DG, Biggs MA, Ralph L, Gerdts C, Roberts S, Glymour MM. Socioeconomic outcomes of women who receive and women who are denied wanted abortions in the United States. *Am J Public Health*. 2018; Mar;108(3):407–413.

The socioeconomic trajectories of women who were denied wanted abortions when compared to women who received abortions show that women denied abortions face more hardships, even accounting for baseline differences. The differences in most economic outcomes such as poverty and employment gradually converge over the five years as women return to working full-time and children enter school; however, as you will see in the next section, there can be long-lasting ramifications of this period of scarcity. Policies that prevent women from terminating unwanted pregnancies result in economic hardship for women that lasts years.

*How does receiving or being denied an abortion
affect women's debt, credit, and economic opportunity?*

Soon after my paper on the effect of abortion receipt or denial on women's employment, income, and poverty came out in early 2018 in the *American Journal of Public Health*, I got an email from Dr. Sarah Miller, an economist I had never met before from the University of Michigan. She had read our paper, and she had a brilliant idea. She suggested that we link the women in the Turnaway Study to data that is contained in a credit report. In contrast to my paper on economic outcomes, which looked at women's own subjective sense of their financial security, the credit report is an objective measure: it's a detailed history of a person's credit use and includes information such as outstanding debt, repayment history, bankruptcy, and how often one has defaulted on a loan. It's created by a credit agency, which doesn't know whether the woman just had a baby or how she's feeling about her ability to support her family. Data from credit reports are crunched into credit scores, which affect women's future economic opportunities—their ability to rent an apartment, take out a mortgage, or get a business loan.

One advantage of credit reports is that we could collect data starting years before the women in the study became pregnant and follow them for a full five years after, even if they stopped participating in the telephone surveys. The only disadvantage is that not everyone has a credit record. People normally show up in credit bureau records when they first get a credit card or a bill in their name.

We went through a convoluted protocol to protect the identity of women in the study, involving requesting data for 50,000 random women with no relation to the study so the credit agency wouldn't know who was in our study. I gave each woman a unique ID number and kept record of which IDs belonged to people in our study. The credit bureau sent back the credit information with the new ID numbers. I sent the data set (without names or other identifiers) to Dr. Miller and let her know which records represented women in the study (as opposed to the 50,000 random women) and whether each one had received an abortion or was denied. Four in five women age 20 and older had a credit score before they entered the Turnaway Study. Dr. Miller brought in her frequent collaborator, economist Dr. Laura Wherry from UCLA, to help with analysis and interpretation. They found that women who received and women who were denied wanted abortions were actually very similar to each other in the three years prior to pregnancy and study enrollment. This is important because the power of the Turnaway Study design stems from the baseline similarity between women who received and women who were denied abortions, allowing us to attribute the difference in their outcomes to whether they got their wanted abortion. As noted earlier in this chapter, one outcome where women seemed to differ one week after receiving or being denied an abortion was employment. This objective data from several years prior to the pregnancy indicate that in fact, even on baseline economic status, the two groups were similar.

Drs. Miller and Wherry separated the credit report data into two types—indicators that showed economic hardship, like bankruptcies, low credit scores, and unpaid debt, and those that showed economic opportunity, like high credit scores and high credit limits. They found that being denied abortion services increased past-due bills by $1,750 on average, a 78% increase relative to the amount that was past due on their credit reports prior to the pregnancy. Over the five years after seeking abortion, past-due bills remained essentially flat among women who received the abortion. The incidence of very bad financial events recorded in public records, like evictions, bankruptcies, and court judgments for bill nonpayment, also increased significantly, by about 81%, for women who were turned away. The differences in credit and financial events persisted for many years following the unwanted pregnancy. See Figure 8, which shows trends in average credit score for both groups. You can see that shortly after giving birth, women denied abortions experienced a shock to their economic well-being and did not catch up to those who received an abortion even five years later.[13]

Figure 8

Trends in Credit Scores Before and After
the Unwanted Pregnancy

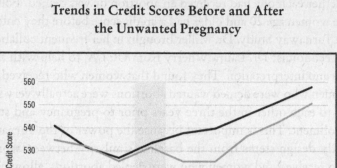

Adapted from Miller S, Wherry LR, Foster DG. The economic consequences of being denied an abortion. National Bureau of Economic Research working paper 26662. Published January 2020.

Using these objective reports of economic well-being shows that being denied a wanted abortion sharply increases the chance of economic hardship, compared to receiving an abortion. And this gap persists over the next five years. We did not find the same gap, however, in measures of economic opportunity—high credit scores, mortgages, or high credit limits—through the credit agency, although these positive indicators were quite low for both groups. These data indicate that receiving an abortion doesn't necessarily increase opportunities, but it often prevents women from experiencing the worst economic outcomes, like bankruptcies and loan defaults.

How does receiving or being denied an abortion affect women's educational attainment?

My colleague Dr. Lauren Ralph, an epidemiologist, is particularly interested in how abortion and early childbearing affect the well-being of teenagers and young adults. There is an unanswered question about whether having children early — while still in one's teens or early twenties — affects a woman's educational attainment and lifetime income. Studies have definitively shown that teenage moms do worse on some measures, including finishing high school or earning higher incomes. But that doesn't mean that early motherhood on its own causes poverty or forces young women to drop out of school. It could be that young women with fewer other opportunities are more likely to choose to become mothers at a young age.[14] With the Turnaway Study, it seemed like we had a perfect opportunity to answer this question of whether carrying an unwanted pregnancy to term versus having an abortion affects educational attainment, because all the women were pregnant and did not choose to be.

At the time of enrolling in the Turnaway Study, a third of study participants were in school, with no differences between those who received or were denied an abortion. However, women who were denied the abortion were more likely than those who received an abortion to be seeking a high school diploma (40% vs. 24% of those still in school) as opposed to a higher degree. This is likely the result of the difference in average age between those who were denied versus those who received (the turned-away women were 1.5 years younger on average). Over the five years the Turnaway Study followed each woman, one-third of the participants who were in school graduated (34%) and a little more than a third dropped out of school (38%). To our surprise, there were no differences in the chance that a woman graduated or dropped out by whether or not she received an abortion. Among graduates, participants denied a wanted abortion were less likely to complete a postsecondary (like college or technical school) degree (27%) than those who received an abortion (72%), but they were also less likely to be pursuing such a degree at baseline. Our finding that abortion versus birth is not significantly associated with women's chance of graduating or of dropping out is at least partially explained by differences in degrees sought at the time of abortion-seeking. In other words, women who received and women who were denied abortions were equally likely to meet their educational goals, but because of the differences in what degree they were seeking, women who were denied an abortion received a lower-level degree than women who received the abortion over the study time period.[15]

The lack of difference we find in graduation rates is surprising. I would like to think that the explanation is that schools are making a big effort to keep pregnant and parenting women in school by providing childcare, flexible schedules, and breastfeeding support. There was a time when as soon as a girl started to show, she would have to leave high school for fear she would inspire other girls to become pregnant, too. These days, laws at the federal and state levels prevent school districts from discriminating against pregnant students and employees and actually require districts to accommodate breastfeeding students and staff.[16] Although there are currently scattered examples of great programs to keep pregnant girls in school, such effective efforts are not yet widespread.[17] And in the last few years, many programs have closed for lack of funding.[18] It is possible that another study, with more participants at each level of schooling, might find a difference in graduation rates at each level of education between those receiving versus being denied a wanted abortion. The Turnaway Study did not.

How does receiving or being denied an abortion affect women's five-year plans?

Recall that at the end of each survey, we asked women how they envisioned their lives, both one and five years later. Dr. Molly McCarthy, then a doctoral student at the University of Nebraska, reached out to me to see if she could use Turnaway data for part of her doctoral dissertation in public health. I gave her a blinded data set (meaning she could not tell who received and who was denied the abortion) containing the open-ended responses to women's five-year plans at baseline. Dr. McCarthy categorized the plans by type and by whether the plan was aspirational. Then she figured out how to measure whether, for nearly two thousand five-year plans, each woman achieved her plan using the women's own survey responses.[19]

Women described 1,864 plans, the vast majority of which were aspirational (91%), an even higher percentage than the 80% of one-year plans that Dr. Upadhyay found were aspirational. Women who anticipate some short-term hardship are nevertheless hopeful that in five years, they will accomplish something positive.

Women who made aspirational plans were hoping for a wide range of positive outcomes—18% of aspirational plans were related to employment; 16% were about children; 15% had to do with education goals; 12% were about romantic relationships; 11% were related to their living situation; 11% had to do with their emotional well-being, such as feeling happier; 7% were related to their financial well-being; and 10% were about other plans. When I matched Dr. McCarthy's coding of five-year plans to the full data set, we found no difference in the type of five-year goals (e.g., education, employment, children, relationships) by whether the woman received or was denied an abortion. For instance, Olivia, who received her abortion, had the long-term employment goal of owning a restaurant. Meanwhile, Tamara, who did not get an abortion, dreamed of starting a nonprofit school.

Consistent with our analysis of women's one-year life plans, we find that women who were denied an abortion were less optimistic about their future. However, looking ahead five years rather than one year, the difference between those who received and those who were denied abortions was a lot smaller. For five-year plans, 83% of women who were denied abortions reported an aspirational plan, compared to 91% of women who received an abortion just under the clinic gestational limit and 93% of women in the first trimester. In comparison, recall that the difference between women just over and just under the limit was 56% versus 86% for one-year plans.

For most five-year aspirational plans (85%), we were able to collect data through our surveys to determine if the goal was achieved. We found that more than half (56%) of these plans were achieved by the end of the study. We found no difference in whether the women achieved a five-year aspirational plan by whether they received or were denied the abortion. Women denied an abortion scale back their one-year aspirations a lot and their five-year aspirations only a little, compared to women who receive an abortion. This study found that overall, women are optimistic about their short- and long-term futures; however, women who do not receive wanted abortions are less likely to set ambitious goals than women who receive wanted abortions.

Destiny, the 30-year-old African American woman from Florida, illustrates how difficult the adjustment to having a child can be but how, over many years, women can achieve their goals. Destiny faced significant challenges in the five years after she was denied an abortion, among them "overcoming homelessness," as she puts it, while she struggled to find a place to live, including a month during which she had to stay in a series of hotels with her two children. But she also told us what she had achieved. "The baby is now five. We moved from the country to the city. I went from being a cashier to running my own business full-time. So, it's not that bad." She even continued to pursue her education. When she first sought an abortion, she was only a couple of months shy of completing an associate's degree. Five years later, she had finished her bachelor's degree and was about to begin a master's program.

Conclusions about Women's Lives

The Turnaway Study shows that women who are denied wanted abortions scale back their short-term plans and suffer economic hardship for years. When pregnant women say they are not able to afford to support a child or another child, we see those concerns realized in the experiences of women who are denied an abortion. Carrying an unwanted pregnancy to term results in reduced full-time employment that lasts about four years; an increase in public assistance that persists until women are timed out of these programs; an increase in household poverty that lasts at least four years; an increased likelihood that women won't have enough money to pay for food, housing, and transportation that persisted the whole five years of the study; and finally, at the end of the five-year period, an increased chance that women are raising children as single parents with no family support. We can see these negative economic outcomes for women denied abortions in their own self-reports, and we can see them through credit-agency reports of debt, bankruptcy, and worse credit.

Of course, not all unplanned pregnancies are bad. Some are happy surprises. Pregnancy can be a meaningful challenge, a chance to reconsider one's priorities and plans. But when the woman explicitly does not want to be pregnant and have a baby, as is the case for most of the women in the Turnaway Study, it can be downright frightening. As you'll hear from Brenda after chapter 9, "Pregnancy is an incredibly scary thing, especially if you cannot trust the person you're with." Unwanted pregnancies carried to term can result in women being stuck in circumstances that are not fun or romantic and hinder opportunities to shape their future. The Turnaway Study findings about economics and life plans strongly support Justice Ginsburg's assertion that abortion is about "a woman's autonomous charge of her full life's course." We'll see other dimensions of a woman's life in subsequent chapters on children and relationships; there, too, we see that abortion presents broader issues than a debate about government control over pregnancy decision-making or the legal status of fetal lives.

My hope is that we will think about pregnancy and abortion in the context of real women's lives rather than just as fodder for political debate. It is important to understand the complicated lives women lead, the competing demands on their time, resources, and affections. Asking women about their life plans reveals their resilience and optimism, the desire to improve their lives—to own a nail salon, open a café, get degrees in psychology or criminal justice or law, or excel in a male-dominated sport. The women who seem to have the hardest time—with abortion, adoption, and parenting—are doing it on their own, sometimes with partners away in prison or the military, and alienated from their families by judgments about pregnancy, abortion, or childbearing. Government, employer, community, and family supports for struggling mothers are already grossly insufficient to keep women and children from deprivation and poverty.

Next you will meet Melissa, who was 26 years old and raising four kids on her own when she found out she was pregnant with a man who was not the father of her children. She is a perfect example of a woman deciding to have an abortion to take care of the children she already has. But she also later decides to carry a subsequent unintended pregnancy to term when the conditions of her life, especially practical support from extended family, improve.

MELISSA

*I knew it was the right thing to do. I didn't need
to bring another kid up into that life.*

My hometown is in Georgia. My mother married a few times,
so we moved around quite a bit. My dad has been in prison
a bunch of times. The last time was for most of my childhood, so
he was really not there. My dad, all I know is that he was an alcoholic. And apparently he got into drugs, and that's what got him
his first conviction.

My grandparents lived in one town, so I always ended up back
there somehow. It was a very small town, and my grandmother
owned a restaurant. Everybody in that town knew everybody;
there were no secrets. My grandmother on my dad's side worked
in health care, and she raised me quite a bit. My mom would leave
me there with her when she'd be in between houses or have problems with her boyfriends or one of her husbands.

At my grandmother on my mom's side, she had a really nice
house. And she wasn't there very much, so when we were there,
you had to go to her restaurant to eat; there was never any food
in the house. But she'd buy you anything you wanted. My dad's
mom, she'd take care of you—she was always tending to your
every need, and she'd cook and clean and she was really interactive with me.

I love them, my grandparents. My dad's mom, she acted more
like a mom to me. She had a stroke when I was a teenager. She

was on bed rest for years, and my grandfather took care of her the whole time instead of putting her in a nursing home.

The first time I saw my dad as an adult is when I was in labor with Eva. She's one now. The doctor was breaking my water, I looked up, and a guy walked in the door right in front of me. And so that was the first time I'd seen him in many years. You can tell that he's been locked away from people, because he acts really anxious around people, kind of shy. But he lives so far away now. I only have to see him every so often, so I don't have to deal with all of the mental issues that he has going on. I'm grateful for that, but, at the same time, sometimes I wish that he had more interaction with my kid.

And my mom, I don't know what her actual medical diagnosis is. I know that she had a hysterectomy in her thirties. And she's been laid up in bed, depressed to the point where she has called and asked for help, somebody to come get her because she didn't want to be alive, that type of depressed. When I was growing up I was an only child until I was a teenager, when she had my brother. So all my life it was just me and my mom. I went through everything she went through, all the marriages and divorces. She was a good mom. She was never depressed and laying in bed then—it was when I got older and moved out. When I stressed her out, it probably helped put her in that state.

Chris and I got married young. My mom didn't like him, and he wouldn't hold a job. I thought I could handle everything and take on the world, so I got a job and I continued school. So not only was I in school, but I was pregnant shortly after our marriage. And I had Jacob—I think when he turned six months old, I was turning 16.

Before I was 20, I bought my own house. I worked as the assistant manager at a pet store, and that lasted a few years. I barely got to see Jacob. I put him in daycare, and Chris stopped going to pick Jacob up on time. I'd get home and be like, where's Jacob? And Chris would've not picked him up. So I had to drive 15 miles back to pick Jacob up—everything that Chris wasn't doing was adding up and stressing me out. I guess it just got old quick. I wasn't even an adult. I was still just a teenager, taking on all of that. So our marriage lasted a few years, and finally I just got sick of everything and realized that I was fighting a losing battle.

The next boyfriend I had, when Chris and I split up, that guy, he beat me up. And my mom hated him, and he was on drugs. After that relationship, I got with another guy who beat me up, because when you hang around a certain crowd, that's what you're around. I think my mom feared for me. She would come in and try and pick me up and take me home, and I would refuse and tell her I was all right. And you know, with two black eyes you can't tell your mom you're all right. That went on for a good five years. Finally she quit trying to talk sense into me and decided that she was going to step away, and she told me that she was going to pray for me. I stopped seeing her for a while.

In the meantime, I had Joshua and Michael and Billy. I got with their dad, Carlos, and he got put in prison twice. So I went through a pregnancy—like, I had Joshua, and he was out. I got pregnant with Mike; Carlos got put in jail. I delivered Mike; Carlos was out by that time, because he only stayed a few months that first time. And then when I got pregnant with Billy, Carlos went to prison for two years. And so I had all three of these boys and had Jacob, my oldest, staying at his grandma's. So I had four kids, by myself, with my old man locked up.

At that point, my mom wouldn't even open the door for me. I could knock on the door, and she'd say, you had all them kids, and you're going to take care of them, because I've done all the raising I'm going to do. That still sticks with me when I talk to her now. One of my mom's former husbands, I remember him blow-drying my hair and stuff when I was little. He'd blow-dry my hair for me and play the guitar. He is the one whose family has stuck with me through all of this. Every time I needed anything, they were like, come on down here with us. I thought they were crazy. I'm not moving 200 miles away, is what I always thought. But a few years ago I actually did. I was like, ahh, something's got to give. And I moved down here, and they've done nothing but help me. They've taken my kids in like they were their own. I'm talking Christmases, birthdays, science projects. You know, everything a family would do, a tight-knit family would do, these people have done for me, and they're not even my blood relatives.

I want to tell the truth about something. When I got pregnant with Eva, as soon as I found out I was pregnant, I freaked out. And immediately, depression. I didn't want to get out of bed. I didn't know what I was going to do. I actually scheduled an appointment for another abortion, and two of my stepdad's relatives show up at my door, and they're telling me, "We'll help you through this; you don't have to do that; you don't need to do this." Because they're anti-abortion all the way. "Why don't we just schedule a doctor's appointment? Maybe it's that girl you want. You know, you've got all these boys; maybe it's that little girl." So we scheduled a doctor's appointment, and I called to make sure I can still have the abortion if I wait that long, and they said yes, I could. We went to the doctor's appointment, and on the first sonogram you could see that it was a girl.

Well, those relatives do not know that I've ever had an abortion in the past. It was nice to know that I would have some support, but the thing is I'm raising all of these kids, and I know my limits. I know when my hands are already this full, the last thing I need is another one. I knew that. But at the same time, they reassured me that it would be easier because they would be there, and I wanted a girl all my life, so I just went for it. The timing was not very good, but I'm not getting any younger. Those family members watch Eva for me every day. I'm in college, doing my prereqs. I have to go to classes all week, and they watch her for me for free every day. And then my kids get out of school, and if their dad's not home from work yet, my relatives will come and get every single one of my kids. It's a group effort.

I was able to get my tubes tied this time, because every other time in the past—with my second they told me that I was too young; with my third they told me that I didn't sign the papers soon enough, for the tubal. That I would have to wait 30 days or something. I ended up just putting it off and never doing it. With the fourth, I think it was the same situation, I didn't have the paperwork signed or something. Every time they told me they couldn't do it. And this time, from the day one when I went into that doctor's office, I was like, "Y'all have got to schedule me a tubal because I've got to get my tubes tied. I can't even fit all my kids in my car!" And, what was it they did to me—they made me wait two weeks after I had Eva to get my tubal. I had to go back and get the IV and do everything all over again. But I actually went and did it. They had me sign the paperwork at the doctor's office, and for some reason the doctor's office didn't get it to Saint Mary's hospital. They were acting like they had lost it or something. I freaked out on these people. I was like, there is no way in the world this can be happening. I've been through that too many times. I don't know if it's because I was on Medicaid; maybe they don't like paying for that? But I would assume that would be better than paying for 15 more kids to be born, right? Obviously if I were able to control it, it would've been controlled by now.

Joshua and Michael and William, they all have the same daddy. When I joined this study he was in jail. In the meantime, a relative of Carlos's was coming over and visiting me all the time. I would work and come home to the kids, work and come home to the kids. He'd be the only one to come around—the only one to check on us, only one to help us, only one to bring Christmas presents, only one to bring birthday presents. So eventually I did let him close. And we did mess around. I ended up getting pregnant, and I didn't tell him until I was in the office waiting on my abortion appointment. He wanted me to get out of there—"Don't do it." And you have to know he didn't have a job and was no better off than my kids' daddy was when he want to jail. So there was no way I was going to listen to anything he had to say. But I asked him if he would help me to pay for it, and he wouldn't. I had a friend who had noticed how depressed I was and came to visit me one day, and he actually gave me the money to do it, and so there I was.

I was living by myself, with just my kids. I hadn't even thought of going to school then. At that point in my life all I was doing was being miserable and waiting for their dad. I did some call-center work, but I only did that for about a year and a half. And then it was just, stuck in the apartment all the time. With the kids. It was rather depressing.

I was ashamed that it was with somebody that was in the family, you know? So that was my biggest concern. And the fact that I could barely take care of the children that I had. I mean, most of the time I wasn't working. I never filed for welfare or any of that, because I didn't want to have to put child support on Carlos and then him get out of jail and have to pay child support. It tends to slow people down, and I didn't want him to feel like I was against him. I was going to three, four different food pantries and struggling to maintain those children. I didn't want any more. So it was panic at first, and then it was depression because I thought there was no way I can pay for an abortion, so I'm screwed. It was bad.

Can you imagine if I'd had that baby and then Carlos had gotten out of jail and I'd have told him whose it was? If I didn't tell him whose it was—heck, they were all going to look alike, they're the same family. There was no way, no way. Oh, it would've been horrible. Can you imagine if I'd have gone to a single family reunion? Carlos probably would've left me; he probably wouldn't have come back. And how would I explain adoption? "You were just pregnant, weren't you? Where'd the kid go?" No, I wasn't doing that. I would always be thinking about a child running around out there that's mine. That thought would eat me up for the rest of my life.

I can't remember how far along I was when I actually had it. I want to tell you it would've been $800, but they gave me some kind of a discount. I think we paid five-something. I was the happiest person in the whole wide world the day I went and did it. I was scared to death to do it, but I didn't have any of those thoughts about what if I regret it or is this not the right thing to do. Because I knew, without a doubt in my mind, it was the right thing to do. I didn't need to bring another kid up into that life.

A guy named Robert, he's an old man. My kids call him Grandpa. He's the one that gave me the money to do it. He was the only one I spoke with about it. I Googled the abortion clinic. He drove me. He took off work, and he gave me the money and he drove me down there. Because he knew all of the people involved. There were ladies outside the front door. You know, preaching. Protesting, I guess. Trying to pray for me. I accepted it and I prayed with them, but I think that you know what's right and wrong in your heart, and I don't feel like God would have any kind of judgment against me considering the situation that I was in.

At the clinic, they were excellent. Nobody was judgmental. They were very professional; they didn't give me any trouble. They didn't try to talk me out of the process, but they gave me all the information I needed if I wanted to go another route. I think they put laughing gas on me. I expected that when I woke up I would probably have pain and crazy amounts of bleeding and things they had told me about some of those side effects, but it wasn't really like that. I didn't have abdominal cramps like I expected. And I think I only bled for three days. So it went really smoothly.

By the way, the guy that I had become pregnant with, David? Today he's a drug addict. He doesn't have a job. He's a mental case now. He lives with his mother; he's 40 years old. It wouldn't have been any good. The decision I made, I just feel like it wouldn't have changed him. He wouldn't have been a better dad. David's never spoke of the pregnancy to me or to anybody else in the family. Thank God. His mother has asked me before if maybe William was his. I guess she thought that because we had been messing around when Carlos was gone, maybe there was a chance there, because she would come around and bring Billy birthday presents. I told her, "No, there's no way, I'm sorry. I'm absolutely certain." I love David's mom to death. I wouldn't mind her being in my life, but no.

I didn't write Carlos letters in jail. I only wrote him letters that asked him what we were going to name Billy. He came up with some crazy off-the-wall misconfounded names. I was like, no, sorry I even asked. Because all my life the only time I interacted with my dad was my dad would send me letters. And expect me to write. I rarely wrote my dad back because I was angry about him not being there with me. It was like living that all over again. I didn't want my kids to live like that. So I told him, "We're not going to write you letters. If you want to be in our life, you best get out of trouble and be free."

When Carlos got out of jail, he started using again. It was just years and years of going through the same crap, over and over. He cheated on me with everybody he could possibly cheat on me with. He got into drugs real bad. And he was never ever home. I want to tell you that throughout most of our relationship, it was pretty obvious I was pregnant. And he'd just leave me. He'd just leave me there for days on end. My mom had given me a car, and he would take my car and stay gone for days. I wasn't financially stable, and I couldn't better myself—watching my kids live through that and watching him run over me? That had to stop. So it came down to this. I told him, "I'm packing up my stuff. I'm moving down there with my family. You can come with me, or you can stay down here in this miserable life by yourself. But either way, you're not going to have a place to live." Because it was my apartment. And he broke down in tears and told me that he was ready, too, and that he'd do anything that we needed to do, that he was ready for a change. We called my relatives; they drove down there and picked us up. We left everything that we owned there. Everything except a backpack full of clothes; that's all I brought. And they came; they had actually already gotten the kids because I had called them weeks before and told them how crazy it was at my house and how I couldn't take it, and they came and got the kids. Then they came and got us, weeks later. We came down here, and it's been great ever since.

I got Carlos in an intensive outpatient rehab, and he went for six months. I got a job the first day we moved down here. I worked all the time. There was no reason, no logical reason for me to stay with the man. Except that I can honestly tell you now what I think that was going through my mind was that I thought

I could fix him. I thought I could get him off the drugs; I thought I could make him better. That's irrational for me to have thought that, but today he's better. He's had a job for three years straight, and he couldn't be any better with the kids. He actually interacts with our kids more than I do.

He's the one that'll take them to the park; he's the one that'll cook them breakfast. I'm not sure if that's because he loves them so much and being a better dad or if it's because he's waiting for me to graduate and he knows I'll make a lot of money. But either way, either way he's a totally different person. I also think it has a lot to do with men after 30, you know. Before 30, I don't think any of them were really any good. But now he's almost 40, and he's realizing he really doesn't have much time to make up for all of that. Basically it's from the time the alarm clock goes off in the morning. I have to be there at six o'clock in the morning. I leave the house at five. So I leave, and he gets the kids ready for school. Then I don't get out of school until five, so he gets home from work at about two thirty or three o'clock, and they get off the bus at 3:45, I think. And he'll do dinner. He does all of the stuff a mother should be doing. He does that.

When we moved to this town, we were having a hard time finding him a job because of the prior convictions on his record. And he didn't have a driver's license. It wasn't until last year that I finally got him to take his driving test. So I went into town for him and asked a man that owned a farm and several businesses. I put the application in at one of his businesses, and the man came up to my work and told me that if Carlos needed a job that he had it and just to get him up there Monday. I told Carlos, and he's been there ever since. He does a bunch of farmwork and any kind of maintenance and catering jobs.

I don't know when I signed up for school, but it took me two years to finish my prereqs. And I got accepted into a four-year college. I got my acceptance letter, which was a really big thing because it was my first time applying. Every day I want to quit, and every day I think it's too much. But so far every test that I've taken I have done very well. My first son got his driver's license and he's in school. And if I graduate when I'm supposed to, he and I will both be graduating at the same time, him from high school and me from college.

As long as I can get through college, we should be okay. I've got four tests Wednesday. I'm kind of leery about it all, but I'm trying, just doing one day at a time. I just want to be able to support my kids. If I get through this program, I'm going to try to go through the next program. It'll only be another year. And instead of an associate's, it'll be a bachelor's. But that would allow me to take on a management position if I wanted to. I want to work in labor and delivery and pediatrics. Just because I've been there a lot. And I can relate.

It makes a whole world of difference when you have a support system behind you. Where I lived before I didn't have any family interaction at all, the family that was down there was so negative, mom with depression, dad with alcoholism, family members with drug addiction. With every man that you ever date having drug addiction, having abuse issues and things like that, it's nothing but a bunch of negativity. I think it made every bit of difference in the world getting away from that small town, where I knew everybody and everybody was so negative. Moving away and being able to start over—not having all that stigma with me has made my life much easier. The people here, all they know about me is that I work hard and that I'm always in a good mood. They don't know anything about my past. That's what's really helped me to be able to change my life. I've always been one of those people that said that I can do it. I can do it by myself. I can handle anything. I'm real hard-headed and strong-willed, so that held me back because I never asked for help. Then I get down here and these people, all they want to do is help. I don't think there's anything else that I could have asked for.

You know, people talk about how you'll regret an abortion all your life? I don't ever think of it. I feel guilty that I don't feel guilty. I don't want people to think that I'm heartless, I'm not—

at all. It just doesn't impact me negatively. If I hadn't had that abortion, I don't think that I would've been able to do anything. I think that my whole life would be in chaos. I'm just grateful it was even an option. If they had made it any harder to have done it, it wouldn't have just changed my life, it would've changed the lives of my entire family. I've never been very judgmental toward anybody that has done it. Sometimes I think, "Oh my gosh, they should maybe stop spreading their legs." I'm one to talk. I could say that I had three kids with the same guy and I came to find myself in a situation where I'm glad that I was never judgmental because it can happen to anyone.

When I was growing up, I didn't want any kids. I didn't picture myself as a mother. And then when I got married, I wanted one. I wanted it to be a girl. I had that first child, and you find out that you love them no matter what; it doesn't matter if it's a boy or girl. You think, there's no way I can love anyone in the world more than I love this baby right here. Then you have another one. And you worry when you're pregnant, am I going to love this one like I do that one? There's no way; you don't want it. Then you have that second one and you love them totally different. There's no amount of love more for one than the other; it's overwhelming. When it's all said and done after you have each child, it doesn't change the way you feel about any particular one; they're all very different people.

I would not take any of it back. If I could I wouldn't have done anything differently. I think that all of the struggles from the past have made me the person I am today and made me able to deal with the things that I go through today.

Melissa, a white woman from Georgia, was 26 years old and 13 weeks pregnant when she had an abortion.

CHAPTER 7

Children

Women's lives—their mental and physical health, their aspirations and economic security—are not the only lives affected by the ability to access abortion care. Nationally and in the Turnaway Study, more than half of the women having abortions are mothers, and their desire to care for the children they already have is a leading reason for aborting a pregnancy. Their unwanted pregnancies sometimes come too soon after a previous birth, or risk upsetting the tenuous day-to-day balance of caring for young children. In addition to the many women who are already raising children, there are women who want very much to become mothers in the future but aren't yet ready to nurture and support a child. For these reasons, you may not be surprised to learn that receiving versus being denied a wanted abortion can have consequences for children—those already born at the time of the unwanted pregnancy; those born because of an unwanted pregnancy; and those yet to be born from a future, potentially more wanted pregnancy. Being denied an abortion negatively affects the development and financial security of one's existing children, the emotional tie to the child born from that pregnancy, and the chance of having a more desired pregnancy later.

There are people who believe that pregnancy is a punishment, the price to be paid for having sex or for failing to use contraception.[1] For people who think that pregnancy is a punishment for carelessness or promiscuity and that women should not be able to use abortion to skirt the consequences, these next results are particularly important. We've already documented the physical, economic, and social hardships faced by women who were denied an abortion. This chapter shows the measurable negative effects on their children as well.

Existing Children

Why might an unwanted pregnancy carried to term affect the well-being of the existing children in a family? If resources—money, time, parents' attention—are fixed, then the more children there are, the less any one of them will receive.[2] When there is not enough to go around, one more mouth to feed, one more body in need of holding and protecting, one more mind to nurture may be more than the parents can provide for. Additionally, circumstances surrounding an unwanted pregnancy may compromise the mother's physical or mental health and make it difficult to take care of more children. That was the situation for Jessica, whose pregnancy presented serious health risks, whose marriage was on the verge of collapse, and whose toddler and newborn depended primarily on her. The father of her children was in jail again and not someone Jessica considered a reliable parent. "[The abortion] was just a sacrifice I had to do," Jessica told us. "If that wouldn't have happened, I might not be here today. Or my kids might be in foster care." Or like Kiara, whose new boyfriend began stalking her around the time she became pregnant. She worried about the safety of her three-year-old daughter from a previous relationship if she remained forever tied to her current, abusive boyfriend. "The situation was just a very bad situation," Kiara said. "I was continuing to try to be a good mother for my daughter and realizing that I was in no way or shape or form wanting to be connected to this person for the next umpteen years of my life."

Outside of a study like the Turnaway Study, it is not easy to determine what effects carrying unwanted pregnancies to term might have on existing children. A family with poor material or emotional resources may not want another child. To the extent that a lack of resources negatively affects existing children, it may be the family finances rather than how intended the pregnancy is that affects children's well-being. In other words, the same circumstances in the family that make a woman want to avoid pregnancy might also cause poor outcomes for existing children.[3]

Another major challenge in determining the effect of an unintended pregnancy on women and children is to define what we mean by "unintended." Not planning a pregnancy in advance doesn't mean that the couple isn't happy to be expecting. But previous work has relied on measures of pregnancy intention that are focused on whether the woman wanted to become pregnant at the time of conception. Lumping the happy surprises in with the total disasters makes it difficult to zero in on the effect of carrying to term a pregnancy that the woman explicitly does not want to bear. Adding to this complication, in many previous studies researchers have asked women to report the intendedness of children *after* the children were born. A woman in a family that thrives in spite of the unexpected additional birth may be less likely to report that the child was unintended than a woman in a family where everything fell apart. In other words, pregnancies where the outcomes were better than expected might be more likely to be retrospectively categorized as intended, hence creating a spurious relationship between intendedness of the pregnancy and outcomes for the child.

We did things differently in the Turnaway Study. I wrote the paper in which we compared the health, development, and well-being of the youngest child of women who were turned away to the youngest child of women who received an abortion.[4] These are children who had already been born at the time that their mother sought an abortion. One week after seeking an abortion, there were almost no differences in characteristics between the children and mothers for women who received or were denied an abortion—not in the mother's age, race, education, or marital status or in the child's age, birth order, development, or health. Women who received and women who were denied abortions had similar incomes by objective measures—the ratio of income to the poverty level. Both groups were, on average, at the poverty level, consistent with national data showing that women seeking abortions are disproportionately low-income.[5] But they had different measures of subjective poverty—one week after seeking an abortion, 96% of those denied an abortion compared to 83% of those who received an abortion reported that they lacked money to pay for basic living expenses, like food, housing, and transportation. That nearly all women denied an abortion reported that they didn't have enough money for basic living expenses may simply reflect the fact that they were anticipating the costs of an additional child.

Although the two groups of existing children were very similar at the time that their mothers sought abortions, over time, the existing children of women who received and of women who were denied abortions fared differently in two areas: economic well-being and achievement of developmental milestones. Consistent with what we saw in our analysis of economic consequences for women, when a child's mother is denied a wanted abortion, the child is more likely, over the next four years, to live in poverty (72% vs. 55%); to live in a household that receives public assistance (19% vs. 10%); and to live with adults who don't have enough money to pay for food, housing, and transportation (87% vs. 70%), compared to children whose mother received an abortion, even though the two groups of kids were initially the same.

Another area where we see measurable differences in the well-being of existing children by whether their mother received a wanted abortion is in the achievement of developmental milestones. We used a measure called Parents' Evaluation of Developmental Status: Developmental Milestones (PEDS:DM).[6] These questions ask about six areas of child development: fine motor, gross motor, receptive language, expressive language, self-help, and social-emotional. For each area, we asked the mother whether the child could accomplish an age-appropriate milestone. For example, we would ask the mother of a nine-month-old whether

her child can recognize his or her name. We would ask the mother of a two-year-old whether her child can point to parts of his or her body when asked. These are examples of receptive language milestones.

Children whose mothers received an abortion were more likely to accomplish these developmental milestones than children whose mothers were denied the abortion (77% compared to 73% of milestones achieved). I don't know the cause of this small but significant difference. Perhaps the family's material hardships impede children's development by reducing the amount of food available or causing housing insecurity. Perhaps the strains on their mother of raising an additional child impacts the next-older child's growth by reducing the amount of time and attention she has to devote to fostering that child's development. Finally, it is possible that a mother who is busy trying to take care of a new baby is simply less able to report on the developmental milestones of her older children. In that case, the observed difference may be due to a lack of maternal knowledge rather than the child's failure to achieve milestones.

The women we randomly chose for in-depth interviews offer some insight into what is happening to existing children when a woman carries an unwanted pregnancy to term and brings a new child into the family. "In the beginning I was doing good," Julia, a 26-year-old Latina who was denied an abortion in Illinois, told us. "I had my job and I had my kids and everything. But the reason why I thought I should have an abortion was for the simple fact that all of a sudden everything came down. I lost my job, my bills started accumulating. So I couldn't do it. I already had four; how was I supposed to do it with another one, without a steady job?" A shortage of both money and time can make a woman feel that she is not ready to have another child and also make it more difficult to take care of her existing children if she is unable to terminate an unwanted pregnancy.

The Child Born from the Unwanted Pregnancy

What happens to children born from a pregnancy their mothers wanted to abort? First, I must emphasize that an unwanted pregnancy does not mean the resulting child is unwanted. As we reported in chapter 4, one week after being denied an abortion, nearly two-thirds of women report that they still wanted an abortion. But six months later, when all had given birth, just one in eight (12%) still wished they could have had the abortion. Five years later, only one in 25 (4%) still said they wished they could have had the abortion.

Most of the women turned away, over time, reported that they were happy they had the baby. Jenny, a 26-year-old white woman from California, started crying at the thought of her then-six-year-old no longer being in her life. "She is just everything to me," Jenny said. Sue from Missouri expressed a similarly fierce love for her second son, whom she conceived within months of delivering her first. It was terrifyingly bad timing for Sue and her young family, but ultimately she's "relieved that what happened happened." "Just all of the cute little quirky things that he does, and how he makes me smile and the things that I would have missed out on, all those things—it breaks my heart that I actually thought about [having an abortion]," Sue said. Again, as our quantitative data show, most women aren't choosing abortion because they don't want or like babies. In fact, many choose abortion with the needs of children in mind. They're choosing because they feel that the timing and/or environment is not ideal or could even be harmful to a future child, or to their current child or children. But once these women are told they can't have an abortion, the majority come to embrace the new child.

However, we do find significant differences in the well-being of children born of this unwanted pregnancy and the children born to women who got the abortion they were seeking and then had another baby at a later date. Children born after a woman received a wanted abortion are the ideal comparison group. One of the most common reasons women gave for wanting to end a pregnancy was "It isn't the right time," second only to not having enough money to support a child. So I wondered if by ending this pregnancy, women were able to have a baby at a better time and if so, if the better timing would translate into better outcomes for the child. In the Turnaway Study, I refer to the child born from the unwanted pregnancy (that the woman sought to abort) as the "index child" and the child born from a pregnancy subsequent to the abortion as the "subsequent child." Comparing the two groups of children enables us to see if being able to have kids when the timing and circumstances are better for the woman improves the child's outcomes.

First, what wasn't different: birth outcomes. Similar to U.S. averages, 10% of these index children were born premature, 8% had low birth weight, and 13% needed to spend time in the neonatal intensive care unit (NICU). Among children who were not the firstborn, there was an unusually high rate (17% of index children and 3% of subsequent children) born within 21 months of a previous child. (The World Health Organization recommends 24 months between births.[7]) Recall that many of our study participants did not realize they were pregnant because they had recently given birth. That was the case for 25-year-old Sue, who was still breastfeeding her first child when she discovered she was 25 weeks along in another pregnancy.[8] Although short birth intervals are a risk factor for poor birth outcomes, we did not find particularly poor birth outcomes (like low birth weight, prematurity, or health problems at birth) among these index children in our study, some of whom were very close in age to their older sibling.[9] Recall from chapter 4 that women who were denied abortions reduced the incidence of drinking any alcohol but they did not reduce drug use. Those with problem drinking behaviors (e.g., binge drinking and drinking first thing in the morning) had difficulty reducing these behaviors. Fortunately, the exposure to substances during pregnancy, which certainly can cause fetal harm, did not result in worse birth outcomes in our study.

What we do find is that when women are able to get an abortion and have a child later, those subsequent pregnancies are much more likely to be planned than the index pregnancy (24%, compared to less than 1% of index pregnancies).[10] See Figure 9. The mother is, on average, three years older (27 vs. 24 years old) at the time of the subsequent birth, compared to the index birth. The household has more economic resources—subsequent children live in households where income is 32% above the federal poverty level, compared to index children who, on average, live at the poverty level. Note that 32% above the poverty level is not luxury living. In actual dollar figures, we're talking about a family of four living on $33,132 instead of $25,100 at poverty level.[11] In fact, households of both index and subsequent children report similar use of public assistance. The big difference is that mothers of index children are more likely to report that they don't have enough money to pay for basic living expenses (72% compared to 55% for subsequent children).

Subsequent children were more likely than index children to be raised in households in which their mother had a male romantic partner (49% vs. 35%). We don't know for sure that these men are the biological fathers of the children because we did not ask, but it is likely most are. Enabling women to have wanted abortions increases the chance that they raise their subsequent children with a male partner.[12]

How do women feel about the children they bore from an unwanted pregnancy, compared to the child of a later pregnancy they chose to carry to term? Early in the child's life, women who were denied abortions report feeling less emotionally bonded to their new babies than women who got the abortion and had a baby later. We used a series of questions known as the Postpartum Bonding Questionnaire to measure maternal bonding for children under 18 months old.[13] Women denied abortions scored significantly lower on this scale of maternal bonding than women who had another child later. For example, women denied were less likely to agree with the statement "I feel happy when my child laughs or smiles" and more likely to say, "I feel trapped as a mother." For

9% of women denied abortions, their answers reached the scale's threshold indicating poor bonding with the index child, compared to 3% poor bonding with subsequent children. So, in the short term, we find that women feel less emotionally attached to the child born of an unwanted pregnancy than women feel to the next child born after having had an abortion.

Figure 9

The Intendedness of Pregnancies: Births to Women Denied an Abortion versus Subsequent Births to Women Who Received an Abortion

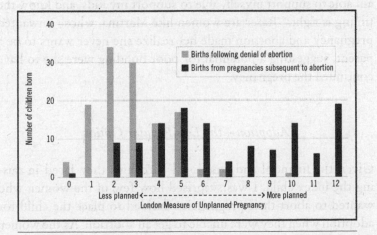

Adapted from Foster DG, Biggs MA, Raifman S, Gipson J, Kimport K, Rocca CH. Comparison of health, development, maternal bonding, and poverty among children born after denial of abortion vs after pregnancies subsequent to an abortion. *JAMA Pediatr.* 2018;172(11):1053–1060.

While this finding is obviously noteworthy, it's by no means a given that a woman who did not want to have a baby cannot forge a loving and healthy relationship with that child, even if it doesn't happen right away.[14] But the finding does underscore the adverse circumstances for the child when a woman continues a pregnancy against her will. Scientific literature on child development shows an association between poor parent-child attachment and children's long-term psychological and developmental outcomes.[15] In the Turnaway Study, women often considered their own mental and emotional state when determining what would or wouldn't be a nurturing environment for a new child. Olivia, for instance, said it would have been "dangerous" for her whole family, including her then-infant child, had she not terminated her unexpected pregnancy. "It would have been probably the worst thing for that child to come into this world because it would have never had the support that it needed. I wasn't mentally stable for that child," Olivia told us. "I do have a one-year-old now, and I am able to support myself, able to support my kids, and know the timing is right." Rarer are women like Martina, whose unwanted pregnancy and abortion made her realize she never wants to be a parent, suggesting a potential for poor bonding were she to have continued the pregnancy.

Adoption—the Less Popular Option

Given the financial and emotional hardships they faced in raising the index child, I was surprised how few of the women who wanted to abort their pregnancies decided to place the child for adoption when they were unable to get an abortion. As the women themselves had anticipated and as the Turnaway Study has shown, their lives became worse in many measurable ways trying to care for a child they weren't prepared for. So why don't more women place the child for adoption?

We asked women who were denied wanted abortions whether they were considering placing the child for adoption. One week after being denied, 14% were considering adoption. My colleague Dr. Gretchen Sisson, a sociologist, found that even when abortion is not available, the vast majority of women do not choose to place their child for adoption.[16] Fewer than one in ten women denied abortion (9%) actually placed the child for adoption. In the in-depth interviews, we asked women (those who received and those who were denied an abortion) to tell us about their decision-making process in their own words, including whether they considered placing the child for adoption. When women decide to have an abortion, they do not want to continue to be pregnant and give birth. When abortion is no longer an option, the vast majority of those who initially chose abortion choose parenting over adoption.

When women who first considered adoption opted to parent instead, it was often because they received more family support than they expected. Or, like Sue, they anticipated feeling a bond with the child after birth. "I actually thought about giving up the child," Sue told us, "but I know how attached I was to [my first-born], and there is just no way that I can go through the whole thing, see the baby, and be able to give it up." Or they anticipated feeling guilty if they placed the child for adoption. We commonly heard women say they could not stand the idea of the child being out in the world without their knowing the child and having some control over how the child was being cared for. Some women expressed fear that the child would find them and confront them, perhaps with an accusation of abandonment. Camila, whose story you'll read next, had felt abandoned by her parents as a child, and this motivated her to choose to parent after the clinic turned her away. "My parents, they—I think they loved me, but it was still hard for them as young people. You know, they wanted to be free. And so they just kind of kept bouncing and kind of dropping me off at each other's houses, and it was just, like, a burden all the time. And I just didn't feel like I wanted my child to ever feel like that," Camila said. "I just felt like I was not a strong enough person to give up my child for adoption."

Some women expressed concern about how people would react if, after being visibly pregnant, they had no baby. Finally, women like Nicole, the 20-year-old white woman from Ohio whose story you heard after chapter 4, reported that they think there are already enough children in need of homes and it wouldn't be right to add to that problem. "I definitely didn't want to do adoption because there are already enough kids in the foster programs," Nicole told us. "There doesn't need to be another one."

Both of the women in our qualitative interviews who placed the index child for adoption had subsequent unintended pregnancies in the course of the five years of the study. One opted for abortion for the subsequent unintended pregnancy. The other is Sofia, whose story is in this book, who decided to carry the pregnancy to term and parent the child. The two women both reported satisfaction with their decision to place the child for adoption from the first pregnancy, yet they opted to do things differently for the next unintended pregnancy. There is also Amy, whose story you read early in the book; she and her young husband initially placed their first child for adoption and then changed their minds and retrieved the baby. That experience made them rule out the possibility of adoption for the subsequent unwanted pregnancy.

Adoption is clearly not an easy solution to the problem of an unwanted pregnancy for women who preferred to have an abortion. Few women choose it and those who do place a child for adoption have the highest incidence of regret and negative emotions about the pregnancy.

Contraceptive Use

Let's take a moment to look at our data on how receiving versus being denied an abortion affects women's contraceptive use. It's relevant to our next set of findings about subsequent intended and unintended pregnancies. As we described in chapter 2, some methods of contraception are associated with lower risk of subsequent pregnancy than others, and all methods are more effective than taking the risk of using none. Does access to abortion make women more careless in preventing future pregnancies? Does either abortion or carrying an unwanted pregnancy to term make women more determined to avoid a subsequent unintended pregnancy? The Turnaway Study provides an opportunity to test these ideas.

The question about contraceptive use after an abortion versus a birth is complicated by women's access to health insurance. The most effective contraceptive methods are expensive if one has to pay out of pocket. One of the ways we thought that women who were denied abortion would be better off was in having health insurance (because Medicaid covers most low-income uninsured women's births), and I found this was true.[17] Women who gave birth after denial of abortion were more likely than women who received abortions to have health insurance at six months (76% vs. 66%), but they did not retain this advantage after a year and a half. After giving birth, a woman whose delivery was covered by Medicaid typically has at least two months of health-insurance coverage that she could use to cover contraception. There is no such special period of insurance coverage after an abortion, of course. The delivery is almost always covered by public insurance (Medicaid) for poor women, but abortion is, by law, usually not. For women with public health insurance living in one of the 33 states where public health insurance is not allowed to cover abortion, even getting contraception covered at the time of an abortion is extremely difficult.[18] Covering contraceptive services through public and private insurance, even if these services are delivered at the time of an abortion, would be an effective way to help women prevent any future unintended pregnancies. In addition to the difficulty many women experience paying for contraceptive methods, some abortion clinics don't offer all methods of contraception. Ninety-six percent of our recruiting facilities dispensed contraception; but only 80% offered a wide range of methods, including over-the-counter methods like condoms, prescription methods like the pill, and methods that clinicians place inside the woman like IUDs and implants. Others offered fewer options.[19]

Dr. Heidi Moseson, then a doctoral student in epidemiology at UCSF and now an associate at Ibis Reproductive Health, analyzed contraceptive use data reported by women in the Turnaway

Study.[20] She found that one year after seeking an abortion, the vast majority of women were using a method of contraception—86% of women who received the abortion and 81% of women who were denied. These small differences continued through the remaining four years. But there were important differences in the types of contraceptives used. Four years later, women denied an abortion were more likely to have received a tubal ligation (17%, compared to 6% among women who received an abortion), while women who received an abortion were more likely to use barrier methods or hormonal methods like the pill, patch, and ring (43% vs. 28%). Just over a third of women in both groups used long-acting reversible contraceptives (LARC) such as the IUD and implant. This is a very high rate of LARC use, twice that of the general population. Overall, women who received abortions were more likely than women who were denied an abortion to use a method of contraception but less likely get a tubal ligation. So although it was known from previous research that women who have abortions are at high risk for subsequent abortions, we find this is not due to a lack of motivation to use contraception, at least compared to women denied an abortion.[21] It may rather have to do with being biologically very fecund (able to become pregnant) and also having poor access to affordable contraception.

Future Pregnancies

Many of the women in the Turnaway Study still wanted to have children (or more children, if they already had them) later. When we compare the well-being of children born after women were denied an abortion—index children—and children born at a later date to women who received an earlier abortion—subsequent children—we see that the latter group do better in terms of economic well-being and maternal bonding. They also are more likely to live in a two-parent household. But what is to stop a woman who is denied an abortion from having the index child and then another, more intended, child later? If you were opposed to abortion, you might think that women should just carry all pregnancies to term and then particularly enjoy the ones that arrive under more favorable circumstances. Well, let's take a look at the data to see how carrying an unwanted pregnancy to term affects future childbearing.

It is clear from our study that abortion does not cause infertility. In fact, we find that women having abortions are at particularly high risk of having another pregnancy. Of the 956 women in the study, 39% had at least one additional pregnancy over the next five years, with an average of 1.5 pregnancies over the time period. Of these pregnancies 15% were clearly intended, 39% the woman was ambivalent about, and 46% were unintended.

Dr. Upadhyay showed that whether women had a subsequent pregnancy was related to whether they received their wanted abortion—44% of those who received an abortion, compared to 32% of women who were denied, had a subsequent pregnancy.[22] The pregnancy rate was higher among women who received an abortion, and it stayed higher for the full five years of the study. You might be surprised to learn that many women who have abortions still want to have (more) children in the future.[23] Dr. Upadhyay showed that women who received an abortion had a higher rate of *intended* pregnancy (7.5% per year) in the subsequent five years than women who were denied the abortion after giving birth to the index child (2.2% per year).[24] In the first two years, women who received an abortion were more likely to be trying to become pregnant than women who just had a baby (which makes sense, given the demands of taking care of an infant). After that, the two groups were similar in desire for pregnancy, but the women who received the abortion were more able to have that desired pregnancy.[25]

In contrast to our findings on future *intended* pregnancies, Dr. E. Angel Aztlan-Keahey, then a nursing graduate student at UCSF, found, as part of her doctoral dissertation, no difference between women who received and women who were denied an abortion in incidence of subsequent *unintended* pregnancy.[26] A third (34%) of women in the study had at least one subsequent pregnancy that was unintended at the time of conception. There was also no statistical difference in the outcome of those unintended pregnancies—29% of women in both groups aborted the subsequent unplanned pregnancy.

The upshot is that, over the next five years, women who received abortions were more likely to have an intended pregnancy than women denied them. Enabling women to have abortions when they want them increases the chance that they will become pregnant later when they are ready and prepared to parent. You read about Olivia, who was able to have an intended child that she and her partner could support because she was able to get an abortion after their first child. Margot, a 30-year-old white woman from Washington, told us, "Well, for one, I sobered up. So that automatically made it a better time to be having a kid."

Conclusions about How Children Are Affected by Abortion and Abortion Denial

Abortion is not just about a woman's rights versus an embryo's or fetus's rights; it's also about whether women get to have children when they are ready to care for them. Everyone cares about the well-being of children, and this study shows that when women are able to decide whether to carry a pregnancy to term, their children do better. This includes the children they already had at the time of the unwanted pregnancy—again, 60% of women seeking abortions are already mothers—and it also includes their future children.

Having a baby when a woman is not ready is associated with bad outcomes for the woman and her children. Women are less likely to be able to financially support that new child, and they are more likely to experience poor emotional bonding with the child. Being able to get an abortion makes it more likely that a woman will have a desired pregnancy later under better circumstances.

The next story you will read is Camila's. She had a partying lifestyle, but the experience of being denied an abortion puts her on the straight and narrow. In many ways, it's a social conservative's fantasy. However, her story is unusual in that Camila doesn't experience the increase in poverty from delivering the unwanted pregnancy that we see among women in the study as a whole. Most women (in the study and in the world at large) do not end up married to men making hundreds of thousands of dollars per year. But I caution against attributing her marriage and subsequent material success to continuing the pregnancy. She might have stayed with Diego even after an abortion. As we'll address in chapter 8, we see no difference in the likelihood of staying in a relationship with the man involved based on whether the abortion was received or denied. Had she been able to wait to have a child, she might not have been alienated from her family or had her first child under conditions of material and psychological hardship. It's also important to note that Camila previously had an abortion; her entire experience of meeting this man in Texas and having a subsequent wanted child might not have happened without the life trajectory made possible by her initial abortion.

CAMILA

I always say giving my child life, I saved my own.
It's just something that opens you up and changes you
when you become a mother.

New Jersey is where I'm from. It's middle class, a little rougher of a community. But it's a beautiful place. When I was born, my parents were really young, and I bounced around a lot. I bounced around to probably ten to twelve schools from sixth grade to twelfth grade. My dad lived in New Jersey. My mom lived in Texas. One year I would live with my aunt, and then one year I would live with my grandmother, and then one year I would live with my other aunt.

I was crazy when I was 21. I was supposed to be going to school. But I dropped out, and I got a job at a pharmacy. I had my two best friends, and we all lived together. I was having a good time with my girlfriends and working and making money—just kind of finding myself. Well, I went to a friend's house in El Paso, Texas, to visit. We went out to eat; Diego served me my steak. I'm not very forward, but I was so forward with him. I said, "After your shift, why don't you come sit down?" Me and my girlfriends were just having a beer sitting there at the bar. He came over, and we had a love-at-first-sight type thing. I fell in love, and I moved to El Paso. It happened super fast.

We had our first Christmas, and then I was pregnant in January. But I didn't know I was pregnant because I still had my period. It was very light, but I still had it. I had such crazy periods, so I didn't think anything of it until I started having other symptoms around four months. I thought that I could take care of it [have an abortion]. I did not know that there was, like, a statute of limitations. I didn't even know really what all an abortion was. I had had an abortion before that, but I hadn't ever thought about it, never read about it, never Googled it. I just knew that it was me not having a baby. Almost like your brain doesn't compute that it's a life and it's inside you. I remember feeling very scared but also thinking like, oh, I can take care of it. It's going to be okay. It's not the end of the world. I wouldn't say I'm ashamed of that feeling, because I was innocent. I didn't know to cherish life the way that we all should.

It was that May I came in and I sought to have an abortion. One big reason was because I had just barely met Diego, it wasn't even a year. I did [consider adoption], but then—I know this is so weird—you know those adoption books or adoption shows? I would always watch them, and I'd always feel such sorrow for that child. Whether the mother came back or not, I felt like that bond—I just couldn't imagine. And a big thing for me was my family. My parents, I think they loved me, but it was still hard for them as young people. They wanted to be free. So they kept bouncing and dropping me off at each other's houses, and I felt like a burden all the time. I just didn't want my child to ever feel like that. That was never an option for me. I felt like I was not a strong enough person to give my child up for adoption.

To have a child with somebody, it was scary. Diego is a good guy. He's wonderful. When I met him, he was a crazy kid. I think he had just turned 21. He's a year younger than me. He had two jobs at the time. He was working at Walmart, and he was working at that restaurant. And it wasn't enough; we weren't making enough.

At the clinic, they were really gentle. I recall them not being snooty or ugly because, you know, we are in Texas, and it does get like that. I love Texas, and I love the way it is here, but, yes, it does get kind of ugly. I expected them to say, what, you're five months? But no. They gave me all the information I needed if I wanted to proceed. They were really helpful. That made it better. Emotionally you feel shock and then you feel anger, and then you're like, what am I going to do? This disbelief. And then you have to make that decision.

Are you packing your stuff and are you going to Albuquerque? Or are you going to have this baby? And it's life-changing. It skips you to the next chapter. This is your new life, and this is what's going to happen. A sense of peace came over me. I didn't let anybody come in contact with me who was going to be negative. I had a conversation with my grandparents and my mom and my dad, all of them. They all told me to have an abortion and to go to Albuquerque. El Paso turned me away, but you could go to Albuquerque for later term. They really urged me to, and after that I cut them off for about a year. I didn't see anybody until Gabriel was five months. That was the hardest point—turning away my family and cutting them off, and not having anybody that supported me because of the decision not to go to Albuquerque. I felt really mad at my parents. I felt like they did not deserve to be in my life. It was really just Diego and his grandparents. The solitude of being by myself with just me and my thoughts, I think that that is something that strengthens you, especially at a sobering time like finding out that you're going to have a baby.

Diego was really like, whatever you want to do. He would be supportive, he would give me anything, and he would do anything, but he did not want to leave El Paso. I didn't know El Paso. I just didn't know if I wanted to raise my kid there, because there wasn't very much to do. It wasn't a prime location. It's the desert. And it's not very pretty. I didn't want to start a family there, but he did. So we did. He is really easygoing. And he's set in his ways. He has things he doesn't like, like me drinking while I was pregnant. I wasn't going to be drinking. Any decision that I ever make, he's really open to it; he doesn't hold too much of an opinion. He's very supportive of me. He's not hands-on with the children at all, but he works long, long, long hours and he's a great provider—a good man that way.

We were living in an apartment. And it was fine, but I was working two jobs. Financially, we weren't doing great. We were living paycheck to paycheck, getting by.

Diego doesn't drink alcohol. He doesn't smoke, which is one big thing—weed or cigarettes. I had just come from partying and being crazy and drugs. When I moved to El Paso with Diego, that was one of the things I was not going to do anymore my whole life. I went completely cold turkey after doing it for four or five years. I think it takes some time for you to completely get off that stuff. He really settled me down and made me view life a little bit differently, love and cherish it a little bit more.

After I cut everybody off, I went into my own, like, little mind, and I got up every morning and had a cup of tea and watch[ed] my baby shows. I got really happy until the last month. The doctor said it was postpartum depression, but before I had the baby, I got so sad. It was absolutely miserable. It was so bad in fact they wanted me to take Prozac. I picked up the prescription, but I did not take the pills. I didn't want that for the baby. I knew that he was already developed and it probably wasn't going to hurt him, but I just couldn't. I would say that I was sad because I was alone. A month later I had Gabriel, and it went away. It was like it never even happened. It was the strangest thing.

I was late. So we had to schedule an induction. I was excited. I had diapers, but I had just enough diapers. I had onesies, but I had just enough. We didn't have a lot of money. I didn't have a baby shower because I didn't know anybody in El Paso. I didn't talk to my family, so they didn't send me anything. It was very tight, down to the penny. I think that having Gabriel and being like that and being really humbled by that, it was still the best experience of my life. Having him, even though I was alone, I had never felt more connected with somebody or something than I did with Gabriel. For a long time it was just me and him every day.

I didn't leave the house. I didn't drive for three months. Diego drove me everywhere I wanted to go after I had the baby. I was so in love with Gabriel. I just wanted to be in my house alone with him. It was the weirdest thing. I almost felt like an animal hibernating with their baby. It was wonderful. Coming off a depression that was so strong, so overwhelming—it was bouts of tears for no reason. Total chemical imbalance. After I had Gabriel, I was so happy. I had this new baby, and it was wonderful. It was just me and him, best friends forever in our little house.

When Gabe was 18 weeks, I started working for Diego's great-aunt. She has a café, and I started working for her. I worked, and I bought it from her in 2012. I became a business owner. That was huge. I didn't go to college; I dropped out. I felt really accomplished. And I extended it and bought a new building next door and made a Christian café. Gabe has been raised in the café. His school bus drops him to and from school there. It's all kind of wonderful. I always say that the café is like a bar with no alcohol. You come in, you sit there, and you can tell me about your mother-in-law or your sister or whatever. And you know it's not going to go anywhere. It's therapeutic to listen to everybody and have conversation. I think that is the best medicine for anything. Time mixed in with being around people. Being alone and being secluded and isolated, it's not a good recipe when you go through things. Having a purpose and knowing that your family is strong, you can keep going.

I did not talk to anybody until that March. So Gabe was five months when I went to visit New Jersey. My grandmother had called me and she had written me messages. She finally left me a voicemail that said, "If you do not call me, I am coming there to see you." I finally called her. She said she was sorry and that she should have supported me. I talked to every one of them except my dad. We still don't talk. Out of all of the relationships, my father's and mine is the only one that hasn't come back healthier and stronger and better than ever. I'm so glad that they now support me. But it did take some time.

One year me and Diego got in a really nasty fight. It was an accumulation of things. He was working 14 to 16 hours a day. He's a lawyer—a long way from working in a restaurant. I wanted a divorce. I felt like it was so hectic, and I felt like he was being really ugly. I didn't want to waste my life. I wanted to be happy. I wanted him to be happy. But we worked through it. We never cheated on each other or hurt each other. I think it was just all of these exterior things that I just didn't like. I didn't like El Paso, and I didn't like some of the things that he did or said. Once we got rid of all of that except living at El Paso, it really changed.

I got pregnant last year. It was wonderful. It was a great Christmas, the best Christmas. Nine months later we had her. I would say that the two biggest accomplishments were the café and then having my daughter. Those are the two benchmarks of life. I had been trying to have a baby since Gabe was three—I'd say, like, two and a half I had been thinking about it, and then three I had decided I wanted one, and we had two losses since then. Gabriel came faster than we could even think it; we thought we'd never have problems getting pregnant. When we lost the first one, I was only eight weeks. It was like a really bad period. The second one was 14 weeks, and I have to say that one was a hard one. I lost that baby. That was a big challenge for me. But I had so much to do. I was at the café. I was working five days a week—six days a week. I brought Gabe on Saturdays, and he went to school Monday through Friday. Getting up, getting your son dressed, going to work, coming home, getting the dogs fed, starting your supper, feeding your husband, going to bed, getting clothes laid out. Just that repetitive day-to-day keeping yourself busy. Keeping yourself busy with outside things, not telling the whole sob story, just being around people. But we tried again.

In one year we lived in three different places, an apartment, a little house, and then a little trailer house. When I had the baby, I was very poor. We were just getting by, not married, not anything. And now, Diego clears over a quarter million dollars a year, and I have no worries at all.

If the café closes, there's no financial headache for us. It doesn't matter. We live very comfortably. Diego is gone still the way he was five years ago. He works long hours. But my life is so wonderful. Having kids has given it so much meaning. And it's so fun. I'm not sure that I didn't love life; I just didn't know how to cherish it when I was younger, when I was blinded by partying and things like that.

You're for yourself, and then in one day or however long you're in labor—for me, two—it's like you do everything for this little thing, and you love it. And Gabe is going to be six this year. I love him for everything he did for me. He truly made me a better person. He made me slow down and think about things when I'm driving. I used to drive like Batwoman, and now I drive like an old lady with a "Baby on Board" sticker. You know, your whole dynamic changes. Everything.

I'm glad it happened, because I think I would have died from being crazy and doing drugs and being wild and reckless. If it wasn't drunk driving, it was smoking weed or meth or whatever was available—whatever my girlfriends had, we were going to do. I don't follow any particular religion, but I think there's something that comes over you that changes when you become a mom.

It was a wonderful story that you don't really hear too often. Every day is like the last for us. Diego goes to work at ten o'clock so we can lie in bed as a family. Gabriel comes in our room every morning, and the baby is already in there. Every morning we try and have that bond with our kids and with each other. We all have a job to do. We all have each other at the end of the day.

I want to be able to dress my kids nice and let them go to a nice school, and I want to be able to afford nice things for them. I just want to be able to afford both of them equally, and I want to be able to give them a lot. If I have more children, I am not able to give them everything that I want to be able to give them. Not just physically or materialistically. Mentally and emotionally, I want to be in tune with my children. I want to be able to give them that attention that they both crave.

I'm going to school. I'm going to learn this stuff to work for a company with my uncle. So right now I'd say I'm closing the café—that chapter. And then doing this chapter. I definitely love businesses. If I could, in the future, I'd love to start them and sell them. Right now my goal is just to feed my children and make them happy and get to swimming class on time. That's my only goal right now. But I do have some entrepreneur goals, I would say.

I could not imagine my life not choosing to keep my baby — to keep the decision that the clinic gave me. And I wish that every woman had a good experience like mine, and I pray that they find that. It was all for the good. I truly believe one door shuts and another door opens.

What I think about abortion has changed over the course of time. Lots of girls did it. I think almost every member out of my family has had one at least. And it was never a problem. It was never a problem until I came to Texas and it came up, and people were so opposing of abortion. It just goes back to the argument about whether it's life at conception or is it life at birth? I always say giving my child life, I saved my own. It's just something that opens you up and changes you when you become a mother. And there's nothing that you can do about it.

Camila, a Latina from Texas, was 22 years old and 18 weeks pregnant when she was turned away.

CHAPTER 8

Men

The Turnaway Study's findings, and the stories in this book, make clear that men play a big role in the lives of women who seek an abortion. One could argue, as the Mormon mother of six Gabrielle Blair does, that men—with their "irresponsible ejaculations"—should bear significant responsibility for unwanted pregnancy.[1] After all, Blair reasons, the most available means to prevent pregnancy—withdrawal and, more effectively, condom use—rely on men taking responsibility.

Men also play a large role in decision-making—sometimes being involved in the decision and sometimes *being the reason* women opt for abortion. We find that few men involved in these unwanted pregnancies are eager or able to accept the responsibilities of taking care of a family. Think of Jessica from Louisiana. At 23, she had an abortion shortly after giving birth to her second child and discovering that she had multiple sclerosis, a neurological disease, and also hyperemesis gravidarum (severe nausea and vomiting during pregnancy), which can make pregnancy and birth risky for both mom and baby. Jessica couldn't trust her in-and-out-of-jail husband to raise their children if something happened to her. She had been in extremely poor health immediately following the birth of their new baby, and she said he only visited her twice during her three-week stay in the hospital. Even more troubling, he saw his toddler and brand-new baby only twice in three weeks. They'd left the kids with a relative. These memories influenced Jessica's choice to abort her third pregnancy. She could not rely on him as a father or a husband and would go on to file for divorce during one of his stints in jail.

In our study, disagreements between men and women about what to do with an unplanned pregnancy were uncommon. I can sympathize with the man who loses out in the pregnancy decision-making. It must be terrible for a man who wants to father a child when the woman does not want to have the baby, or a man who emphatically does not want a child when the woman does. But, as Martina says, since it is the woman's body sustaining the pregnancy and demanding her physical and emotional resources, it is the woman who should decide. In response to the lack of power in the decision, some men walk away. But this study shows that most of the time, male partners play both direct and indirect roles in the decision-making and in accessing care.

Before I get to our findings, I need to acknowledge that we did not, as part of the Turnaway Study, ask men how they felt about their partner's receiving or being denied an abortion or look at men's outcomes over time. This chapter contains women's reports of their own relationships and their impressions of the opinions of the men involved at the time of abortion decision-making.[2] To directly contact and interview men, we would have needed their consent to participate in the study. Even if we had tried to recruit male partners in the waiting rooms of abortion clinics, which is where we recruited women, the subset of men who accompany women would not have been representative of all men involved in unwanted pregnancies. Men's experiences with unintended pregnancy and abortion is clearly an important topic and one that is worth investigating further.

The Role of Men in Decision-Making

The vast majority of men actually do participate in the decision about what to do with an unplanned pregnancy. We find that four in five (83%) learn about the pregnancy when the woman is still deciding what to do. About 7% find out after the fact. The remaining 10% are kept in the dark about the pregnancy and abortion entirely, in rare cases (1% of women) because the woman is not sure who the man involved is (including women who were raped by a stranger).

When the man involved in the pregnancy knew at the time of decision-making, 43% of women report that he was unsure what he wanted to do, or left it to her to decide. Almost a third (31%) of women reported that the man wanted her to have an abortion.[3] About one-quarter (26%) of the women reported that the man wanted her to carry the pregnancy to term and raise the child. Nicole told us her abusive boyfriend "tried to talk me out of [abortion] a few times." Among men as among women, adoption does not seem to be a popular choice. Less than 1 percent (0.7%) wanted the woman to carry the pregnancy to term and let someone else raise the child.

One of the more concerning stories we heard of a man trying to influence a woman to have his baby comes from Sydney. She told us her verbally abusive boyfriend had tampered with their birth control and gotten her pregnant intentionally, and against her will. "Me and him wasn't seeing eye to eye," Sydney said. "Around that time when I did become pregnant, we were wearing condoms, and one night I guess he decided to poke a hole in it, take it off, or whatever. . . . It may have slipped off, or he may have taken it off. I have no idea what really happened because he was trying to get me pregnant, you know, he wanted me to have his child, and I kept saying no, I wasn't ready for that." She opted not to tell him she was pregnant, or having an abortion, until after the fact. Otherwise, she said, "It would have been chaos."

In concealing the fact of her pregnancy until it was terminated, Sydney intuited that disagreement with the man involved can significantly slow women down in getting an abortion. Almost one in five women (18%) reported that such discussions or disagreements delayed their abortion. Many times in these stories, we see that men's lack of support around the pregnancy or failure to take responsibility seemed to confirm women's decision to abort.

Additionally, men's failure to help women access abortion services suggested to these women that the man in question was not reliable enough to be a father. These issues show up in the stories of Sofia and Martina.

Sofia, a 19-year-old from California whom you'll meet after chapter 10, wanted an abortion because her boyfriend was unsupportive of her and of the prospect of their becoming parents together. The day she found out she was pregnant, she was bleeding excessively and scared, but she said he refused to drive her to the emergency room. In the end, Sofia was too far along to get the abortion and she had to continue the pregnancy. Yet she says she was considering his needs when she decided to place the baby for adoption. "I didn't want to force him to be a father if he didn't want to be a father."

And remember what happened when Martina, whom you met after chapter 3, told her boyfriend that she was pregnant? He reminded her he had to work out of town the next day. " 'Do you want me to stay?' " Martina remembers him saying. "And I was like, 'Well, no. I'll just deal with it myself.' Like, the fact that you're even asking me if you need to stay tells me that I'm just going to do this by myself because you don't care. There should have been no question of, do you need to be here?" Her boyfriend was already a father, and Martina had been far from impressed by his parenting skills during the brief tenure of their relationship. But the complete lack of urgency or interest on his part when Martina announced she was pregnant with his child was the clincher. She knew he would not be a reliable father to this child, and she did not want to be a struggling single parent at 22 years old.

Men as a Reason for Abortion

The public health scientist Dr. Karuna Chibber, who at the time was my colleague at UCSF, looked at the role of men in women's abortion decision-making.[4] She found that almost a third of the women in the Turnaway Study (31%) reported that their reason for wanting an abortion had to do with the man involved. Let's break it down: A third of women in that subset said their relationship with the man was not good enough. That was the case for Margot, who fought often with her alcoholic and "verbally nasty" boyfriend. A quarter of them said their partner would not or could not support the child, which was the case for Jessica, as well as Ariela, who loved her high school sweetheart but was barely in college herself and worried that her boyfriend would not be able to be a good parent at that point in his life. One in five women who said their partner was a reason for abortion said the man was just the wrong guy to have a baby with—for example, because he was already married, incarcerated, or was using illicit substances. Again, Melissa did not want to have a baby with her incarcerated husband's relative, a decision she remains happy with years later.

Carrying a pregnancy to term can result in a long-term connection to the man involved in the pregnancy, which many would like to prevent. Margot reported that she felt her abortion helped her dodge a bullet. Soon after, her alcoholic ex-boyfriend ended up going to prison for driving drunk and seriously injuring another person. "I was, you know, kind of thankful that I didn't have a kid with him because then I would have been attached to him for, well, pretty much the rest of my life, because you are never really done with your kids." And then there's Jenny, who became pregnant at the age of 20 after having sex twice with a neighbor. By the time she sought an abortion, she was too far along. Soon after the baby arrived, Jenny and the man involved broke up and he was sentenced to 25 years to life for child molestation; we don't know if the baby or another child was the victim. She's since obtained restraining orders against him, and he is now out of their lives. She married someone else and says her child calls her husband "Daddy." Jenny is grateful she had her daughter, but she does not like being tied to the man who got her pregnant.

Among the 31 women who participated in qualitative, in-depth interviews, two said their then-boyfriends pressured them to have an abortion. Guadalupe attests that when she was 18, her then-boyfriend insisted she have the abortion, found the information, and took her to the clinic. A young immigrant from Mexico City who was already a parent to a toddler and had no family support, Guadalupe said she felt helpless against her boyfriend's strong opposition to the pregnancy. Adrienne was 34 and living in Chicago with her young daughter when she discovered she'd become pregnant after reuniting with an old boyfriend. She wanted the baby. He didn't, and his method of letting her know was calling her every day and telling her to get an abortion. "I really don't want the baby. I hope you die," she recalls him saying. However, only one woman in our entire study reported that pressure from the partner to get the abortion was her *only* reason for getting an abortion. One of the major justifications for parental-involvement laws—laws that mandate that young women inform or even get permission from a parent before getting an abortion—is that involving parents might protect a young woman from coercive pressure from an exploitative older man.[5] However, in this case, the woman reporting coercion from a man was 30 years old, not a teenager. The study I led at one large clinic in the Midwest showed that when young women report being pressured into having an abortion, it is much more often a parent than a boyfriend who is doing the pressuring.[6]

Violent Relationships

Brenda spent her early twenties often broke, drinking, and trying to escape a violent relationship with, she says, "an asshole." He'd beat her. She'd hit back. They'd break up. She'd eventually tire of sleeping in her car and go back to a relationship she knew was no good for her. And then . . . "When I found out I was pregnant, oh my God. I was horrified. I was absolutely horrified," Brenda told us. "I really, really, really did not want to have a child with that person." But, as I described in chapter 2, Brenda found out too late, and several abortion clinics turned her away.

You'll read Brenda's full story in her own words after chapter 9. Assuming you've already read 20-year-old Nicole's story after chapter 4, you know Brenda's is not the only pregnancy conceived in a violent relationship. Nicole's boyfriend wanted to control her. He prevented her from studying. He prevented her from breathing clean air, by smoking constantly in their apartment despite her chronic asthma. He regularly coerced her into sex, applying both emotional and physical abuse. "He would just come in randomly, and if I didn't give in to him, we'd end up fighting," Nicole described. And, as you read after chapter 2, Jessica's husband, in addition to being an absent father, physically abused her.

A small minority of women seeking abortion (2.5%) in our study cited partner abuse as the primary reason for seeking an abortion, very similar to what is found among abortion patients nationally.[7] However, twice that many had experienced recent violence. At the time they sought an abortion, 1 in 20 women in the Turnaway Study reported that the man involved in the pregnancy had pushed, hit, slapped, kicked, choked, or otherwise physically hurt them within the past six months. Another 1 in 30 reported a fear of such violence in their relationships. You may note that abusive relationships are more common among the ten women profiled in this book than among abortion patients in general. I didn't select the stories on that basis; instead, I was looking for the strongest voices and a range of experiences and perspectives. For women like Brenda, Nicole, and Jessica, who have become pregnant with a violent man, their desire for abortion is about not wanting to tether themselves to an abusive partner and not wanting to expose children to a partner's violence. That was also true for Shawna, a white woman from Oregon who participated in one of the in-depth qualitative interviews. At 33, Shawna was a single parent to a daughter and in a very new relationship. Suddenly she was pregnant, and after the shock wore off, she knew she wanted to have the baby. She felt she could handle it, financially and emotionally. But then she told the guy. "And the second he freaked out and I saw his true colors, it scared me so bad that I literally the next day called and made an appointment." He later flip-flopped and wanted her to have the baby, but experiencing his volatile behavior frightened Shawna. "I thought, he's either going to kill my kid or me at one point or something, and it's not safe for any of us. . . . And to be tied to a man like that and have his child would have been a living nightmare." She'd go on to have another child with someone else the following year, telling our team, "It's not that I didn't want more kids; I just didn't want one with him."

At the time of abortion-seeking, there was no difference in experiences with abuse between women who received versus those who were denied an abortion. But for women who received the abortion, there was a dramatic reduction in the incidence of violence that was not experienced by women who were turned away. It took Nicole about a year after her abortion to leave her abusive boyfriend. But when it was over, it was over. Shortly after Jessica's abortion, her husband went back to jail—to her relief. She sought the help of a university law program that assists domestic violence victims and filed for divorce. And Brenda? After she was turned away, her boyfriend stopped hitting her, but only for the duration of her pregnancy. She wanted to place the baby for adoption, but her boyfriend was against it. After the baby was born, the violence resumed. "I went to a job interview with a freaking black eye," Brenda told us.

My colleague Dr. Sarah Roberts, who you may remember also analyzed the data on substance use in pregnancy, found that after two and a half years, women who were denied an abortion were more likely to experience violence from the man involved in the pregnancy than women who received an abortion.[8] The explanation is that women who are denied an abortion have ongoing contact with the man involved, even if they aren't in a romantic relationship with him, and it takes them years to extricate themselves. In the meantime, they have continued exposure to the risk of violence. As Dr. Roberts puts it, denial of abortion care can result in women being tethered to violent partners.

What happens to the relationship?

Based on our data, the majority of men involved in pregnancies that women sought to terminate weren't eager to take on the role of father. And many had a very tenuous romantic attachment to the woman. Sofia, whom you will meet after chapter 10, had a rocky relationship with a man she couldn't rely on to get a ride to the hospital when she was bleeding. When she called from the emergency room to tell him she was pregnant, he hung up on her. When he called her back later, it was to urge her to get an abortion. At the time of conception, four in five of the women in the study (80%) were in a romantic relationship with the man involved. Just one week after the women sought an abortion, a quarter of those relationships had ended, leaving three in five (61%) still in a relationship.

Since poor romantic relationships prompt women to seek abortion in the first place, one should not be surprised by the steady dissolution of relationships. Two years after seeking an abortion, just under two in five (37%) women were still in the relationship that conceived the pregnancy, and by five years, it was almost down to one in four (26%). We don't find any evidence that abortion is the event that causes couples to break up. Rather, it's the bad relationship that prompts the decision to terminate the pregnancy. Of course, there are exceptions among the women we interviewed. Single mom Kiara, whom you heard from earlier, had been wanting to leave her boyfriend. The relationship had turned scary—he'd started stalking her, she said. But it was the unexpected pregnancy and her immediate decision to abort and cut ties that helped her exit. "I knew that making this decision would be my way out of this relationship and I could close that chapter and go forward and not have to look back or have any strings holding me back." The fact of the pregnancy also ended Shawna's relationship with her boyfriend. Not only did she deem him unfit as a coparent, but now she felt he threatened the safety of her and her child. Most often, as our stories indicate, the actual breakup happens months later, as it did for Jessica, Martina, and Nicole.

You might think that carrying the pregnancy to term and having a baby together would keep couples in a relationship. In fact, relationships dissolve even when the pregnancy continues and the woman parents the new child. Recall Amina, one of our qualitative interview participants whom I talked about in chapter 6. The boyfriend that Amina became pregnant with stayed with her for two years after the baby was born. But the relationship wasn't great, and she said he had no interest in being a father. For the Turnaway Study, University of California, Berkeley, public policy professor Dr. Jane Mauldon looked at women's relationships in the two and a half years after they had sought an abortion. She found no significant difference in being in a romantic relationship at two years (40% among those denied the abortion and 39% among those who received the abortion just under the limit). In those intervening two years, there may have been a slower dissolution of the relationship among those who were denied, but by two years, there is no longer any difference. Dr. Mauldon also didn't find any significant differences in marriage rates or relationship quality for women who were still in relationships with the man involved in the pregnancy. Only 3% of women denied abortions got married within the next two years. Coincidentally, 3% of those who were married at the time they became pregnant got divorced over that time period.[9]

What is clear is that carrying the pregnancy to term results in women having ongoing contact, if not a romantic relationship, with the man involved in the pregnancy. Dr. Mauldon found that at one week after seeking an abortion, 90% of women kept in contact with the man, with no significant difference for the abortion or turnaway groups. However, after two years, 79% of women denied the abortion were still in contact with the man, compared to 68% of those who received an abortion just under the limit. My colleague Dr. Ushma Upadhyay looked at relationships again once the full five years of data had been collected and found that at no point was there a significant difference between women who received and women who were denied a wanted abortion in the chance that they were still in a romantic relationship with the man involved in the pregnancy.[10]

Dr. Upadhyay pointed out that our measures of romantic relationships gathered during the first two years of data collection were not sufficient. They focused solely on the relationship with the man involved in the pregnancy and not on subsequent romantic relationships with men or women. Given the rapid dissolution of relationships, this was a serious oversight. So, starting at the two-year mark, we added questions about whether women were in a romantic relationship with anyone and the quality of that relationship. Because these questions weren't in the first few interviews, we don't have data to know the full trajectory, but we can say whether there were differences after the first two years.

This is what Dr. Upadhyay found: There were no differences in rates of being in an intimate relationship between those who received and those who were denied a wanted abortion—both groups had an equal probability of being in a relationship. However, those who received an abortion had a greater probability of saying their relationship was "very good" up to three and a half years later. Among those who received an abortion, 47% were in a very good relationship at two years. Among women denied, only 28% were in a very good relationship at two years.

So what does all of this tell us? Forcing women to carry unwanted pregnancies to term is not, it turns out, a good strategy for producing strong relationships and families. In the previous chapter on children, we showed that children born after denial of abortion will likely not be raised by two romantically involved parents. That was certainly the case for Brenda's child, who in the end wound up living with neither parent, thanks to too many domestic violence incidents requiring visits from the police and Child Protective Services. Brenda said she would have ended things much sooner had she been able to obtain an abortion. "I stayed with [my ex-boyfriend] way longer than I intended to because we had a kid together—a bond. And then it turned into, oh well, I've been with you so long I don't know how to be by myself, on both of our parts. So it lasted way longer than it had to. I mean, I think that if I hadn't found out I was pregnant and it was his, that probably would have been it. We would have split up for good the year I started this study."

Providing abortions increases the chance that women will find healthier and happier relationships in the future. Such was the good fortune of Guadalupe, who told our team that the man with whom she became pregnant in 2009 strongly pressured her into having an abortion. "Then I met my current partner, who taught me that all men aren't the same," she said. "He showed me that; he gave me the opportunity to see that I could have a second chance. With him I have a two-year-old son . . . For me it was a blessing to be pregnant again. This time, planned and with a partner who really cared about having a family with me."

Supportive Men

Our interviewers on the Turnaway Study heard a lot of stories of men behaving cruelly and violently. We also heard a lot of stories of men being thoughtful, kind, and supportive, both those involved in the pregnancies and other men in the woman's life, who gave her the financial and/or emotional help she needed either to access abortion or, if she was denied one, to navigate adoption or parenting. Sofia's boyfriend might not have given her the support she needed—remember, he wouldn't even take her to the hospital when she was bleeding profusely—but her male best friend did. He went with her to the abortion clinic and, after she was denied, was the only person she confided in about her plans to place the baby for adoption. "He was there for me when I was signing the papers for adoption," Sofia said. "He was there when I had to choose the parents. When I went to the hospital, he was actually the person who took me when I was going into labor." Years later, even after their lives drifted in different directions, they would always reconnect on the birthday of the child she placed for adoption. "He's an angel for me," Sofia said of her friend, noting she couldn't have gotten through this challenging time in her life without him.

Male friends also came through in big ways for other women among the ten profiled in this book. Melissa was struggling to feed her four children while scrambling to abort the pregnancy conceived with her incarcerated husband's relative. Her friend—an older gentleman her kids nicknamed "Grandpa"—noticed her desperation. He not only paid for the procedure but drove her to the clinic. Nicole couldn't afford the abortion she desperately needed to break ties with her abuser. When she asked an ex-boyfriend for help, he wired her several hundred dollars.

Camila's story may sound like a fairy tale—a struggling young couple accepts they cannot get an abortion and turns things around, settles down, and makes good. They went from struggling financially to living better than comfortably. Camila described her partner as "set in his ways" and somewhat disengaged when it comes to parenting, but mostly a loving provider. They would go on to have another child after the unexpected first. "I would say he's very supportive of me and when I had the [first] baby," she said. "He's not hands-on with the children at all, but he works long, long, long hours and he's a great provider—a good man that way."

To me, the greatest redemption story is that of the man in Melissa's life. Her husband seems to have been the worst possible partner—cheating, drug-abusing, untrustworthy, dishonest, and cruel. But after he got out of jail and agreed to move to a new town, he turned himself around. He became a responsible parent, enabling Melissa to go to college. Note, though, that he wasn't the man involved in the pregnancy she aborted. Regarding that man, Melissa is sure she did the right thing because even if she'd had the baby, "it wouldn't have changed him. He wouldn't have been a better dad." Most of all, Melissa's husband is a counterexample to all the men that seem hopelessly irresponsible. His reform couldn't have come as a bigger shock to Melissa. "There was no reason, no logical reason for me to stay with the man," she said. "Except that I can honestly tell you now what I think that was going through my mind was that I thought I could fix him. I thought I could get him off the drugs, I thought I could make him better. That's irrational for me to have thought that, but today he's better. He's had a job for three years straight, and he couldn't be any better with the kids."

Conclusions about Men and Abortion

In the Turnaway Study, the vast majority of the men involved knew about the pregnancy prior to the abortion, but few wanted the pregnancy carried to term. There is widespread support among men for women's decision to end a pregnancy. Only a quarter of men wanted the woman to have the baby, and preferring adoption to abortion was extremely rare. We find that men are often the reason women choose to have an abortion, sometimes explicitly because the relationship is not strong enough to support a child. So it is not surprising that the relationship with the man involved slowly dissolves. However, remarkably and contrary to what many would assume, whether the woman ends the pregnancy or has a baby makes no difference to the chance of an ongoing romantic relationship. For the one in twenty women who experience abuse from the man involved in the pregnancy, being turned away and giving birth increases the duration of ongoing contact, with the result that the incidence of violence is higher among women who are denied an abortion compared to those who received one. A pregnancy carried to term that is with the wrong man or comes at the wrong time has reverberations for the woman's future relationships. In the long run, being denied an abortion reduces the chance that women are in a very good relationship years later, further evidence of the role of abortion in enabling women to set their own life course.

Now we turn to Jada, who was 19 and living in Illinois when she had a second-trimester abortion. As with the other women we've referenced in this chapter, Jada considered her relationship to the man she became pregnant with as an important factor in her decision.

JADA

I was really sad and disappointed and hurt. Even if I had wanted to keep the baby, which I knew I wouldn't be able to, it was just knowing that the father would be him, and that I would be doing it basically by myself.

I was born and raised on the South Side of Chicago until I was about 18 and I moved to the North Side. I grew up in a single-parent household, like, just my mom. My father was present, but he wasn't as present. And now I live with my mom and my aunt.

Where I grew up, it's an urban area, so there's some good, but it's mostly known for its crime. It wasn't as bad then as it is now. I went to a private school in the area. I wasn't really exposed to much crime. I just really heard about it in, like, the newspaper or the news. We have a lot of Boys & Girls Clubs, different programs for the kids. And there are different parades every year for the kids to participate in and the different high schools. So there's good. But it's really known for the crime. People like to focus on the negative.

My mom raised me. She's in law enforcement. And my father is in law enforcement as well. He wasn't a bad dad, but he just wasn't as—he wasn't around as much because he had other kids and he also got remarried. My aunt lived around the corner from us, like, not even two minutes walking. So we were close. That's why she moved north with us. We were trying to get out of the area because it was getting worse as time progressed.

I was living in the North Side of Chicago around the time I got pregnant, but I was still dealing with the guy who I was with when I was living in the South Side. So it was a back-and-forth thing. Like, he would come visit or I would come visit him.

I met him when I was in high school, and our relationship was just, it was really immature. We were together maybe almost two years off and on. I guess I thought we were serious, but now looking back it wasn't as serious. And we weren't practicing safe sex, which was not so smart on my end. But I was in love, so I thought I really didn't care. I really didn't even think about the fact that I would get pregnant. It's just something that happened. Even up until the time that I knew I was pregnant, I was in denial.

For so long my friends were asking me was I pregnant, because I guess they saw the changes in me, but I didn't see it. And when I finally got confirmation that I was pregnant, it was just kind of a relief knowing that I was and ready to figure out what I was going to do next.

I instantly knew that I was going to get an abortion. I didn't think of anything else like adoption, having the baby. I just instantly went to abortion. And I didn't grow up around people who had abortions. So it's not like it was just something that I knew. It was just, like, there was no other option.

In a week's time, I found out about the pregnancy and I had the abortion. I was almost 20 weeks, and I didn't even know because I was in so much denial. I knew I didn't have much time to make a decision. And if I wanted to get an abortion, I would have to do it right away. If I waited any more weeks, then I probably would have had to give birth to a baby and then I would have had to figure out my life and someone else's life.

I kind of handled everything on my own. I had insurance through my father, so I had to ask him for the insurance card. I didn't tell him what it was for. But I had to get my insurance information and then look around for places that would do an abortion. I didn't know when I got pregnant, so I just had to make an assumption of how far along I was. The only help that I did get was from my father's insurance, but everything else as far as looking around and calling places I did all on my own.

I didn't speak to anyone about the decision because I already knew what I wanted to do. I had one friend that knew. She found out that I was pregnant because the day I decided to go and figure out if I was pregnant or not, she came with me, and we found out together. She didn't really say much about it. And I really don't even remember the conversation. The decision was totally mine.

I don't know how the process is for anyone else. But for me it was fairly easy. I just looked around, called, gave them my information, and then they called back, and they set up an appointment, and that was it. I was treated—it was decent. The wait was long, but everyone was nice. They made sure that everything ran smoothly. There weren't any difficulties or anything.

The day of the abortion was pretty emotional for me because the whole time that I was pregnant, I didn't know. There weren't any symptoms or signs or anything. But on the day that I went to get an abortion, I started to feel some kicking. It was like someone telling me not to do it. But I just knew I had to. There was no turning back from then. And then it was a two-day process. So it was like—it dragged on.

By the time that I had the abortion we were no longer in a relationship. I didn't even speak to him. At the time I didn't know that he was doing some illegal things, but it was brought to my attention after we had broken up that he was doing some not-so-nice things. I was really sad and disappointed and hurt. Even if I had wanted to keep the baby, which I knew I wouldn't be able to, it was just knowing that the father would be him, and that I would be doing it basically by myself. I didn't want to disappoint my mom, either; she was a factor in my decision.

The worst part of it is the emotional aftereffect. Like, you realize that you did it. I didn't really have a connection with the pregnancy, so that's why it was just so easy for me. I found out, and I got it done. I'm glad I did it. I'm not a monster, so I knew that part of it was wrong. But it was just something that I had to do to have a better life.

So that was the emotional part of it, knowing that I could have had a baby. But I didn't. Now what if I can't have a baby? Because they explained you might have difficulties with an abortion where you can't get pregnant anymore, and then as you get older your body changes.[11] You can develop certain things. It's just being paranoid.

I still feel like it was the right decision to do it. It was the right decision because I was still a child myself. I wasn't financially stable. It wasn't really smart for me to bring a child into this world to struggle along with me and put them in a position where it would have to want for things. It wouldn't have been fair. I had the decision to choose a lifestyle where I'd have to struggle with a child and to not have to struggle. I didn't want to be selfish.

I haven't talked to my mom about it ever.

Right now I currently work for the city, as a dispatcher, so that's a pretty good place to be at this moment. It's kind of like a career, but I still want to go back to school and maybe figure out how to do something else. Just get a degree. I'm not sure. I'm still trying to figure that out. But I am not in a relationship. I am just trying to live life while I still can.

I still live in the same place that I was living when we started the study. Living with my mother and my aunt. Hopefully by next year I'll be moving out, and I'll have my own place. That's the goal.

I'm not as trusting when it comes to men. Like, I'm not as naive. I think I'm a bit smarter. So I don't just have unprotected sex. Even back then I wasn't having unprotected sex with just anybody. But even when I am in a serious relationship, I still have protected sex until we're both ready to bring a child into this world. But I just practice safe sex all the time. I'm just really more cautious with who I lay down with and get into a relationship with.

I'm happier now. I'm more mature, and I'm coming into my own. And I know what I want from life and who I want it with and what kind of men I want to spend my life with. And I have goals for myself. I want to move into my own place hopefully by next year and go back to school. And I want to open up a business maybe within the next five years and just be financially stable and become closer with family members and travel.

I want a man that's family-oriented and financially stable and secure and what else? Caring, supportive, that type of man.

My father, he eventually found out, and so that kind of made us closer when we finally spoke about that. He was a little bit sad. But his main concern was how I was feeling, and I told him that I was okay, and then we moved on from there. I became closer to my family after that.

Life went on. It wasn't any dramatic changes or anything because it didn't really disturb anyone else's life but my own. We didn't dwell on it. Anything that I was dealing with I dealt with on my own. I didn't share it with everyone.

I had a journal. I wrote in my journal, and then I listened to music. That's just how I deal with anything that happens in my life that's tragic or hurtful or happy, whatever it is, I write about it and listen to music. Yeah. That's what I did.

The abortion made me more of an emotional person. I just became really sensitive to different life events. And when it came to children, it would just be different whenever I was around babies or when I saw babies on TV.

Sometimes I just feel sad. I'll feel numb or emotionless, but I just try not to think about it. I'll see someone with a baby and think like, "Oh, I could have had a baby." Just random moments. Not all the time. I'm not trying to put myself into a depression.

But I just try to think positively because it has been over five years. I've grieved, and I've been depressed, and I've been emotional. I've been sad. Now I'm just kind of moving on with life and hopefully will get pregnant again later on and start over.

It was a natural process. It wasn't over-the-top depression. It was just, like, a natural reaction. And then I got over it. It didn't last for that long. Maybe a few weeks. That initial part of it, like, oh, I just had an abortion, but after that I tried not to think about it.

You have to be careful who you lay down with and who you give yourself to. That's what I try to tell my little cousins. Like, you have to be careful because you can get something that you can't give back. And you can get pregnant. And it just so happens that everything was convenient for me. I had the insurance. It just happened so quick. But I could have been in a situation where it didn't happen like that and I would have had to have had a baby.

I was going to look into different school programs to see if I wanted to go back to school. I was going to look up to see what I would have to do to be able to open up my own business. But that's for maybe next year. Not right now. I still have to figure out if that's what I really want to do, because that's an investment, and I don't want to go into it and then not finish it out. I wanted to open up a salon for nails, hair, waxing, that type of thing. I wanted to open up that kind of salon.

I just hope that I can find a man or a man can find me, and he finds me suitable to be a wife, and he's a suitable husband. And that we can have kids. That's how I want my life to be. But God has other plans. So I'm not even going to think and plan out my life knowing that anything can happen at any time.

I'm really hopeful. I'm optimistic about everything. And I try not to think negative about things because just no point to always be negative.

Jada, a black woman from Illinois, was 19 years old and 23 weeks pregnant when she had an abortion.

CHAPTER 9

Reactions to and Reflections on the Turnaway Study

I f you've heard of the Turnaway Study before picking up this book, perhaps you saw—maybe in the *New York Times*, on Fox News, or in dozens of other national and international news outlets—our most eagerly awaited results, that abortion does not harm women's mental health. We published this evidence in the prestigious medical journal *JAMA Psychiatry* in February 2017, too late for Koop, who died four years earlier at age 96.[1] Maybe you've heard the often-cited statistic that 95% of women who have abortions felt their decision was right for them, a fact known only because of the Turnaway Study.[2] Since we started releasing results of the study, there has been a lot of media attention—more than 360 news articles. Most articles have focused on the rarity of mental health problems and negative emotions after abortion.

There has been comparatively little attention to the findings about the harms of denying someone an abortion: the economic harm to women of being denied a wanted abortion, the detrimental effect of abortion denial on women's existing and future children, and the lasting physical health consequences for women of carrying an unwanted pregnancy to term (including two women's deaths in our study after abortion denial).[3] The relative lack of attention is particularly surprising since, in these areas, we found significant long-term differences between women who received and women who were denied an abortion. While our leaders and lawmakers and newsmakers regularly speculate about deaths from unsafe abortion, they overlook deaths from childbirth. I believe that consequences of abortion denial received less attention than articles about the emotional and psychological consequences of abortion did because the supposed mental health harm from abortion was already part of our national conversation. Our media and our society are slow to present more complicated ideas that change the frame of the conversation. We are still talking about whether abortion harms women and not whether lack of abortion harms women and children. I hope this book helps us see another side of the issue of abortion.

One Turnaway Study article in particular has attracted undeserved attention. Anti-abortion journalists and activists seized on one sentence in the introduction to a paper I published with sociologist Dr. Katrina Kimport in the journal *Perspectives on Sexual and Reproductive Health* titled "Who Seeks Abortions at or after 20 Weeks?"[4] Academics can keep track of how often their papers are cited or mentioned by the media. I would be proud to announce that this one paper is now one of the Turnaway Study's most influential papers as measured by the number of citations and media mentions, except that many people citing this sentence are willfully misinterpreting it. This one particular sentence is the only evidence I have ever seen cited to support the claim that most third-trimester abortions are not done for reasons of fetal anomaly and maternal health, with the underlying assumption that other reasons are more frivolous. Unfortunately for those taking that position, that isn't what the sentence is about and, as far as I know, that isn't true. Want to know how it feels to lead a team of scientists for over a decade, produce nuanced and important findings about abortion's impact on women and children, and then have the most media attention paid to one sentence used as documentation for a claim that isn't true?

It's really, really frustrating.

So let me set the record straight. In the introduction of that paper, we write, "But data suggest that most women seeking later

248

terminations are not doing so for reasons of fetal anomaly or life endangerment." Introductions of scientific papers describe what is already known about a topic; they don't contain the findings of the study in question. In the article we define "later abortion" to be 20 weeks' gestation or later. The purpose of the paper was to describe who would be affected by now-ubiquitous 20-week bans; the paper focuses on women having abortions in the second trimester.

Data on women having abortions in the second trimester don't tell you anything about abortions in the third. Again, the number of abortions drops sharply with each week of pregnancy—90% of abortions occur in the first 13 weeks of pregnancy and only 1.3% occur after 20 weeks.[5] In the introduction of this paper, we explain that the women in our study represent the vast majority of those who are affected by 20-week bans, even though the study includes very few women who received abortions in the third trimester. Why? Because the women at 20 to 25 weeks' gestation (whom we now know a lot about) vastly outnumber those at 26 weeks and beyond (whom we still know little about). Even if all women in the third trimester were having abortions because of fetal anomaly and maternal health indications, our statement would still be true of women having abortions after 20 weeks, simply because women in the third trimester make up a small fraction of those having abortions after 20 weeks.

So the purpose of our statement was to say, if states pass 20-week bans, the bulk of those who will be affected are not women who might receive a "life or health" exception because they are seeking an abortion for reasons of fetal anomaly or life endangerment; they are women like the women in our study. We found that gestational limits will disproportionately affect teenagers, single mothers, women with mental health and substance-use issues, women experiencing domestic violence, and women who were already slowed down because of the many existing barriers to getting an earlier abortion. Sadly, there is no sign that the conservative columnists who cited that one line of our paper absorbed any of the rest of it.

Other people, who may have actually read our Turnaway Study academic papers, have raised criticisms of the study that are important to address.

Objectivity of the Study

First, critics who are politically motivated by anti-abortion stances have suggested that my university and I are too biased to produce valid data. The University of California, San Francisco, is one of the top medical schools and research universities in the world. It is also a major center for abortion training and research. Very few universities study abortion at all, and once a university is known for specializing in a topic, it attracts funders, faculty, and students interested in that topic. Researchers at the UCSF Bixby Center for Global Reproductive Health consider abortion an important, legitimate topic of study. The Bixby Center conducts clinical research into contraception and abortion, and it also trains clinicians to provide family planning procedures like intrauterine device placements and abortion. I am also part of a large social science research group within the UCSF Bixby Center called Advancing New Standards in Reproductive Health, better known by its acronym. ANSIRH studies models of service delivery to improve access to family planning services and how abortion restrictions affect patients, practice, and safety. We at UCSF benefit from having so many experts in close proximity. Our department produces leading research on a wide range of topics, from infertility to fibroids to cervical cancer to the basic science of yeast cells.

I have a doctorate from Princeton University in demography, formally the study of statistics about birth, death, and migration. In practice, it's a field where one can study sex, contraception, marriage, education, employment, poverty, race, health, parenthood—everything measurable that is important to understanding human life.

As it happens, the research I have done over my career at

UCSF, where I began as a staff statistician and am now a full professor, has likely contributed to the prevention of tens, and possibly hundreds, of thousands of abortions. Evaluating Family PACT, California's state family planning program in the late 1990s and early 2000s, colleagues and I showed that providing contraceptive methods to low-income women and men who wanted them saved the federal and state government millions of dollars in averted medical costs for pregnancy.[6] My work demonstrating the cost-effectiveness of contraception in a real-world program likely helped convince the federal government to subsidize this program, which turned it from a politically vulnerable state-funded program to a well-entrenched expansion of Medicaid. The federal government then went on to support similar programs in 25 states, buoyed by our estimates of the cost-effectiveness of doing so. The Guttmacher Institute, a private reproductive health research institute, estimates that these family planning programs avert more than 2 million unintended pregnancies—including more than 700,000 abortions—each year.[7]

I am also responsible for the research showing that when women are given a one-year supply of oral contraceptives, they are much less likely to become pregnant—and less likely to have an abortion—than if they are made to return to a clinic or pharmacy every month or every three months for a resupply.[8] I did this work because California's state government was trying to reduce costs and thought a one-year supply could be wasteful if women don't use all the pills they are given. But because of my work, California decided to continue allowing a one-year supply. And subsequently, 19 states passed bills (whose sponsors cited my research) that now allow a one-year supply of contraception.[9] To be sure, it takes a lot of people—lobbyists, policymakers, health professionals, journalists, and so on—to apply new scientific evidence to medical practice and policy. It's not as if one day we publish data in a respected medical journal and then the next day all medical care is based on this new evidence. But my work has made a contribution to reducing the need for abortion.

Still, the fact that my research has likely prevented abortions doesn't put me in the anti-abortion camp. It was not my primary goal to prevent abortions, though I am very happy that my research has prevented the need for some of them. But when someone feels they need to terminate a pregnancy, I support their right to do so. And when someone becomes pregnant unintentionally and wants to have a baby, even if a partner or parent objects, I support their right to do so. Both of these scenarios have occurred in my own family.

My team and I designed this study to be rigorous and objective. I wanted to measure all the effects of having an abortion and of being denied an abortion. When crafting the survey questions, I put myself in the shoes of someone who was concerned about the harms of abortion, because it was important for the study to address those concerns. So I didn't shy away from asking about the struggles a woman might go through after an abortion—in fact, we asked about more negative emotions than positive ones (so many that one woman said she wouldn't answer any more questions unless the interviewer assured her we weren't using this information to prevent women from being able to get abortions). Given how common abortion is, if it hurts women, I wanted to know. Likewise, I know that raising children is both difficult and rewarding and I wanted to understand how the balance shifts if the pregnancy is unwanted. We specifically asked about life satisfaction hoping to detect a larger sense of accomplishment that might help women transcend the daily hardships that many new parents experience in taking care of a baby.

Representativeness of the Study

The other criticism of the Turnaway Study has to do with whether it is a representative sample. One way bias could arise is through a low participation rate. About a third of the women we approached agreed to participate in the study. Of the 3,045 women that clinic staff approached, only 1,132 women (37.5%) agreed to hear more about the study by phone from UCSF staff, went through the informed-consent process, and enrolled in the study. Just under a thousand (956) completed a baseline interview one week later.[10] It is legitimate to be concerned that those women who agreed to participate do not represent the experiences of all women who have abortions.

One reason women may have declined is that it was a big ask. We were asking them to do 30-minute- to hour-long phone interviews every six months for five years. And we wanted all of their contact information, including phone numbers, email addresses, home addresses, and even the names and numbers of others we could contact if the woman was unreachable. Unsurprisingly, not everyone was up for this level of commitment and disclosure. Our participation rates are similar to other longitudinal studies, but that doesn't entirely reduce the concern.[11] It could be that a woman who felt a lot of shame about her abortion would not want to be reminded of it and would not want anyone else to know she had had one. (In fact, very few of the questions in the follow-up surveys are about the abortion itself, but the women wouldn't have known this at the onset.) A woman who was denied an abortion at the clinic where she was recruited for the study might not want to spend the time signing our informed-consent form because she may have felt that finding an abortion elsewhere was a much more urgent task. On the other hand, a woman who was having trouble processing her abortion or facing anxiety about having to continue the pregnancy, like Sofia, whom you will meet later, might want to talk to someone about it and might be more likely to participate.

I don't think our participation rate was unduly affected by the topic—that women were declining to participate because they did not want to be in an abortion-related study. The rate of participation did not vary by whether the woman received or were denied the abortion but it varied tremendously by recruitment site. The top three sites enrolled two-thirds or more of their eligible women. The bottom five enrolled fewer than a quarter.[12] It is not the case that sites located in more liberal areas had higher recruitment than sites in conservative areas. I attribute the difference by site entirely to the dedication and charisma of the clinic personnel who approached women. For example, Tammi Kromenaker, our energetic and enthusiastic clinic contact person in Fargo, North Dakota, told women that studies often only recruit from clinics on the coasts and this was their opportunity to have their experiences represented. Her clinic achieved one of the highest participation rates.

I have conducted one-time surveys in abortion-clinic waiting rooms where we asked for no contact information and where 80% of women agreed to participate.[13] So I believe the lower participation rate in the Turnaway Study is more a function of the recruiters' enthusiasm and people's willingness to give contact information and commit to repeated interviews over years than of a reluctance to be in an abortion-related study. We have tested whether our results change when we limit the data to just those sites with more than 50% participation rates. When we do this, our findings are the same, although we sometimes lose statistical significance because the number of observations is smaller. The sites that were best at recruitment had people working at the clinic who really embraced the idea of their patients participating in research: California, Georgia, Kentucky, New York (until halfway through recruitment when the initial contact person left), and, of course, North Dakota.

We do have some ways to check how potential participation biases might have influenced the study. We can compare our sample to national studies of women getting abortions from either the Centers for Disease Control and Prevention or the Guttmacher Institute to see if there are biases in who signs up. Is our sample older, younger, poorer, or less educated than women getting abortions nationally? I was relieved to find that the answer is no. The women in the Turnaway Study almost exactly match the demographic profile of women seeking abortions nationally. But I wondered if women's emotional reaction to abortion might have affected their agreement to participate in this study. To check this, I compared our results to those of a separate study in the Midwest, in which women seeking abortions reported, on clinic intake forms, how they felt about their decision. Again, one of our most talked-about statistics from the Turnaway Study is that 95% of the women in our study reported that having an abortion was the right decision. This finding mirrors what I found in that separate study of more than 5,000 women who sought abortions in one year from a large abortion clinic in the Midwest: 94% say, "I am sure of my decision to have an abortion," while 95% indicated, "Abortion is a better choice for me at this time than having a baby."[14] To the best of our knowledge, attitudes about abortion among our participants are very similar to study samples where there was no possibility of selection bias.

Another criticism is concerned with whether women who are denied an abortion and carry the pregnancy to term are representative of those who might lose access if all abortions were made illegal. Of the women initially turned away, 30% sought and received an abortion elsewhere. The comparisons in this book, other than the credit report study, focus only on those who carried the pregnancy to term. It could be that the 70% of women turned away who had a baby just didn't want an abortion as much as the 30% who got an abortion. This seems to be partially true for Camila, who opted against traveling three hundred miles to Albuquerque to get an abortion and views having the baby as her choice rather than a forced decision. The study could be underestimating the harms of abortion denial by following only women who didn't want an abortion badly enough. We reduce this problem somewhat by excluding from the longitudinal analyses women from one site (the site where the gestational limit was lowest, at 10 weeks) where nearly all women turned away got their abortion elsewhere; this brings the proportion who carried the pregnancy to term after being turned away up to 80% among all the remaining recruitment sites. Even without the data from this one site, women who got an abortion elsewhere after being turned away were earlier in pregnancy than women who carried the pregnancy to term and so traveling to another facility was still an option. In my view, the validity of the study rests on whether the women who received an abortion and the women who carried a pregnancy to term after being denied were similar. On measures of how intended the pregnancy was and how difficult it was to decide to have an abortion, they are the same.

Having addressed these study design critiques, I want to point out that the Turnaway Study is very strong on a number of methodological fronts. It is large in terms of the number of women who participated and geographic coverage. The women in this study closely reflect what we know about people seeking abortions in the United States as a whole. We retained 95% of study participants from interview to interview. Moreover, their likelihood of remaining in the study was not affected by how they felt about their pregnancy and their decision to obtain an abortion. The study design was a success: Women who received abortions and women who were denied abortions were remarkably similar at the first interview. Their lives diverged thereafter in ways that were directly attributable to whether they received an abortion. Forty-one researchers from nine universities and four research institutes from across the country analyzed Turnaway Study data, giving credence to the conclusions drawn from the study.

Purpose of the Study

The final critique is about the purpose of the study. There are people on both sides of the abortion debate who do not think it is relevant whether women's outcomes are better or worse if they receive or are denied an abortion. For those who believe an abortion is a matter of bodily autonomy, a woman should have a right to end a pregnancy whether or not it leads to better outcomes for herself and her children. When I report that all the concerns women raise about why they don't want to carry a pregnancy to term are borne out in the experiences of women who are denied abortion, this sounds to such critics as if I am asking women to justify their decision. On the other side, I had a UCSF colleague who was opposed to abortion who told me before I began collecting data, "No matter what you find, abortion is still wrong." She intuited that carrying an unwanted pregnancy to term would bring increased hardships to women but that did not affect her belief that abortion is immoral. To both of these groups of people I say, this study is about the lives of women and children and how they are affected by access to abortion services. I am not attempting to engage in a moral or political argument, though people will, of course, bring their own beliefs and perspectives to the issue of abortion. But it is important for our opinions to be grounded in an accurate understanding of reality. The purpose of the Turnaway Study is to provide, as concretely as possible, an understanding of how unwanted pregnancies and abortion affect the lives of women and their children.

Before I began the study, I also heard from some skeptics who thought that women seeking later abortions would have lives that were such a mess that whether they got an abortion or not, their lives would be miserable. These people were firmly proven wrong. Yes, women seeking later abortions are disproportionately low-income (about two-thirds are below the poverty level, compared to half of women having first-trimester abortions). But in all other ways—in reasons for abortion, decision-making about the pregnancy, and life aspirations—women having later abortions are similar to women having early ones. This is because the leading cause of being late is delay in realizing you are pregnant, followed by logistical challenges that are exacerbated by not having health insurance or cash to cover the cost of the procedure and transportation. We find that both women having early abortions and women having later abortions set ambitious plans and are equally likely to achieve those plans. There may be relatively few people who seek abortions after 20 weeks (about 1.3%, nationally) but for these people, receiving or being denied an abortion has large effects on the trajectory of their lives and the well-being of their families.

Unexpected Study Findings

I was not surprised by our finding that there is no mental health harm following an abortion. This is consistent with many high-quality studies — based on registry data from Denmark, prospective cohort studies in the U.K. and Netherlands, and national longitudinal studies conducted in the United States. Most of these studies did not have a comparison group of women who carried similarly unwanted pregnancies to term. They showed that mental health problems occur at a similar rate before and after an abortion and that women obtaining an abortion are not at higher risk of experiencing mental health problems than other women.[15] The one study that included people denied an abortion, a study of 13,000 women with unplanned pregnancies recruited between 1976 and 1979 in the U.K., found that women who were denied an abortion were not at higher risk of subsequent severe mental health problems (as reported by their physicians) than women who never sought an abortion, after adjusting for previous mental health history.[16]

In the Turnaway Study, I was surprised that we didn't actually find higher life satisfaction among women who were denied the abortion and chose to raise the child. I have a theory about why. Raising a child is difficult and, although it may bring joy, the joy may be offset by the additional difficulties that stem from having a child under less than ideal circumstances. Meanwhile, the women who got abortions are not sitting around thinking about their abortions. In fact, most rarely think about their abortions unless someone calls them every six months asking about it. Instead, they go on to do other things they want to do, sometimes including having a birth under better circumstances later. Pursuing these other life aspirations is apparently giving those who received an abortion similar levels of life satisfaction as those who carried the unwanted pregnancy to term.

Our most unexpected and truly tragic finding is the high level of maternal mortality among women denied an abortion. I did not expect to find even one maternal death in a study of 1,000 women, given that the U.S. maternal mortality rate is on the order of 1.7 per 10,000.[17] Maternal mortality is three times higher among African American women (4.2 per 10,000) than among white women but differences in access to and quality of care by race/ethnicity do not explain our findings.[18] Neither woman who died was African American. But it is not difficult to imagine that the social stressors and discrimination that play a role in African American women's experiences may also be factors for women of other races/ethnicities who are facing stigma and isolation after carrying a pregnancy to term that they feel they cannot support.

My Family Story of Abortion and Unwanted Pregnancy

I can personally relate to the findings of the Turnaway Study, even though I don't have any of my own abortion stories. I did have a pregnancy scare early in my relationship with my husband. We'd had sex when I (mistakenly) thought it was a safe time of the month. I remember the feeling of dread that, within my body, something serious and out of my control and possibly life-changing was happening. I turned out not to be pregnant and never needed to consider having an abortion. When we decided to have children almost ten years later, I was thrilled. Being pregnant felt powerful and extraordinary. I felt a deep appreciation of and connection to the thousands of generations of women whose bodies carried out this astonishing feat before me.

Although I never experienced an unwanted pregnancy, it doesn't take too much looking in my family to find women who did. Sally, my Jewish grandmother on my father's side, had an abortion during the Great Depression and later went on to have three children. With my grandfather, she traveled from New York City to Puerto Rico to get an illegal abortion. She passed away when I was in high school, and what I remember about her was that she loved shopping, had lots of friends, and told great jokes. The abortion was not an open topic in the family. So it was quite a surprise when my grandfather announced that in lieu of flowers when she died, donations should be made to Planned Parenthood. I would like to know how she knew to go to Puerto Rico, what the journey was like, whether the provider there was kind, whether she had complications, how she felt about her experience. Was the decision to donate to Planned Parenthood hers and a result of knowing what an absence of legal abortion is like?

On the other side, my maternal grandmother, Dorothy, became pregnant when she was a 19-year-old in Southern California. As she grimly put it, her golf instructor "taught me more than I needed to know." When she told him she was pregnant, he told her that if she ever told anyone that the baby was his, he would get all his friends to say it could be theirs. So that's my charming biological grandfather. Apparently he already had two sons and was in the midst of a separation from his wife.

Dorothy was raised in a very strict Christian home and her parents were furious about her out-of-wedlock pregnancy. They pressured her to have an abortion. At that time (1940), abortion was illegal but commonly performed. Dorothy's mother had had two abortions herself after getting married but before having Dorothy, because, not unlike many women who choose to have an abortion today, she felt she and her husband could not afford to raise a child. So it was not abortion that was stigmatized; the premarital sex and out-of-wedlock pregnancy were the scandal. Dorothy resisted getting the abortion, and her parents sent her to the Salvation Army Home for Unwed Mothers in San Diego. She stayed there for the rest of her pregnancy and then had a very complicated delivery. Unable to walk, she couldn't go home. Her parents did not visit or check on her after dropping her at the maternity home, so she wasn't sure she would be welcomed back by her parents. Instead, she went home with a fellow new mother she met at the Salvation Army. While she was recovering from childbirth at this friend's place, her new friend's brother raped her. Dorothy later told me that what hurt the most from the whole experience was how she felt after being raped. The man said he raped her because she was "already no good." This idea that she was spoiled or tainted and so had lost all claims over her own body is a theme that one hears regarding unwanted pregnancy as well— that if a woman became pregnant without intending to, she loses all say over what happens to her body.

My mother was placed for adoption with a Unitarian family—a marine biologist father and ornithologist mother—who raised her to care about science and humanity. My son's middle name is Marston in honor of my mom's thoughtful and peace-loving adoptive father, a man who witnessed the effects of testing of the atomic bomb on the Bikini Atoll in the late 1940s.

Dorothy, meanwhile, went on to have a very interesting life. In her first marriage, she spent years trying to become pregnant to no avail. The marriage ended in divorce when she discovered that her husband had, unbeknownst to her, had a vasectomy years before. Between her marriages, she supported herself—getting a paralegal certificate and owning several businesses, including a beauty salon and an insurance company. In her midforties, she married into an Italian family that ran the Los Angeles County Fair. Her new husband was decades older than she and had never been married. He told her that if she married him, she would never have to work again. To her surprise, she found herself working harder than ever in his family's business after the marriage. When she pointed this out, he clarified that he meant she would never have to work for *pay* again. This second husband died of cancer ten years later. During those ten years, they worked for just a few months each year on the fair and spent the rest of the year traveling around the world by ship.

I know all about Dorothy because my mother found her when I was twelve years old. Dorothy was sixty-four then, and my mom was forty-four. A friend of my mother's who was interested in genealogy found Dorothy through the information on my mother's birth certificate. Modern birth certificates have the adoptive parents' names, but in 1940, the birth mother's name was on the birth certificate of an adopted child. Dorothy was happy to be found, in contrast to how many women in the Turnaway Study anticipated feeling if they had chosen adoption over abortion. She hadn't had other children. She lived in a cozy former hunter's cabin in the hills of Santa Cruz, California. When I finished high school in Maryland and moved to Berkeley for college, Dorothy was my closest relative. She picked me up from the airport in San Francisco and drove me to my dorm on the first day of college. She set up a small camper trailer on her property for me to sleep in on my visits. I spent many happy weekends with Dorothy over the next few years—walks in the woods, the county fair in San Jose, dances in Boulder Creek. I loved her and loved spending time with her.

One funny thing is that Dorothy was not a feminist by today's standards. She felt that a woman's greatest achievement was to marry a man who would take care of her. I believe this ideal was unattainable to her and seemed like an easier path than the one she took. All of the things she accomplished—getting a professional position in the 1960s, owning her own businesses and a rental duplex—these were things she had to do because she hadn't managed to find a provider husband. On the other hand, she was completely in favor of abortion rights. Yet she never explained to me why she resisted getting one herself when she was pregnant with my mother.

As an adult, I settled in the San Francisco Bay Area and visited her, sometimes bringing my son and daughter. Later, when she was quite senile, she always recognized me, but she often seemed to think I was still a college student. In her last year, I moved her closer to my house and was able to be with her more frequently. I was with her when she passed away peacefully at the age of 92.

My own personal life and my family reinforce the findings of the Turnaway Study. Clearly, people often have sex without any intention of having a baby. As in my experience, they usually get away with it without becoming pregnant. But unintended pregnancy can happen to anyone. Women who do experience unwanted pregnancy are no different from the rest of us. Based on my paternal grandmother's experience, abortion is such an important part of being able to plan one's life and family that women will go to great lengths to get one. Usually, they feel no regret and instead are able to go on and accomplish other life goals, including having wanted children later. What I learned from Dorothy's early experience is the importance of choice and the power of stigma. Abortion isn't right for everyone. And as Dorothy also experienced, birth is associated with great physical risk. The punishments for women who are known to have any stigmatizing reproductive experience—premarital sex, out-of-wedlock childbearing, adoption, abortion, infertility—can be severe. And yet, in the stories of the women in this study and in the lessons from my own grandmothers, we see that women can triumph over great adversity.

Dorothy refused an abortion, and gave birth to my mother. If she'd had an abortion, I would not exist. Sally overcame great obstacles to get a wanted abortion, then later gave birth to my father. If she had not had an abortion, I again would not exist, because my father would most likely not exist. You often hear the argument that abortion should be banned because we were all once fetuses in utero and that each fertilized egg with unique DNA should have the opportunity to be born. But abortion has been legal for more than 45 years and was actually quite common before that. Many of us are alive today because our mothers or grandmothers were able to avoid carrying a prior unwanted pregnancy to term. While an abortion ends the possibility of one life, the Turnaway Study shows that it also enables a woman to take care of the children she already has, and—if the woman chooses—it makes it possible for her to have a baby under more favorable circumstances later.

To me what matters is not whether or not an abortion occurs. It's whether women are able to chart their own life course. I happen to be the granddaughter of two women who were able to make their own choices. I am certainly not unusual in having relatives who experienced an unwanted pregnancy and decided to have an abortion. Abortion is common; based on current rates I estimate that one in every three women has an abortion in their lifetime in the United States and one in two women worldwide.[19] It is very likely that someone in your family has a similar story to tell. On our slow and very bumpy road to making the world a better place, increasing women's ability to plan the circumstances, number, and timing of their births is an important goal. The Turnaway Study shows that women and children are better off when women have some control over their childbearing.

Brenda, the next woman you will meet in this book, is trying to make decisions in the worst possible circumstances—her life is full of drug use, alcohol abuse, material hardship, and physical violence. Her sharp intelligence does not enable her to transcend this chaos. Having a baby when she preferred an abortion did not set her on a path toward a better lifestyle. And caring for a baby in her situation was just not possible.

BRENDA

It is very, very difficult to find a job when you're
pregnant, to keep a job when you're pregnant,
and to find or maintain a job with a baby,
especially if your partner is a douchebag.

I was born in the South, and I lived there until I was a toddler. And then because my mom's family is from upstate New York and my dad got sick, she decided that we were all going to move to New York, so that she could have some help, because she had a husband who had a terminal illness, a baby, and me.

So for a while we lived with my grandparents until my dad eventually passed away. And then we got our own place. And growing up in upstate New York was, it was fun. My mom made her money differently than other people did, so it was a little awkward sometimes just because, like, don't get me wrong, my mom makes good money, but she's a janitor. And at one point she worked as a janitor at my school, and that was a little awkward. But she works hard. She does good. And I never went without stuff. You know, I grew up riding horses.

I rode horses until I was a teenager. I had a bunch of them. Not all at the same time obviously, but, you know, sequentially. And I guess I was a little awkward socially because I spent most of my time with animals, but I had fun. And that's pretty much what mattered. It was always go to school, get your work done, do your homework, and go to the stables. Eventually it got to be a little too much for the budget with everything that was going on. So I ended up selling my horse because we just could not afford for me to ride anymore. It got to be where the horse board was almost as much as our rent. So at that point, something had to give.

I was kind of ready to give it up anyway because I wanted more of a social life when I was a teen. And I was ready to start dating, meeting boys, that sort of thing. Then I found something that I liked riding more than a horse. Yeah. I got a little bit into partying. Anyway, I had a healthy little social life there. I did that for a couple years. Then my mom kind of had enough of it and shipped me off to a lockdown in Texas, in the middle of nowhere. It was horrible. I was not allowed to go anywhere. They kept us all in the same room, all the doors locked, fucking, yeah, horrendous.

Well, now my mom admits that it was absolutely the wrong thing to do, but she says that her motivation at the time was that she was worried about me, and she was convinced by a sales rep for that place that this was the best thing to do. And she just got suckered into this thing that cost me 18 months of my life. All the money that I had from selling the horse plus a bunch of money that she borrowed from someone at work and never paid back, plus everything that I was getting in survivor's benefits from Social Security, my entire college fund, all went to that.

I was a couple months short of 18 and super unhealthy overweight because I wasn't allowed to go anywhere or do anything or exercise really. So that's how I was when I started college. When I was in the lockdown I didn't give up. I kept doing the whole school thing. Obviously I was getting good grades even though it was independent study, and I later came to find out that they're not even an accredited school, so I don't have a high school diploma. But the university I went to overlooked that. I took my SATs from captivity, and I got into college. I turned 18, and then a couple days later I was down there. And I told my mom to fuck herself for a good two years. I was back in shape, going to school, and partying as much as I wanted.

At university, I was in political science. So that's why I work in restaurants now, because there is no job market for that. Not when you have any sort of a record, which I do. I have DUIs. I have driving-on-suspended-licenses. I have domestic violences, although to be fair that was, like, mutual combat, where I pled the Fifth because I didn't want to just be like, "Oh, it was all him; take him to jail." But that's what he did: "Oh, it was all her; take her to jail." Except for the time I was bleeding, and they took him. So, anyway, that's why I can never join the military. I also have violating-court-orders. And I think there's an old possession case, but that about sums it up. It's all misdemeanors. But there's so many of them that it would just look really bad in politics.

So, anyway, at university I did most of my research in politics and communications. I did some research on my own, and I also worked as an assistant for one of my professors on a book. I would make extra income by writing people's papers. You know: "You can give me money. You don't have to do your schoolwork. Let your parents pay for everything." That is what I did in college. I lived on frat row for a while. That was fun.

When I became pregnant I was back and forth between my kind-of boyfriend at the time. Matt and I had been together for a while, and we kept breaking up because he's an asshole. It was usually my decision. He'd flip out, and I'd leave. But then sometimes I would stay at my mom's house in the spare bedroom until she decided I couldn't stay there anymore. I was not working. I had absolutely no money. And I am not even sure how I managed to buy myself cigarettes, honestly. Like, to this day, I can't even imagine. When she was like, "No, you can't be here anymore," I would go sleep in my car. It was kind of stressful. And I tended to drink a lot. And yeah, the relationship with the person who did that to me, who got me pregnant, was incredibly tumultuous. I would go weeks ignoring his calls until finally I just straight needed a place to stay, and I was sick of sleeping in the car, and I would agree to take him back for a couple days so that I could go stay with him and his aunt.

It had been physically violent with him for, I would say, about a

year when I got pregnant. And that stopped for a while once he figured out that I was pregnant. Once the baby was born, he was right
back at it. I didn't find out I was pregnant until, I would say, four
months. And at that point it was too late to do anything about it.
And, you know, I really, really, really did not want to have a child
with that person. When I found out I was pregnant, oh my God. I
was horrified. I was absolutely horrified. I mean, I was relieved that
I wasn't just fat, don't get me wrong, but I was just overwhelmed. I
was just wondering, is this because I have been drinking too much?
I'm getting a beer belly? No. Once I found out that I was pregnant,
I had to quit drinking. And that was really hard, especially when,
like, he was getting drunk in front of me half the time.

Once I found out I was pregnant, I was right down there at the
abortion clinic. I was like, stick it in me. You know, I cannot afford
this. I cannot do this. The likelihood of this kid having fetal alcohol syndrome is incredibly high. I mean, thankfully he doesn't,
but still it was the worst thing that could possibly be happening.
The abortion clinic turned me away and said that I had to go to a
hospital. Then, when the hospital turned me away, I was heartbro-
ken. Because I was in no position at all to even think about raising a kid. I could not afford diaper number one. So what helped
me stay positive was learning that I could get my teeth fixed with
Medicaid because, since I was pregnant, I got Medicaid. So, at that
point, like, my teeth were awful—totally fucked in the front and,
like, just a disaster, cavities everywhere. So that's what helped keep
me motivated and stay positive. I got to have all of my dental work
done. I had my whole mouth fixed up, even though they wouldn't
give me good painkillers because I was pregnant, I was cool with
that. I needed that work done so badly, and it kind of gave me a
second lease on life, if you will.

Anyway, so I kind of felt like some of the people at the abortion clinic were just, like, how could you not know you were pregnant when you're this far along? You're such a fucking idiot; you
missed four periods? And I was, like, well, you know, I haven't
been having periods for a while. I just thought it was nothing new

because really I hadn't had a period for, like, eight or nine months at that point just because I was kind of underweight—like, almost all of my calories came from booze. I just wasn't having them. I thought it was nothing new until I felt something kick. I felt like I was being considered the dumbest person in the room who doesn't know she's pregnant for four months. I had taken one of those Dollar Tree pregnancy tests, and it said I was fine. So obviously that's a defective product. They were like, "Well, we can only do this up to seventeen weeks, and you are way past that." I was freaking out. I was absolutely freaking out, you know? Being homeless and pregnant fucking blows. I went to a hospital after the abortion clinic. And they're like, "Well, you can go to Georgia." And I was like, okay, I think we're done.

I mean, I had no money, no employment prospects, because you're not going to hire someone who is fucking four months pregnant, five months pregnant. People just don't do that. So that left me entirely dependent on him for my income. And that was a very bad thing. It did motivate him to agree to pay rent somewhere so that we didn't have to live with his aunt. Because I adamantly refused to be living with his aunt in her Section 8 house, having to follow her rules, listening to her bitching all the time, and me having a kid. I pretty much told him that either we would move out and get a place, or he can stay with his aunt and rot. So he decided to go with me and the baby. I really wish he hadn't.

I cried for days. I didn't want to talk to Matt at all, but I kind of had to. And I wanted to drink so fucking bad. I did a couple times. But really, once I learned I was getting Medicaid and that I could get my mouth fixed up, I was, like, okay, it's worth it. I can do this for a little while. And then thank God he came two weeks early because at that point I was already miserable. I didn't even want to have a baby shower, but my mom kind of threw a baby shower, and I had to go.

My mom was super excited that she was going to be a grandma. And she was like, "Oh, this is perfect. This is wonderful. This is going to fix everything." And I'm like no, it's not. She's like,

"Maybe having a baby will make you settle down." No. "Oh, maybe Matthew is going to be nicer to you now that you have a baby." No. It doesn't work like that. It doesn't work like that at all.

Matt started getting real possessive—just super possessive and controlling, wanting to know where I was all the time, what I was doing. And at that point I had to distance myself from him a little bit emotionally just because it got to be too much. It really did. I understand that I don't have a father, but I do not need a father figure. I'm an adult. Especially with someone that I'm seeing. That's just weird. I cannot be with someone who is that controlling. Matt was dead set against adoption. He's like, "If you're having a baby, that's my kid. I'm keeping it. If you don't want it, I'll take the kid and leave and go move in with my mom."

What ended up happening is he kept beating up on me with the kid once I wasn't pregnant anymore, and we had the cops over there all the time. By the time the baby was a year old, we had both been to jail a couple times. And my mom sued for custody and won outright. We, at that point, were getting evicted. I got served with the court papers for custody in jail. I mean, that didn't look good. There was a restraining order between me and Matt. And that meant that I had to go sleep on my friend's couch because I wasn't allowed in my own house. So once that restraining order came down, one of my family members, who owned the property that we had been living at, said, "Okay, well, if she can't stay there, nobody can. Evicted. You both are." So at that point, there was just no way.

Matt didn't even show up for court because he's such a fucking genius that he thought he could evade the process server and just run away from the guy and make the hearing not happen. Which is totally not the case. And my mom and I came to terms with the fact that this is not really a healthy environment for a child. CPS investigated us a couple of times just based on his domestic violence arrest, my domestic violence arrest, like, everything. When we got arrested for having drugs, CPS investigated again. It was pretty clear that we could not have a child.

Brenda

It was an official adoption. I was served with papers suing me for custody. And then I was served with papers again to terminate my parental rights. My mom is Anthony's legal parent. Honestly, I think I did the right thing. He has a nice place to live with my mom. He's five. He's in kindergarten. He loves it. He's happy. He's healthy. He goes to the local schools, which are incredibly wasteful financially for the city but good schools.

For the baby's first year, my mom was taking the baby for, like, three days at a time. And then she'd call and she'd be like, "Oh, well, Anthony is sleeping. I can't bring him home." So sometimes he'd be staying with my mom for a week. I mean, it almost felt like I was coparenting, but not with Matt, with my mom. So as Anthony started staying over there more and more and more, my mom got more and more and more attached. To this day, Anthony does not know that I am his mother. He calls my mom "Mom." He has no idea. Yeah. And if I mention anything even alluding to the fact that, you know, I'm somebody's mom, my mom freaks out, and she positively hits the roof. Like, "You fucking bitch, shut the fuck up." She will go off on me if I even mention it.

Now I'll see my son every so often. Like, he doesn't like to talk to me anymore. He used to, but now, I don't know, like, it's different. It's that age, I guess. But I do know that my mom tells him things about me that I am not necessarily pleased with. I guess even though they can't have the "I'm not your biological mother" talk, they can have the "You should never drink alcohol because Brenda drinks too much" talk. At four, apparently, is when they had that talk. And I'm just like, what is wrong with you people? You need to tell my four-year-old this so that he can be more alienated from me? Thanks.

My mom does help me financially now because I told her I need a little bit of help. Now, like, my mom helped me out to get me a place. So I'm renting a room from someone. She is paying— well, she paid all the rent last month, but it's going to be part of the rent this coming-up month because I'm working.

Looking at my lifestyle since the adoption, I am 100% certain

271

that I did the right thing. I mean, Matt and I kept fighting. It got worse. It didn't get better. And that continued until we broke up. I went to a job interview with a freaking black eye. I was amazed that they still hired me. I've been in and out of jail. Not for long periods of time, but, like, a month at a time. But still, that's not good for a kid. He'd be staying with my mom anyway. You know, being homeless and being in an RV, I literally lived at the parking lot at work. I was living in abandoned buildings right after we got evicted from one place. Doing that with a kid would be absolutely insane. I absolutely did the right thing.

I did the right thing for them because they are happy together. Anthony is spoiled as shit, and my mom is feeling a lot more youthful because she's taking care of a kid. Really that's what she wanted since she first found out I was pregnant. She wanted the baby. And now she got it. So everybody is happy. I mean, sometimes I'm a little regretful, and sometimes I'm a little bitter about it, just because of the shit that they're saying about me and that I'm not allowed to say.

In the past five years everything has been constantly up and down—just constant. Like, the only thing I can really depend on is that things will be completely different a month from now, just because that's the way it has been. That's the way it has always been. I would say I maintained a residence for a while until, like, a few years ago. And, you know, then I went to jail, and we lost the place, and I lost my job. And Matt didn't have a job because he decided that unemployment was fun.

I've been working at numerous different restaurants. I don't tend to stay at jobs very long, but I would like to not change with this one because I like it there. It's really, really easy, and the people I work with are really cool, and I know the bus schedule. I used to drive. My car got impounded because I haven't had a license in years. But right now I am not driving because I just need to save up money to buy a vehicle.

I had a scare, like, a few weeks ago because my period was way late. I missed one. But I tell you, I have never been more grateful to start bleeding at work, you know? I was thrilled. I had the conversation with the guy that I'm seeing now. I had the conversation. I was like, "Well, my period is late, I took the Dollar Tree store pregnancy test, and it says that I'm good, but there's still the matter of the missing period. So, would you be okay if I didn't keep it; what would you like to do if this is the case?" He was like, "I don't want another kid, and I know you don't, either." And I was like, "So, if I go find out for sure with a medical test, I should just not even tell you and get it done?" He's like, "No, you should tell me. I want to at least go with you when you get it done." But I was like, okay, whatever. And then my period came a few days later, and I was thrilled.

I'm using an IUD. So that was another conversation. He said, "Well, you should have them take that thing out and give you the shot instead because sometimes I get poked with the wires." I'm like no, no, no. The implant thing or the shot, those are all bad. They are full of hormones. The IUD is good. The IUD is staying. End of conversation.

We're—it's nothing official. The guy that I'm seeing now, Jason, comes over on my days off and stays with me for a few days, and I'll hang out with him, and it's like I'm dating my really good friend. Honestly. We don't argue. We just have fun when we hang out. I've got my own place. He's got his own place—he's living with his ex and his daughter and her parents and her other kid. I say, "Let's just hang out at my place and, you know, go into town and enjoy our days off together." We're into the same things. It's not like me and Matt, where it was a constant battle, and he never wanted to like do anything except fucking sit around. Jason is really nice. He went out and bought a lock and fixed my door just because I was like, oh, it's not working. Okay. I'm not used to that really because, like, the whole time I was with Matt, it was always a struggle to get shit done—anything. Jason just does stuff like that. And I really like him.

I think I'm happier, but it took a while to get there. I mean, when I first joined the study my life was just a mess—an absolute wreck. And everything was in crisis mode. Just 100% of things were going wrong. So little by little it started to get better, and even though things aren't perfect now, I would say that, yes, I'm much happier, and it took a significant uptick when Matt and I split. I stayed with Matt way longer than I intended to because we had a kid together—a bond. And then it turned into, oh well, I've been with you so long I don't know how to be by myself, on both of our parts. So it lasted way longer than it had to. I mean, I think that if I hadn't found out I was pregnant and it was his, that probably would have been it. We would have split up for good the year I started this study.

Having my son sent my life completely off the rails. Between having him and then losing him, I went a little crazy. You know, I did. I was with someone that I really should not be with. We were fighting all the time. And I was pretty significantly unhappy with that guy, I must say.

On the other hand, about the upsides of having had a kid, getting my teeth all fixed up made me employable. If I hadn't gotten my mouth all fixed up, fuck, man, I don't even want to think about what it would have been like. I'd be one of those people fucking holding up signs, you know, because when you have a super, super fucked-up grill, people think you're on dope, which is not the case. It's like an immediate turnoff. It kills your personal life. So, yeah, I mean, getting my mouth all fixed up—props.

I love my son. I'm really, really, really glad that my mom got to the courthouse before Matt's mom did because, I mean, it's kind of a near miss in the sense that he very well could have been growing up with some fucked-up, backwater, crazy-ass people. And that's his family. Because when I went to jail and my mom sued for custody, she was in line at the courthouse just before Matt and his mom. So I feel relief about the adoption. I only had the baby for a year. I have maybe a greater understanding of people with kids.

I can take out my IUD anytime I want, but I'm not ready yet. My current partner is not ready. And I figure I have five more years to make up my mind. Then I'll be in my midthirties, and then it's very risky. In five years I will probably have progressed a lot. I would like to work on a book. I think I've got something there, and it's a healthy outlet to express myself. It's incredibly entertaining just for me to write it, to come up with a story and edit all my shit. So that's my recreational goal. My work-related goal is to keep my job, perhaps get a second one as a supplement to my income.

Right now, I have a surrender date for either 90 days of home confinement or 33 days in custody, and I think I would go crazy in home confinement. Plus it's incredibly expensive. And it's so easy to mess up that it's almost asking for trouble to do that for three months when you're me—just because I don't think that I would be able to sit around that house for three months and do nothing but go to work. So I need to clear it with work to do my 33 days in custody and come back and keep my job, because I am not doing home confinement. If I did home confinement, I am going to get violated for something that other people are doing or for something that other people are using, and that is not cool. Those rules are for anything that's in the house. It is automatically assumed to be mine because it is in my house. So I don't want to get violated. I don't want to have to do the whole 90 in jail, so I need to have a conversation with my boss about how we're going to arrange this. They seem to really like me at work, and I think I might have a good shot at keeping that job. So that's my goal, just to get through it. And my goals on a personal level, I don't know, I'd like to get out of the house more, save some money, maybe eventually rent an apartment instead of just a room in someone's house. Yeah. Just kind of keep trying to pretend to be a grown-up, really.

I'd like to move out of the area and start a business. I don't know what yet, and I don't know where. I would like disposable income to go on vacation and travel and get drunk in really exotic places. I would like to have my book published. I would like to sell some more of the songs that I've written, and maybe someone might record some of them. That would be cool. Whatever happens in the next three or four months will probably determine it, because if I am able to just do the jail time and keep the job, things are looking pretty good.

You really feel the impact of pregnancy when you think, oh my God, I might be pregnant again. And then you start freaking out if your period is a week late. I mean pregnancy definitely has a negative impact on people's financial well-being. Because it is very, very difficult to find a job when you're pregnant, to keep a job when you're pregnant, and to find or maintain a job with a baby, especially if your partner is a douchebag and doesn't want to help. So, I think that on that end, that the incidence of domestic violence skyrockets because you're financially dependent on your partner because you have to be home with the kid.

And then, we all know that a major contributing factor in domestic violence is being financially dependent on the person. Where you're like, oh no, I don't want to be homeless. I can't be homeless with this kid. I need him for money, and then he can do whatever the fuck he wants because he's a douchebag. Having that kind of control can make people into douchebags. Pregnancy is an incredibly scary thing, especially if you cannot trust the person you're with.

Brenda, a white woman from New York, was 24 years old and 24 weeks pregnant when she was denied an abortion.

CHAPTER 10

The Turnaway Study
and Abortion Policy

There are more restrictions on abortion in 2020 than there were in 1973, when the U.S. Supreme Court first affirmed access to abortion as a constitutional right in *Roe v. Wade*. In the intervening decades, conservative state lawmakers have ushered in over a thousand restrictions on abortion, limiting who can provide the procedures, in what types of facilities, at what point in pregnancy, and for what reason. Some state laws dictate what doctors must say to the woman seeking an abortion, even requiring physicians to tell outright lies about the procedure, like that abortion causes breast cancer, suicide, and infertility. Other state laws mandate how long the woman has to wait and even whom she has to tell.[1]

Abortion rates nationwide have plummeted in the past 30 years from a high of almost 30 abortions per 1,000 women ages 15 to 44 in the early 1980s to 15 per 1,000 women in 2014. Some of this decline may be good news, the result of the development of better methods of contraception and better access to them. But the number of facilities that provide abortion has also declined dramatically. It peaked at approximately 2,700 in the early 1980s and has dropped to roughly 800 at the time this book was written.[2] Several states have only one clinic left. Difficulty getting to a clinic and the cumulative effect of all of these restrictions, especially those that shutter clinics, very likely explain some of the decline in the abortion rate.[3] In other words, more women would get abortions in clinics if they could.

While it is clear that the politics of abortion make it more difficult for women to access these services, women in the Turnaway Study rarely mention the politics. Abortion rights are a political cause, but this is not how most women with unwanted pregnancies experience abortion—as a pursuit of their "right to privacy." In our interviews with hundreds of American women seeking abortion, we never heard anyone say, "I want to exercise my constitutional rights." They didn't dwell on politics or their state's particular abortion restrictions or the future of *Roe*. They talked about their own difficult situations. You just heard from Brenda, who studied politics in college. But she was thinking only about her own desperate situation when she sought an abortion. As we saw, 3% of women in this study report that they are opposed to abortion being legal in all situations; a larger number (20%) have some moral reservations about abortion. Women like Jessica, who said, "My whole life I've been totally anti-abortion," put aside political views when they are faced with their own unwanted pregnancy. But what we learn from their experiences has important implications for which policies might harm or benefit the well-being of women, children, and families.

Let me say here that there is one type of policy that I hope will not come from the Turnaway Study. I hope that the Turnaway Study is not used to push poor women to get abortions for economic reasons. This study has shown that health and economic outcomes are better when women who want an abortion, perhaps in part because they can't afford a child or another child, can get one. The emphasis needs to be on wanted abortions, not coerced abortions. This study does not say that a woman who is trying to decide what to do about an unplanned pregnancy will necessarily end up poor. We did find that, on average, women seeking and denied abortions were disproportionately low-income, consistent with national data. Women who decide to have an abortion because they feel they don't have enough money are correct to be concerned. But any one person's situation is unique. One may, like Camila, end up doing very well financially because of or despite carrying an unwanted pregnancy to term. For a policymaker who wonders about the impact of implementing some abortion restriction that raises the cost or reduces accessibility for women who have decided that they need an abortion, the answer is clear. That policy will cause greater economic deprivation for women and children.

This raises the question, would making abortion more readily available solve the problem of poverty in the United States? No. And let me tell you why. Women having babies make up a tiny fraction of the population of people who are poor.[4] Women becoming poor for a short time after having a baby does not explain poverty in America. Making abortion more available will help individual women who are experiencing an unwanted pregnancy, but it will not solve widespread problems of low wages, discrimination, structural racism, lack of health care, and low-quality education. Greater support for new mothers—subsidized childcare and health care, welfare, and paid parental leave—would, on the other hand, make life easier for all women with infants, regardless of whether they ever considered having an abortion.

Reproductive Justice

Our findings about women's participation in the labor market, access to credit, setting of aspirational plans, ability to establish quality relationships, and ability to plan future pregnancies all point to the important role of abortion in achieving life goals. Abortion rights are clearly central to equal participation in society. But women and people who are trans and nonbinary with less privilege and less opportunity are rightly concerned with a larger set of issues. Abortion and contraception won't solve all their problems. The single-minded focus on abortion rights risks overlooking the full scope of challenges people face. Recognizing this, in 1994, a group of black feminist activists and scholars gathered together at an abortion-rights conference in Chicago. They are credited with coining the term "reproductive justice," the idea that personal bodily autonomy is a universal human right, as are the rights to have children or not have children, to parent in safe communities, and to access all types of reproductive health care.[5] This framework intentionally centers women of color, women who are incarcerated or otherwise marginalized, and trans people. Reproductive justice addresses and highlights a range of reproductive health and justice issues disproportionately faced by women of color in America, such as a maternal mortality rate among black and indigenous women that is *three times* the rate among white women.[6] The reproductive justice framework acknowledges that the problems are systemic: laws, policies, and practices that systematically block women of color from living and raising their families in health and security.

Reproductive justice organizations don't focus only on abortion rights because they insist on the right to choose to carry a pregnancy to term and parent the child as much as the right to end one. Everything the Turnaway Study has found about abortion denied—including increased physical health risk, greater chance of being in poverty, lowered opportunities for other life goals, and reduced chance of having a wanted child later—was true for women of all race and ethnic groups: African American, Latina, Asian American, American Indian, and white. But in the Turnaway Study, we only examine the consequences of not being able to terminate an unwanted pregnancy, and not the very important questions of how women fare when they cannot bring forth the children they desire or are unable to raise the children they already have.

The reproductive justice framework is more than just about expanding the number of outcomes that women should have the right to pursue. The important emphasis is that real reproductive rights stem from people being able to pursue their own personal desires and goals. Looking at international family-planning programs, alternate justifications for abortion rights still predominate, sometimes and in some places, because the radical idea of providing abortion care because *that is what women want for their lives* is not politically feasible. "Legalize abortion because otherwise, women will die of illegal abortions" comes from a public health rationale. "Fund contraception and abortion to lower population growth" is a demographic argument. "Every dollar spent on family planning reduces public expenditures on medical care for unwanted pregnancies" is a fiscal argument. "Legalize abortion to reduce carbon emissions" is an environmental argument. Note that none of these were mentioned as reasons for wanting an abortion by the women in our study.

There may be benefits to the economy, the environment, or government budgets from providing access to contraceptives and abortion. But I believe that these are not good motivations for providing clinical care to women. Low-income women and women of color express historically justified distrust of family-planning programs. Birth control advocacy in the United States has been tainted by its association with eugenicist ideas about who should reproduce.[7] There is a lengthy history in the U.S. of forced contraception and sterilization, and unethical birth control trials, all targeting women of color and those with disabilities.[8] Studies have shown that people want more control over contraceptive decision-making compared to other types of medical care.[9] Any hint that the services provided are for anything other than voluntary achievement of one's own individual childbearing goals sows distrust. The amount of mistrust that already exists is serious. The only way to inspire trust is to have the goal of the clinician be to serve the interests of the patient, rather than the interests of the taxpayer, the environment, or the church.

The Potential for Scientific Evidence to Shape Policy

One of the greatest moments in the (relatively short) history of research on abortion arrived on June 27, 2016, when the U.S. Supreme Court announced its decision in *Whole Woman's Health v. Hellerstedt*. This was a case about two abortion restrictions the

Texas government enacted as part of a new law in 2013. And as far as restrictions go, these were major. They required all abortion clinics to meet the physical requirements of ambulatory surgical centers, essentially mini-hospitals. And they mandated that all physicians performing abortions obtain admitting privileges at a hospital within 30 miles of the abortion facility. A group of abortion providers in Texas sued the state, challenging these new laws. Because while these restrictions might sound like they were proposed to improve health outcomes, the Texas legislature had provided no real evidence that they would. Meanwhile, the plaintiffs argued, these new rules were clearly onerous and designed to close abortion clinics. A law that appears to bring no health benefits to patients but makes abortion harder or impossible to access violates the "undue burden" standard that the Supreme Court has used to evaluate abortion restrictions since deciding *Planned Parenthood v. Casey* in 1992. Back then, the majority on the Court decided that abortion restrictions must not create a substantial obstacle for a woman seeking an abortion before her fetus is viable (i.e., could survive outside the woman's uterus).

The plaintiffs, it turns out, had a very good case: After just the admitting privileges law went into effect (the mini-hospitals requirement never did), about half of the 40 abortion facilities in Texas closed, primarily because hospitals flatly refused to grant admitting privileges to doctors who provide abortion. Abortions in the state declined by 14%.[10] If the ambulatory surgical center requirement had been allowed to take effect, fewer than ten abortion facilities would have remained in the whole state. As the Texas lawsuit and other state lawsuits over similar restrictions began wending through the courts, state attorneys kept arguing that these laws were necessary to save women's lives and improve their health. But there was no actual evidence that transforming abortion clinics into full surgery centers or requiring all doctors working in abortion clinics to have nearby hospital admitting privileges would increase the safety of a procedure that is already extremely safe.

The Supreme Court struck down the Texas laws as unconstitutional in *Whole Woman's Health v. Hellerstedt*. Abortion-rights advocates rejoiced. And abortion researchers like me rejoiced at one particular piece of this decision. After decades of restrictions on abortion passed with no consideration of the actual impact of these laws on women's health, finally the Court ruled that, going forward, an abortion restriction whose stated purpose is to protect women's health must be based on demonstrated benefits and not just on the stated intent of the lawmaker. In other words, if some state legislature wants to institute a new requirement for abortion providers, *claims* that the law would improve women's health are not enough. To survive constitutional scrutiny, the Court ruled, there has to be valid data or empirical studies to indicate that this new law would actually improve women's health. This decision directed courts to start looking at data like ours. My hope was that this momentous Supreme Court decision would incentivize legislatures to make abortion-related laws *based on evidence*. *Whole Woman's Health v. Hellerstedt* filled me with hope that the Turnaway Study could eventually positively impact abortion-related policy all over the United States.

I was so naive.

About five months after the *Whole Woman's Health v. Hellerstedt* decision, Donald Trump became president of the United States. Trump chose his two (so far) Supreme Court justices—Neil Gorsuch and Brett Kavanaugh—from a roster of conservative judges whom he said would overturn *Roe*. As I mentioned earlier, in state after state, anti-abortion legislators began passing new restrictions, seemingly without regard to what is known about their potential impact. It was clear they wanted these new laws to be challenged all the way to the Supreme Court, at which point the new appointees might abandon *Whole Woman's Health v. Hellerstedt*'s requirement to consider the evidence.

Of course, if policymakers and judges and Supreme Court justices care about scientific evidence, they can choose to reject restrictions that do not improve women's health. What the Turnaway Study shows us is that making abortion harder to get does not improve the health and well-being of women and children. Denying women access to abortion services results in worse physical health, poorer economic outcomes, and reduced life aspirations, including the chance to have quality relationships and wanted pregnancies later. It is yet to be seen whether lawmakers and courts will consider our evidence. The team of scientists working on the Turnaway Study have shared our findings with legislative and judicial bodies all over the world. And while we've seen some positive outcomes, the power of politics over science can be discouraging.

That was my feeling after I returned home from a visit to Washington, DC, in the spring of 2016. I had flown to the nation's capital to testify before the United States Senate Committee on the Judiciary during a hearing on a bill sponsored by Republican senator Lindsey Graham, evocatively but inaccurately named the "Pain-Capable Unborn Child Protection Act" (along with a bill titled the "Born-Alive Abortion Survivors Protection Act," sponsored by Republican senator Ben Sasse). Graham's legislation proposed to ban abortion at and after 20 weeks across the whole country on the unproven speculation that fetuses can feel pain starting at 20 weeks. I read my written testimony alongside one other expert opposed to the 20-week abortion ban and three experts in favor of it. I reported on the results of the Turnaway Study—that denying women access to wanted abortions jeopardizes their physical health, economic security, and the well-being of their children.[11]

After I concluded my testimony, there was an audible gasp as politicians and advocates on both sides realized they had a shared goal of improving the well-being of women and children. Those in favor of the ban suddenly realized how harmful it would be, so they retracted the bill and dismissed the hearing. Everyone was hugging and crying, and we all left best friends.

Just kidding.

What really happened after we all finished our testimony is that there was an almost immediate shift of attention to one of the ugliest of fake scenarios—that abortion involves killing babies who are already born. Louisiana Republican senator David Vitter asked, "Do any of you, including the minority witnesses, disagree that any child born alive, whether after a failed abortion or not, should get all available medical care for survival?" I waited, hoping that I would not have to weigh in, but eventually I spoke up. I had in mind the scenario of a wanted pregnancy and a fatal fetal anomaly: The mother wants to spend what little time she has with her baby, and so the doctor makes every effort to bring her fetus out alive. In these cases, the child may show signs of life and, because the child is already known to have a condition incompatible with independent life, this may be the only time that the parents will have with their child. Intervening in a futile attempt to extend the baby's life simply robs the parents of the few moments they have with their child. There are heartbreaking stories of parents in just this situation.[12] So I said that I disagreed with the senator. "I can imagine situations where the doctors and nurses have decided that there is not a point in medical intervention, and by whisking the baby away you've taken away a woman's chance to hold her child and say goodbye," I said.[13]

The senator probed on: "If the [medical] care could lead to survival, do you think that that should be able to be denied?" I replied, "I think that doctors and nurses and women themselves know best whether care would lead to survival. This bill doesn't allow that judgment to be made." Though I didn't explain the scenario I was envisioning, conservative news sites, including *Breitbart*, reported on the hearing and wrote that I had testified in favor of denying medical care to babies born after a failed abortion.[14] What I had intended to say is that I was in favor of making the inevitable end of life for a very sick newborn as warm, loving, and gentle as possible, rather than doing chest compressions or intubations on a baby that everyone recognizes cannot survive. For the next week or two, I received a huge amount of hate mail, calling me a monster and worse.

Fortunately, Turnaway data has had much more impact in other cases and settings. Turnaway Study papers have been cited in U.S. district courts to explain why women are delayed into the second trimester and why such government-mandated restrictions as waiting periods, ultrasound viewing, and state counseling scripts are not needed to prevent abortion regret. In striking down a 72-hour waiting period, the Iowa Supreme Court noted that the plaintiffs "offered expert testimony, which the State did not contest, that the vast majority of abortion patients do not regret the procedure, even years later, and instead feel relief and acceptance."[15] Before Turnaway, there was simply no way to prove—or even know—that this was true.

In August 2017, my colleague Dr. Antonia Biggs testified before Chile's Tribunal Constitucional, the country's highest court, which was considering lifting a total ban on abortion. Dr. Biggs, who is a dual citizen of Chile and the United States, led most of the mental health–related analyses of the Turnaway Study, and she testified about the lack of mental health harm from abortion. Chile's tribunal heard testimony from more than 130 people over two days. Human-rights advocates and lawyers from all over the world testified in favor of liberalization; deans of Catholic universities testified against; and politicians, clergy, health care providers, and social service organizations from all sides provided testimony. A few days after hearing all testimony, the court approved decriminalizing abortion in three narrow circumstances: 1) to save a woman's life; 2) when her fetus will not survive the pregnancy; and 3) for pregnancies due to rape. In its ruling statement, the court declared that most women feel relief following abortion, a statement that can be traced to Dr. Biggs's testimony about Turnaway Study findings.[16]

What would happen if Roe v. Wade were overturned?

As I am writing this in 2020, the U.S. Supreme Court has enough justices who have professed or signaled opposition to abortion rights to overturn *Roe v. Wade*. That famous ruling recognized that the Constitution protects the right to abortion, and it set up a trimester system whereby states could not restrict abortion in the first, they could impose some restrictions in the second, and they could ban abortion after viability (around the start of the third), except in cases where abortion was necessary to preserve the life or health of the woman. In 1992, the Supreme Court case *Planned Parenthood v. Casey* retained *Roe*'s prohibition on banning abortion before viability but discarded the trimester framework, allowing restrictions on abortion throughout pregnancy so long as they don't put an "undue burden" on women. To overturn these decisions, the Supreme Court would have to agree to take an abortion-related case—as they have with the upcoming *June Medical Services v. Russo*—and rule that the Constitution doesn't actually protect the right to abortion or they could support such weak protections that almost any restriction is allowed. Anti-abortion advocates are hoping the Court will take up recent state laws that ban abortion before viability, like Alabama's ban on nearly all abortions regardless of gestation, which was signed into law in May 2019 but has not been enforced.

So what *would* happen if the right to abortion was no longer guaranteed at the federal level? One scenario is that decisions about whether and when abortion is legal would revert to the states. Some states would ban it and others would protect it. If this happens, women with resources who live in states with bans would be able to travel to states without bans. For women who travel, abortion would cost more, take more time, and be more stigmatized. But they would get their abortions. Women with internet savvy would likely order pills online. Currently many abortion pills ordered online have been shown to have the right medication in the right doses so they might be safe even when taken without clinician oversight.[17] The risk to the purchase of pills online (it isn't illegal everywhere, but I am going out on a limb here to suggest that if a state has made abortions in clinics illegal, it will probably outlaw self-sourced pills as well) is that women will be prosecuted. Already there are women in the United States who have gone to jail for using on their own—or providing to their daughter—the same pills they can legally be given in abortion clinics.[18] So I anticipate there would be an increase in prosecutions of women in some states for doing something that may be legal in other states. Some women might do extremely dangerous things—like drink toxic substances, insert foreign objects into their uterus, or have someone punch them in the abdomen—to end their pregnancies. But I don't think that deaths from illegal abortions will reach the number seen prior to legalization of abortion in New York in 1970, because desperate women will have these other aforementioned options.[19]

Finally, if *Roe* were overturned and legality reverted to the states, the Turnaway Study suggests that a large fraction of women (my estimate: between a quarter and a third) would carry unwanted pregnancies to term. This includes women who don't have the information or money to travel or order pills online. And for those women, all the burdens outlined in this book—worse physical health, reduced life aspirations, higher exposure to domestic violence, increased poverty, lowered chance of having a wanted pregnancy, worse outcomes for their other children—will result.

And here's an even darker scenario. *Roe* and *Casey* say that abortion has to be made available before viability. If *Roe* falls, then there won't be anything to stop Congress, if it had the votes, from passing a nationwide 20-week ban. Or even a nationwide six-week ban. Or a total ban. It seems unlikely that people who believe abortion is murder would be content to say, okay, murder is illegal in my state; I'll just let other women in other states make their own decisions. If this sort of laissez-faire, let-others-decide-for-themselves attitude were feasible, they wouldn't have to change any laws at all. They could refuse to have any abortions themselves and let other women follow their own consciences. So if *Roe* falls and scenario one happens, where the decision to ban abortion reverts to the states, what are all those anti-abortion advocates and politicians going to do? Rest on their laurels and allow women in other states to pursue different options? I doubt it. The end of *Roe* could cause a cascade. Some states would pass laws that make abortion illegal or begin enforcing laws that are already on the books but aren't in effect because of *Roe*. Other states would pass laws protecting abortion rights or even try to expand access with proactive laws that increase affordability and the number of providers. This patchwork scenario would likely prompt anti-abortion activists and legislators to push for nationwide bans that, if passed, would mean that women would have nowhere legal to go in the United States.

Remember how some of the Turnaway Study's findings have been willfully misinterpreted and taken out of context? Well, I have no doubt that will continue to happen. Some people will want to use Turnaway Study results to justify abortion restrictions and bans. They will point to the lack of long-term mental health harm of carrying an unwanted pregnancy to term to say that women are resilient. They might characterize the years of financial deprivation associated with raising a child compared to having an abortion as a small price to pay for bringing forth new human life.

This is not an accurate takeaway of the policy implications of the Turnaway Study.

Yes. Women are emotionally resilient. But emotional resilience does not pay rent. Women who are denied abortions continue to report that they do not have enough money to pay for food, housing, and transportation for the full five years of the study. We do not know how long that experience of not having enough lasts, but the credit report study findings indicate that the economic consequences extend beyond our study period. There is not a short-term fix to welfare policy that will eliminate this hardship, although removing heartless welfare time limits and caps on the number of children covered would be a good start, regardless of the legality of abortion.

Beyond the financial burden, taking away women's agency to determine when and with whom they have children fundamentally changes their life trajectory. The Turnaway Study finds that women denied abortions scale back their life plans and end up in relationships that are not as good, even when they don't stay with the man involved in the pregnancy. In part because a stable, financially secure life doesn't materialize, they don't get the opportunity to have wanted children under better circumstances later, like Kiara and Melissa did. We find that many women experience intimate partner violence, as Brenda did, that they might have evaded if they had received their wanted abortion.

Preventing women from accessing abortion subjects them to the very serious risks of pregnancy against their will, threatens their health, and, in a few cases, causes their deaths. The health risks of pregnancy are far from trivial and last long after birth, as evidenced by women who were denied an abortion reporting worse health five years later compared to those who received one. There is no amount of emotional resilience that could have saved the two women in this study who died as a result of childbirth and who left behind grieving families to cope with the loss of their daughter and mother.

Next you will meet Sofia. Her story shows in sharpest detail the importance of social support. She feels isolated and rejected by her partner. Financial circumstances keep her from putting additional stress on her close-knit family. Sofia does not tell those close to her that she is pregnant or even that she has given birth and placed the baby for adoption. Despite her gratitude to the agency involved, we also see the challenges of adoption. Her subsequent pregnancy and birth following similar circumstances shows that the importance of family support is key in meeting financial and health challenges. No story is typical. The unusual aspects of this story—her late recognition of both her pregnancies and her total isolation from family—help us appreciate the range of women's experiences.

SOFIA

*The adoption did affect my life because it's still
something that I can't talk about with anybody.*

I actually grew up in Los Angeles. When I grew up in the '90s,
it was mostly a Hispanic neighborhood. Then I moved when I
was about ten years old over to a completely different neighborhood, mostly Caucasian. Back in the day if you didn't know English, it was pretty hard for you to get around. Me coming from a
Mexican background, my mother doesn't speak any English what-
soever; it was pretty hard. It was really tough for her, so she really
depended on me and my siblings to get around. We were pretty
much her support group.

My father had gotten incarcerated, so that caused us to move.
And that completely changed our lifestyle. It was three of us, and
my mother was raising us on her own. We couldn't afford to live in
the place that we were living in. We had found something cheaper
in a different neighborhood. We're a really strong family. Whenever a situation happens, we have a lot of family that supports us.
When my mother was raising us on her own, they would always
pitch in, lend a hand and watch over us. While my mom was at
work, my grandma would cook for us.

My mother comes from a Catholic background, so I was raised
as a Catholic. And church was a must every Sunday morning. For
us Hispanics, the Virgin Mary is something really big for us. We
really do take just that one day to attend church. Growing up you

don't really understand the point of being at church. You don't really want to be there. You're young, you want to be out with your friends, or you just want to be home watching cartoons. So it felt like we were being forced to go to church. But as we kept growing up, all the events that happened made us turn to the church because we depended more and more on the church support group.

After my father got incarcerated, things got pretty tough for my mom. She had to work two or three jobs at times to put food on the table and put clothes on our backs. My mother lost one of her jobs. So then, we felt just like the world was crumbling down on us. She was doing her best to provide food for us and clothes. And she did a very good job, because now as we're older we take care of her. She's not old, but we just want to take care of her the same way she took care of us.

I haven't seen my father in several years. He was released from prison and ever since then I haven't really spoken to him. I really don't know what he was incarcerated for. My mother never spoke to us about it. She always told me, if your father wants to speak to you about why he got incarcerated, then he's more than welcome to. But, when I went and asked my father what he was incarcerated for, he just couldn't look me in the eye and tell me. He would always change the conversation. It's something that I'm still struggling with because I just want to know. He reaches out to us, but if I can't get an explanation, then I really don't think there's much to talk about. It's something I still can't completely forgive him for, but I'm trying.

I actually met my boyfriend through mutual friends. He was having a welcome-back party because he had come back from serving in the military. When I got invited, my friends were like, "Let's go. You don't really go out." I met him that day, and it was just like we connected right away. From that day on, it's like we were inseparable. I was 17 or 18 years old when I met him. He's eight years older than me. I was still in school. I was working. And he wanted me to spend as much time as I could with him. When I came out of school, he wanted me to spend time with him. Or when I was in school, he would text me and say, "Well, can you get out of school early?" And I would get upset because you're older and wiser, and you should know that without an education it's really hard for somebody to be something in life. So it was not just work that I felt like he was making me leave, but it was school and my brothers and my sister, which is something that I didn't want to do. But I think not having my father around made me seek the love from other men. It felt like he was making me choose either him or my life. And I practically dropped everything that I was doing to just be with him. I knew I had to do for my siblings because if I didn't, then nobody else would. It's like they depended on me so much, and I couldn't fail them.

I actually found out I was pregnant when I was about five to six months along. I didn't know I was pregnant because I was still menstruating. I didn't get nauseous. I wasn't vomiting—all the things that I knew were symptoms of a pregnancy. I would see it on TV, but you think it can never happen to you. So I was actually with my boyfriend at the time when I started bleeding. And I just felt like, okay, it's just my menstrual cycle. I didn't think anything of it. But when it wouldn't stop, it felt like I was—every time I walked or every time I sat down, it felt like I was urinating on myself. And I knew that wasn't ordinary.

I told him, "I think I need to go to the hospital." And we were already drifting apart, so he didn't come along. And I went to the emergency room because I didn't know what was going on with me. I told them I'm bleeding excessively, which is something that is not normal for me. I was on the verge of having a miscarriage. The first thing they asked me was if I was pregnant. And I said, no, not that I know of. I'm not having any symptoms, any normal pregnancy symptoms. But when they did a pregnancy test, it came out positive. And I couldn't believe it. So they did a sonogram on me, and they told me I was already five months pregnant. At that time I was ecstatic. I was really ecstatic.

I called my boyfriend and I told him, "I have to tell you something." When I told him, he hung up the phone. And I didn't get a call back until the next day. He told me, "Well, I don't think it's the right moment. I really think you should get an abortion." He said, "I'll pay for half of it and you'll pay the other half." When I heard that, I knew that bringing a baby into this world wasn't such a good thing as I thought it would be. When I asked him to come over and maybe we could talk about it, he came over and he kept insisting that an abortion was the best option because our relationship was rocky as it was. And maybe bringing a kid was not going to be so helpful, either.

I was devastated. I didn't want to force him to be a father if he didn't want to be a father. That's when I started looking into abortion. I knew that an abortion was not an option anymore; I was just hoping for somebody to tell me different. So it was really hard. I knew financially I wasn't stable. I had a part-time job at the time. In school, I was really struggling to keep up. I was really focused on working because I saw my mother, and she would struggle at times to put food on the table. Things got really rocky, and we actually got evicted. So we had to leave. And that was another thing that was going on. So it was tight as it was. And just bringing a kid into there, I felt like that would be a burden to my mom because she's raising already three kids, and then one more baby would just be heartbreaking. I know she would have helped me in every way possible. I just didn't want to break her heart.

Deep down inside I felt happy because I knew I was bringing something so beautiful into this world. And then when I stopped and thought about what happens if he doesn't want to be a part of the baby's life? What am I going to do? Everything's going to fall on me. I saw my mother struggle. Do I really want to go through this? Is this the right moment? So many questions popped into my head at that very moment, and I was just confused. My two minutes of happiness that I first felt drifted away when I started realizing that bringing a kid into this world would be a lot harder than I thought. So that's when I started looking into maybe having an abortion.

I actually went to an abortion clinic. I set up an appointment.

They did a pregnancy test. And they pretty much assured me that an abortion was not possible. I just was devastated at that moment. But then they had me speak to a counselor about maybe adoption, putting the baby up for adoption. And I knew that was the best and only option that I had. At that time when I was there with the counselor, she presented the idea and she pulled out the pamphlet. I just broke down because the first thing that came to my mind was, what are people going to think of me? What is my family going to think of me? I knew there were other cousins around me that have had kids, but their boyfriends were there with them to help them raise the babies. And I just felt like this was just going to be a burden on my mother. Things were rough as it was, and me bringing a kid into this world would just be that much more worse.

I really broke down because I didn't know how my family would look at me. I didn't know if they would turn their backs on me. I just didn't know what would happen. And I was just scared of rejection because I already felt rejected from my boyfriend at that time. My best friend, Jose, was the one person that I was able to confide in. He came with me to the abortion clinic. He was just there for me throughout this moment. So I was lucky enough to have my best friend there for me even though I would have wanted my family. But I felt that my family would really look down on me.

Emotionally, I don't think I ever prepared for having a baby. I just started going to my doctor's appointments. I know the doctors were pretty mad at me, but it's not like I knew I was pregnant, because I wasn't having any symptoms. And I didn't have a belly. You wouldn't think I was pregnant, so I guess that's how I fooled my family. My first appointment, when the doctor walked in, he said, "Wow, I can't believe you waited so long to get prenatal care." He was like, "What kind of mother are you?" So when he said that, I broke down because he didn't know the situation that I was going through. He just assumed that I didn't seek prenatal care, which was not the case at all. When that happened, I walked out of the office. If I didn't feel comfortable, I was not going to stay with that doctor.

It was really tough on me. I wasn't able to concentrate anymore on school or even work. And my relationship after that just completely fell apart. Well, it was fine for two months. And then he just told me he wasn't ready for a family. So at that moment, I told him, well, there's nothing that I can do. I'm already too far along, and I'm going to go through with it. But I never mentioned to him the option of adoption, either. So he assumed that I was going to keep the baby. I ended up leaving school because I felt that people could see. I was paranoid because I was thinking, maybe people do know that I'm pregnant, and maybe that's why they're treating me different. But I think it was just all in my head. So it was really tough for me. What made it that much harder for me was I had to look at my mother every day, and I just felt like I couldn't tell her. That was the worst part, not being able to tell my mother, the one person that I always confide in, the one person that I always looked to when I was upset. So it was really hard. And I felt like I had to hide all my paperwork, all of that stuff, because I was scared of anybody finding out.

To this day I haven't told anybody about my adoption. The only person that knows is my best friend. We've drifted apart a little bit. But we still keep in touch. Every year when we hit the day that my son was born, we just reconnect. We just get together. And when I need to cry, even if we don't speak a word, he's just there for me. And I'm so grateful for that because he didn't look down on me. He didn't treat me differently. And he just made the whole situation so much easier instead of having to go through it by myself. He was there for me when I was signing the papers for adoption. He was there when I had to choose the parents. When I went to the hospital, he was actually the person who took me when I was going into labor. He was like an angel. He's an angel for me.

That day, I didn't know if I was going into labor or not. But I was just having really strong back pains. And I couldn't explain it. And I just remember calling my friend Jose and telling him, well, I feel like something's not right. So the first thing he said was let's go to the hospital. He came and he picked me up, and we went to the hospital. And that's when they told me that I was already in labor. My water had not broke, but I was going into labor. When they told me, I was so scared, not because I was going to have a baby, but what was going to be my excuse at work? I had to be at work later on that day. I didn't know what I was going to tell my mother. Why am I in the hospital? Because she doesn't know that I'm pregnant.

My friend was there with me. He was just there when they were checking me, through the whole process. If he could have been in the surgery room, I think he would have been there. But he wasn't able to because it was a higher-risk pregnancy. My blood pressure was going up because I had all these emotions. I had so many things on my mind. And it was kind of—it was really hard. So all I remember telling him was, can you please call Lisa, who was the lady in charge of the adoption. He called her. She met us at the hospital after I had already had the baby.

I remember after they told me that I was pregnant, I went over to the adoption agency.

They told me it was going to be a long process. I met with Lisa. She just pretty much told me the process and the steps. And my mind had still not settled that I was going through with this, and it just seemed like I wouldn't have enough time to do everything before the baby came. I got a complete surprise when the baby came a couple of weeks early. So that's when Lisa really stepped in. After the baby was born, they took the baby to the agency, to their nursery, and she just made everything so much quicker. She helped me pick out a family that I thought was going to be perfect for the baby, and she was just a blessing. I told her that I wanted to be able to keep in touch with the adoptive parents, so I chose for an open adoption. I have no contact with the child, but I do have contact with the adoptive parents. And they're just awesome. We try and keep in touch as much as we can. One thing I did ask them for was for him to learn his culture and know where he comes from. I just wanted for them to keep that culture alive in him. And they've been doing a great job at it.

I'm happy that I went through this, that I went through with it. I felt like it's the best decision I've ever made because I look at the pictures that the adoptive parents send me, and he's very healthy. He's very happy. And seeing him happy makes me happy because at that moment I knew I wasn't going to be able to make him happy the way they're doing it.

After I had the adoption, I reconnected with my boyfriend. I didn't tell him. I pretty much lied to him about what had happened. I felt like that was the best because I didn't know what his reaction would be. I actually told him I had a miscarriage, because he knew that I went to the hospital. After that, things were going good. And about a couple of months later when we reconnected and we got back together, I became pregnant with my second child. And it's like the whole process of him not wanting a family happened again. But this time I was older and wiser, and I had already gone through one situation and I didn't want to go through that again.

I knew that my family wouldn't look down on me, because I approached my mom about it and I told her—I had to confess to her that I was pregnant. I just had to tell her. I couldn't keep another secret from her. I just couldn't. It was breaking my heart just keeping one secret. So I knew I had to tell her about this pregnancy. And she was just ecstatic about it. She was happy she was going to be a grandmother. At the end of the day I'm always going to be her daughter, and she's always going to love me no matter what I do or what I say. She's always going to have my back in whatever decision that I make.

This pregnancy with my daughter was the same thing as my first pregnancy because I didn't find out until I was about almost five months. But I knew I wanted to have my daughter, even if her father was not going to be around. This time around I had my mother there for me. So it was so much easier. Even if I didn't have the support from my boyfriend, I had the support from my family to back me up. It was still really rough because I had preeclampsia. It was a really, really tough pregnancy. My mother attended every doctor's appointment with me. And that made it so much easier.

At times I wanted to tell her about my first pregnancy, but I just couldn't open my mouth and just tell her. I just didn't want to feel rejected from her. I've always kept that a secret from her.

My life is actually going pretty good. I adore my daughter, and she's made me—she's changed me in every possible way that I can think of. She's made me a better person. She makes me see life different. I've always loved kids. So finally having one of my own, I've learned so much. I've struggled so much with my daughter because she was always getting sick. And she was always at the hospital. There was always something wrong with her. When doctors told me that she probably wasn't going to make it past her first year, I was devastated. When I was pregnant with her, I would catch seizures. When I was giving birth to her, I had a C-section and I caught a seizure. Having the high blood pressure throughout my whole pregnancy, doctors said that that was maybe a reason for her poor health. That was something that affected her as well, not just me. But they really couldn't diagnose her with anything at that moment. Her oxygen level would always drop. She would have respiratory problems. And she was always getting sick. Her immune system was really weak. And doctors just couldn't give me a reason why. But as she got older, her immune system got stronger. She got stronger. And it was just, like, a miracle because she didn't get sick anymore.

I'm just so glad, and I'm so thankful to God for giving me another chance to become a mother and making me realize how beautiful life can be, how much joy they can bring to you. She knows how to make me smile. She knows when I'm upset. She can read me so well. And when I'm upset or when I'm sad, she just comes over and lays down with me and tells me that everything's going to be okay. So she's a blessing to me.

Every year that my daughter is getting a year older, I get emotional. So it's really tough on me seeing her grow up and develop her own personality, her becoming independent. When I tell Isabella, "Please stop growing up," she responds, "It's okay, Mommy, I'm still your baby." So it's like she knows exactly—she's a very smart kid. She's actually very healthy. I kind of got in trouble when I took her to the doctor because the doctor said she was a little bit more on the chubby side. But she's very active. She's pretty tall. And she gets that from her father. So that's one reason that the doctor said that her weight is okay, because of her height.

Her father is not really around. But him not being around has made me that much stronger. There was a time where he was living with us and everything was going perfect. But I guess he hasn't reached the point of maturity that he should be at. He's just not ready for commitment. And I just want my daughter to have a stable relationship, a stable family, a stable house. Now I have a completely different job. I'm still not in school like I would like to be. I would like to continue my studies. But right now raising my daughter and putting a roof over her head is what's mostly important to me. Just enjoying her now, it's like she's growing up so fast.

Overall, the adoption did affect my life because it's still something that I can't talk about with anybody, just my best friend, Jose, who was there with me through the whole process. It really did mess me up in a way emotionally because I just didn't know how to respond to it. I was confused at that moment. It was, like, a big confusion. Little by little it just got easier and easier. Having my best friend with me and him telling me that everything would be okay, just having that one person made a big difference, because I really don't know if I would have been able to do it by myself. I have a lot of positive emotions—well, yeah, positive emotions—because it taught me so many things. It changed me completely as a person. It matured me so much more. It made me realize that I needed to consider contraception. It helped me become a better person, not take things for granted, and just it made me become closer with my family.

If adoption was not an option, I think me raising him would have been really tough. It would have been very hard. And that's one thing that I was scared of, that I wouldn't be able to provide for him the things that he needed, and then him later on in his life hating me for not being able to give him everything that he wanted. I'm so happy that I placed him for adoption. I'm so thankful for the adoption agency, for the couple that took him in and are making him so happy. I feel relieved. And I don't feel bad at all. I don't regret it. I look at it as a life lesson.

I actually would like to have one more just because I wasn't able to keep my first child. And I think it would have been perfect if those were my only two kids. But because I wasn't able to keep him, I want to have a boy. And at times I feel like my daughter is lonely. She doesn't have anybody to play with. And I feel like maybe one more kid would be perfect, would make my life perfect. That would make my family that much more perfect. I'm trying to make things work with my boyfriend. I just feel like people would look down on me if I have a kid by somebody that isn't my daughter's father. It's been really rocky. And if it doesn't work, then it doesn't work. Having a kid is not my main priority right now, so I can wait on that.

I'm actually looking into going back to school, getting a better job. I'm an overnight manager. I work the graveyard shift, which is pretty tough because I come home early. I work from ten to seven. So when I come home, my daughter is already awake. And she's up and running. I'm just so drained out from work that sometimes I can't spend as much time as I would like to with her. But the pay is really good. And I think that's what's making me keep that job for now. I was actually going to take a test next week for a job working for the city. I definitely want to go back to school. I just really want to have my own house, even if it's a little house, just something that I can say is mine that I've worked for. And I want to see my daughter happy. If she's happy, I'm happy. But having a house and a place to call mine would be a big achievement for me.

I felt like there was a time and point where I felt like there was nobody out there that would help, because we had gone through so many struggles, and there was people in my lifetime before that had rejected us. And I felt like the whole adoption was something incredible. The people behind it that made it so much easier. They're a blessing, because you would never think that there's people out there that were not knowing you and they would care about you so much. It just really changed my perspective on people.

Sofia, a Latina from California, was 19 years old and 26 weeks pregnant when she was denied an abortion.

CHAPTER 11

Next Steps for Science

Many of the often-repeated arguments about abortion have no basis in evidence. I am not talking about moral or religious arguments that do not admit proof or disproof. I am talking about beliefs and assertions about the role of abortion in our society and its effect on the lives of women and children. These are things that can be measured and tested, such as the idea that abortion hurts women. Here is the scientific evidence from the Turnaway Study that busts common myths about abortion that you hear from both abortion-rights supporters and opponents.

1. Only poor, childless, teenage, irresponsible, nonreligious, [fill in your stereotype] women have abortions.

The only kind of person who can count on never needing an abortion is one who can't get pregnant. All types of people get abortions. These include people from all walks of life, ages, races, ethnicities, incomes, religions, political beliefs, sexual orientations, gender identities, and even those who are opposed to abortion on principle. Having great access to contraceptives, liking the available methods, and being meticulous about using them reduces one's chances of an unintended pregnancy. But not to zero. Those seeking abortions are disproportionately low-income people, people of color, and people in their early twenties. This is likely due to worse access to and more distrust of contraceptive methods and/or health care providers. And for some, less autonomy in their lives over whether to have sex and use contraception. See chapter 2.

2. Abortion is always a difficult decision. Women need more time.

The Turnaway Study finds that for about half of women seeking abortion, it is a straightforward, even easy decision, and for about half it is difficult. That a woman makes this decision easily does not mean she takes it lightly. Instead, the choice may be clear when she considers her options and circumstances. When we ask women why they want to end a pregnancy, we see that all the concerns they have are borne out in the experiences of women who are denied an abortion. Women are making very thoughtful decisions. Mandated delays by the government are unnecessary, frankly patronizing, and cause abortions to occur later in pregnancy. Gestational limits run the risk of making women rush their decision in trying to meet a deadline.

Sometimes people wanting an abortion *are* in a hurry. The largest cause of delay is not realizing one is pregnant. That can happen when one has few symptoms of pregnancy or has health conditions that make one feel tired or nauseated or miss periods, and as a result, not realize that one is also pregnant. The second most common cause of delay is raising the money to pay for the abortion and expenses, as well as traveling the distance to get to one of a diminishing number of abortion facilities. See chapter 2.

3. Adoption is the solution.

Few women (9%) will choose to place a child for adoption if they can't get an abortion. Asking women to go through the physical experiences of pregnancy and childbirth and the emotional experience of placing a child for adoption against their will puts women's health and lives at risk. Women who preferred to have an abortion but placed a child for adoption had high levels of regret about not having received the abortion. See chapters 4, 5, and 7.

4. Making abortion illegal doesn't stop it from happening. It only makes it unsafe.

The first part of this statement gives the impression that regardless of the law, women find a way to end unwanted pregnancies. We know that is not always true. Just making abortion unaffordable stops it from happening for many women. Probably as many as a quarter of women who want an abortion but can't afford it carry the pregnancy to term. In the United States, state law and clinic gestational limits alone prevent at least four thousand women from getting wanted abortions each year. The Turnaway Study would not have been possible if everyone were able to magically end unwanted pregnancies without access to abortions in clinics. See chapter 3.

The second part of this myth implies that illegal abortion is always unsafe. Illegal abortion can be unsafe—when women try something very dangerous, like douching with bleach, putting sharp objects in their wombs, or seeking care from untrained providers. However, the availability of medication abortion pills, online and across borders, means that abortions managed by women themselves can be safe.

Finally, this whole argument suggests that unsafe abortion is the only bad outcome from women not having access to legal abortion. If abortion was illegal, many women would carry their unwanted pregnancies to term. They and their children would experience all the physical health and economic hardships documented in this book. See chapters 5, 6, and 7.

5. Abortion is physically risky.

The complication rate for abortion is very low, lower than for wisdom-tooth removal and tonsillectomy. More relevant for those who are unwillingly pregnant, the complications and risks from childbirth far exceed those of abortion. Not only is the risk of death 14 times higher for birth than for abortion but also we find that women's health suffers for years when they are denied an abortion and have to carry the pregnancy to term. There is no evidence that having an abortion is associated with greater chance of subsequent infertility. See chapter 5.

6. Later abortions are always for fetal anomaly or maternal health.

If "later abortion" means the 1–2% of all abortions that occur beyond 20 weeks, this statement is not true. Most women having abortions beyond 20 weeks are between 20 and 24 weeks. In addition to those with maternal or fetal health reasons for abortion, there are women who are late in discovering they are pregnant or who experience significant barriers to getting an abortion. A tiny fraction of abortions occurs beyond 24 weeks. No data currently describes the reasons for abortion or for delay after 24 weeks. In most states, third-trimester abortion is banned except for fetal and maternal health reasons, which suggests that many patients over 24 weeks are seeking abortions for these reasons. But our fixation on this question implies that only maternal and fetal health abortions are acceptable. Given the physical health, economic, family, and life-course consequences of carrying an unwanted pregnancy to term, it is clear, from a health and justice perspective, that maternal health or fetal health reasons are not the only valid reasons for seeking to end an unwanted pregnancy. See chapters 2, 5, 6, and 7.

7. Women who have abortions regret their decisions, experience post-traumatic stress symptoms, use illicit substances to cope, and are depressed. Or the opposite myth: *If you think having an abortion makes you depressed, having an unwanted baby is much worse.*

We find no relationship between the outcome of the unwanted pregnancy and long-term mental health outcomes like depression, anxiety, suicidal ideation, substance use, or post-traumatic stress. Being denied an abortion is associated with short-term experiences of heightened anxiety and low self-esteem compared to getting a wanted abortion. Women are resilient. That doesn't mean that unintended pregnancy is easy. But other stressful events, like physical and sexual abuse and past mental health problems are much more closely associated with experiencing later psychological distress than unwanted pregnancy, abortion, or birth. Symptoms of depression and anxiety gradually improve for women over the five years, regardless of the outcome of the pregnancy. See chapter 4.

8. Having a baby (from an unwanted pregnancy) brings a couple together.

We find that relationships gradually dissolve whether the woman gets a wanted abortion or carries the unwanted pregnancy to term and raises the baby. At no point over five years are women who have babies more likely to be with the man involved in the pregnancy than women who have abortions. However, being denied an abortion results in continued exposure to violence for women in abusive relationships. See chapter 8.

9. Women are selfish when they choose to have an abortion. Women who have abortions don't want to be mothers.

Most women seeking abortions are already mothers (60%). When women decide to end an unwanted pregnancy, they are often considering the needs of their existing children or thinking about the better life that they could give to a future child. The Turnaway Study shows that women's existing children do worse when their mothers are unable to get a wanted abortion, measured in slower achievement of developmental milestones and an increased chance of living in economic deprivation. For women who want to have more children, ending an unwanted pregnancy makes it more likely their next child will come from a planned pregnancy, live in financial security, and be closely bonded to their mother. See chapters 6 and 7.

10. Women's lives are harmed by abortion.

This is the big one. Abortion is associated with better outcomes for women and children compared to carrying an unwanted pregnancy to term. These include lower immediate physical health risks and improved health outcomes for women over the next five years; greater likelihood of having a wanted child at a later date; happier romantic relationships; lower poverty and less need for public assistance; greater ability to take care of existing kids; and a greater likelihood of setting and achieving aspirational life goals in the coming year. A small minority of women regret their decision to have an abortion, just as a similar percentage continue to wish they could have had an abortion after being denied one and having a baby. See chapters 5 through 8.

Changing the Conversation about Abortion

The point of the Turnaway Study was not to just correct commonly stated falsehoods about abortion. We have studied women who have later abortions for reasons other than fetal anomaly or maternal health. These are the most stigmatized, least socially acceptable abortions. The stories in this book show that women who have later abortions are just like people you know. They have hopes and goals, responsibilities and challenges. If we can see these women as people and their decisions as valid, maybe we can resist the temptation to think that the government can make their decisions for them.

The media often presents the issue of abortion as a debate. An article about abortion is very likely to include pictures of protesters, and for the really balanced news sources, also counterprotesters (at least when they are not running a picture of a pregnant torso). We are so focused on the question of whether women should be allowed to get an abortion, we have missed the question of why they would want to and what the consequences are when they cannot. In our rush to make moral judgments, we have presented the issue as abstract and not one that affects millions of real people—women, men, nonbinary people, children, and families.

Next Steps for Research on Abortion

Until 2007, when I first conceived of the Turnaway Study, I knew little about abortion. The demography and public health academic conferences that I'd attended up to that point in my career treated abortion as a fringe topic. To the extent that women's reproductive health was covered, it was about prevention of unintended pregnancy rather than treatment for unwanted pregnancy. Those few researchers who studied abortion risked being considered activists rather than scientists. All that changed in 2005 with the launching of the Society of Family Planning, a professional organization whose members now include about 800 researchers from nearly every U.S. state, along with the District of Columbia, Canada, and Latin America, who study contraception and abortion. Members include epidemiologists, sociologists, demographers, public health researchers, legal scholars, nurses, and doctors. In the past 15 years, more universities and research institutes have taken on the study of abortion and abortion provision in response to the urgent question of the effect of hundreds of abortion restrictions passed in that time period.

As for me, my two new studies address other questions left unanswered by the Turnaway Study. In truth, the Turnaway Study never reached the people who were most isolated financially and socially. All of the women who participated at least made it to an abortion facility. Some people, and we don't even know how many, have unwanted pregnancies but never show up at an abortion clinic because they cannot raise the money to pay for an abortion, cannot get there, cannot face the condemnation of abortion protesters, or don't even know abortion is legal. My new study with epidemiologist Dr. Corinne Rocca is recruiting women across the southwestern United States to examine the impact of unintended pregnancy on women's lives, whether they decide to seek an abortion or not. We chose the Southwest because neighboring states have diametrically opposed political climates—for example, New Mexico has a libertarian, hands-off approach, while Arizona has passed every restrictive law in existence. This study is an opportunity to see who decides to have an abortion and whether state restrictions actually prevent women from getting wanted abortions.

I am also launching a Turnaway Study in Nepal with demographer Dr. Mahesh Puri from the Center for Research on Environment, Health and Population Activities (CREHPA) in Kathmandu. Nepal has legal abortion up to 12 weeks, up to 18 weeks in cases of rape or incest, and at any time if the pregnancy poses a danger to the woman's life or physical or mental health, or if there is a fetal health indication.[1] Since 2016, the Nepali government has been providing abortion services from public health facilities free of cost. Among the many things that are different in Nepal than in the United States, maternal mortality is astronomically higher—a lifetime risk of one in 150 in Nepal versus one in 3,800 in the United States.[2] The physical health consequences of not being able to get an abortion and carrying the pregnancy to term may be much greater. Also, use of abortion services outside of legal providers is very common.[3] The study is a chance to see how women find out about safe versus unsafe abortion after being turned away from legal providers.

The consequences for children resulting from women's access to abortion services may be quite different in Nepal than in the United States. Here, we find that existing children do worse when their mother is denied an abortion in terms of child-development milestones and being raised in a household with enough money to pay for basic living necessities. In Nepal, the stakes are even higher. Over a third of children under age five experience stunted growth due to insufficient food over a sustained period of time.[4] And an additional facet that is different: Nepal is a country where there is a strong preference for sons over daughters. Some women in Nepal seek abortions when they suspect that their fetus is a girl. My previous work with Dr. Puri reveals that this is not necessarily due to intrinsic misogyny but a response to a patriarchal society and economy that provides more opportunities and a better life for boys and men.[5] As one woman seeking an abortion in Nepal told us, "We have to educate daughters more than sons because I had to face so many hardships, as I was not educated. So I thought I would not be able to educate the child, and I also felt like, what would we do with three children?" Understanding the effect of legal abortion access in Nepal can help direct limited health care funding to women and children at greatest risk of poor health outcomes.

Trust Women

Abortion providers give up a significant amount of peace and security in their own lives to improve the lives of women and the lives of their existing and future children.[6] My observations from visiting clinics is that the people who provide abortion services are kind and caring people. The oldest generation of doctors was around before abortion was legalized in the U.S. in 1973, and they are often motivated by what they saw on the sepsis wards of hospitals—young women who lost their uteruses or even their lives from unsafe abortions.[7] They give off a paternal vibe; they are there to save women's lives. Younger providers, both doctors and nurses, are more likely to be women themselves. They are compassionate, calm, and capable people; they listen to your problems and can help you solve them. Abortion providers of all generations are among the bravest and most dedicated people I've met.

Dr. George Tiller was a physician in Kansas who provided abortions, including third-trimester abortions, until his assassination in 2009. He was one of a very small group of doctors in America able and willing to provide later abortions. Like many abortion providers before and since, Tiller, his family, and his staff endured constant protest and violent threats. His clinic was firebombed in the late '80s. He was shot and wounded in the early '90s. But the threats and the violence did not deter him. He continued providing abortions that women felt they needed, until one Sunday when an anti-abortion extremist showed up at Tiller's church and shot the 67-year-old doctor dead.

Long before his assassination, Tiller was a hero to many abortion providers and advocates. At abortion-research meetings I've attended, family-planning providers and researchers would talk about his bravery, his generosity, and his philosophy. Dr. Tiller's most famous motto is "Trust women," a message posted on the wall of his Wichita clinic and on a button I saw that he wore on his lapel.[8] As sociologist Dr. Carole Joffe, who studies abortion providers, wrote days after his death, "I have been struck that although all reporters mention that he offered [third-trimester] abortions, as a way of explaining his notoriety in anti-abortion circles, remarkably few of these print or radio and television journalists explained why Tiller did this, and who actually were the recipients of these procedures. The fact that so many of those reporting on Tiller were so oblivious of the circumstances of his patients is in itself a powerful indication of the marginality of both abortion providers and patients in American culture."[9]

I hope that this book has provided some insight into why women have abortions and the consequences when they cannot get a wanted abortion. Tiller's philosophy of trusting women is the take-home message from the Turnaway Study. Our study produced strong evidence that women are able to make thoughtful and deliberate decisions about their bodies, their families, and their lives. They are weighing their own burdens, their responsibilities to others, and their aspirations for the future. We learned that enabling women to make important personal decisions about childbearing protects their own and their children's health and economic security. Being able to access abortion gives them a greater chance at developing quality relationships and ending abusive ones, setting and achieving personal goals, and for some women, having a more wanted pregnancy later on. To paraphrase Justice Ginsburg, abortion is not just about fetal versus women's rights, or even the government's role in private childbearing decisions.[10] It is about women's control over their financial security, health and bodily integrity, ability to care for their existing children, prospects for healthy relationships, and their plans for the future. It is about women's control over their own lives.

Afterword

The year this book came out, 2020, was a tragic and politically tumultuous year that had profound effects on all of our lives. Of course, when I turned in the finished manuscript, I could not foresee the impending disasters and political upheaval. The global pandemic caused the deaths of millions of people in a crisis exacerbated by the failure to universally implement public health measures such as testing, contact tracing, and quarantines that might have slowed the spread of COVID-19. The familiar clash between science and ideology that characterizes the debate on abortion also defined the debate over the pandemic and hampered the response. At the same time, the pandemic deepened the conflict over abortion rights by giving politicians another opportunity to restrict abortion while making access to care more fraught and risky. The civil rights marches to support racial justice brought long-overdue attention to fundamental and systemic inequalities, many of which also echo in the experiences of people of color who become pregnant and need medical care. And finally, the death of Justice Ruth Bader Ginsburg and the appointment of an anti-abortion justice in her place has dramatically reshaped the U.S. Supreme Court and the prospects for abortion access in the future. All these events of 2020 make the findings of the Turnaway Study even more relevant and pressing.

The coronavirus pandemic raised so many themes that we see in the debate over abortion, right down to whom to blame for unintended pregnancy. For example, a Facebook post making the rounds quipped, "Seeing how some people wear their masks, I now understand how contraceptives fail." I admit that the number of people wearing masks with their noses poking out over the top is alarming. People aren't entirely consistent with either their face masks or contraceptives, perhaps for similar reasons. Both offer uncertain protection against an unknown level of risk. Many people take a chance in having sex without contraception and don't become pregnant; some use a method every time and still become pregnant. Likewise, some people don't practice social distancing, don't wear masks, and don't get the virus. Some do everything they can to avoid becoming infected and, despite that, still come down with COVID. Wearing a mask and social distancing, just like using a contraceptive method, reduces risk but provides no guarantee. And yet, at least when it comes to the coronavirus, I think we can agree that everyone, no matter how carefully they socially distanced or wore a mask, deserves access to medical care if they become sick. I wish the same spirit of generosity were granted to those who experience an unwanted pregnancy.

The most ironic twist of the mask debate is that anti-maskers have adopted the language of abortion rights advocates, carrying signs that say "My Body, My Choice." Concern about infringements on one's bodily autonomy by government overreach is understandable. So what distinguishes government mandates for mask-wearing from government mandates for pregnant people to carry unwanted pregnancies to term? Science and data. In the case of mask-wearing, the infringement is minuscule, and the public health benefit is large. In the case of abortion, government intervention into private decision-making around childbearing is not a small intrusion. Furthermore, the Turnaway Study shows that unwanted pregnancies carried to term have profound effects on women's immediate and long-term physical health, their economic security, and the well-being of their families. Any exercise of governmental authority over people's bodies and lives should be supported by good science addressing both its impact and its necessity. That scientific basis is strong for coronavirus abatement.

But science does not support restrictions on abortion or imposition of obstacles on people's decision-making around pregnancy, as the Turnaway Study thoroughly documents.

The COVID-19 pandemic had a direct effect on the provision of abortion services, highlighting both how uniquely vulnerable and how essential these services are. Provision of abortion care requires a lot of travel—one in five abortion patients travels more than 50 miles each way to access care.[1] There are 27 large cities across the country that have no abortion facility within 100 miles.[2] Clinicians also travel to provide the services—many clinics in conservative states contract with doctors living out of state to fly in to provide care.[3] All of this travel became much more difficult and dangerous during the pandemic. Meanwhile, staff at clinics faced the same disruptions to childcare and school that we all experienced, which made continuing to work while caring for dependents nearly impossible. Combined with COVID illnesses, quarantines among staff, and demands for their clinicians elsewhere, many facilities struggled to continue to provide abortions. More than a quarter of clinics canceled or postponed abortion services for some period during the pandemic.[4]

Adding to the problems caused by the pandemic itself, some politicians took the opportunity to make abortion even more difficult to access. Between March and May of 2020, 12 states temporarily declared abortion a nonessential service, meaning that clinics were not permitted to remain open.[5] The stated justification was that abortion facilities used personal protective equipment (PPE) that was needed in hospital wards that treat COVID-19 patients. Of course, the idea that a pregnant woman can simply wait to have her abortion until the end of a pandemic is absurd. Most of these designations were short-lived; they were immediately challenged and courts struck them down.[6] Except in Texas, where abortion services were halted for an entire month.

Texas state officials designated abortion as a nonessential service, resulting in the closing of abortion clinics in the state between March 22 and April 21, 2020, and providing striking evidence of how vulnerable the system of abortion delivery is to bad public policy.[7] In the month of April, the number of abortions dropped by almost 2,000 (38%) compared to a year earlier. The number of Texans getting abortions in neighboring states shot up to almost 1,000 that month, five to nine times as many as usually travel out of state, but nowhere near high enough to offset the drop in in-state abortions. Many abortions that might have occurred in the first trimester were delayed into the second.[8] And finally, thousands of people in Texas likely shared with the women in this book the experience of needing an abortion and being unable to get one.

It turns out that abortion facilities use very little PPE, and during the pandemic many abortion facilities found a way to use even less. A rule imposed by the Food and Drug Administration (FDA) required women to travel to a clinic to receive the abortion pill in person from a clinician.[9] There is no medical justification for this rule. Screening for eligibility for a medication abortion can be done over the phone, and the extra risk from travel and from spending time inside a clinic made even less sense during the pandemic. In response to the increased risk of travel for women seeking abortion services, a federal court ruled in July 2020 that the FDA's in-clinic requirement was unconstitutional, reducing this burden in states where other laws do not prohibit telehealth for abortion.[10] Across the country, provision of abortion dramatically changed to reduce travel and in-person visits, streamlining access to medication abortion. A study of abortion providers across the country showed that 87% of providers altered their care, including many who turned to telemedicine, using internet and phone communication instead of in-person visits.[11] Professional medical organizations endorsed the practice of "no-touch" medication abortion provision.[12] For half the year, pregnant people in most states could call an abortion clinic, be screened for medication abortion, and pick up their pills in the clinic or curbside, or even have those pills mailed to them.

In January 2021, the Supreme Court reversed that ruling, again requiring in-person dispensing, despite the fact that the risk of COVID-19 exposure and the dangers of travel had only intensified in the intervening months. Why did the Supreme Court step in to make abortions more difficult to access during a pandemic? Because it could. The death of feminist hero Justice Ruth Bader Ginsburg on September 18, 2020, and the very rapid appointment and confirmation of Justice Amy Coney Barrett marked a major shift in the Supreme Court and created a six-to-three anti-abortion majority. The death of RBG hit people who care about abortion rights particularly hard. Prior to her death, it was reassuring that a senior member of the court understood why abortion rights are so important—that "in the balance is a woman's autonomous charge of her full life's course."[13] I feel no such assurance that this viewpoint will be well represented in the new court. In its first case involving abortion with Justice Barrett on the bench, the Supreme Court reinstated the policy that required patients to travel to receive medication abortion pills in person, in a predictable six-to-three ruling.[14] As this callous decision foreshadows, this new Supreme Court may bring an end to a nationally protected right to abortion.

Some pro-choice advocates seem almost eager for the challenge to *Roe v. Wade*.[15] Perhaps they hope that allowing local control over the abortion issue will reduce controversy, as decisions won't be seen as coming from outsiders, imposed by the federal government. There is the hope that shifting the debate to the state level will reveal the clear majority of Americans who support abortion rights.[16] And in terms of national politics, the Supreme Court overturning *Roe* could spark a political backlash that would defeat the anti-abortion movement by inspiring massive street protests, like the ones that successfully demanded the end to longstanding abortion bans in Argentina and South Korea in 2020.[17] Any major new Supreme Court restriction on abortion would go against an international trend that has been overwhelmingly toward abortion legalization.[18] But I believe that looking forward to the end of *Roe* for these political reasons is deeply problematic. Any political gains from a renewed public debate comes at the expense of people who need abortion care, specifically in the twenty-one states with laws banning abortions—laws that are currently unconstitutional but may go into effect if *Roe* is overturned.[19]

As described in this book, the Turnaway Study shows that when people are unable to get abortions and instead carry unwanted pregnancies to term, they face major negative consequences for their physical health, economic well-being, and the trajectory of their lives. Government restrictions on abortion impose an unfair burden—making the lives of people who can bear children more difficult and precarious than those of people who cannot. Barriers to abortion also disproportionately affect people of color, who make up more than half of those seeking abortion care.[20] When people are unable to dictate the conditions of their lives and create safe, economically secure environments for their children, everyone is worse off. The most important message of this book, when considering the role the government should play in reproductive choices, is that people are able to make good decisions about their bodies, their childbearing, and their lives. People understand the consequences of abortion and the consequences of ongoing pregnancy and childbirth, and they can make that decision for themselves. I hope the government will turn to science and evidence in the coming years, when we are faced with the next public health crisis and as we inevitably turn our attention to the question of abortion policy and rights. The health and integrity of our bodies, the economic security of our families, and the well-being of our children depend on it.

Diana Greene Foster
January 20, 2021

Acknowledgments

Science is a collaborative effort. Throughout this book, I have referred to scientific papers by the name of the person who took the lead on each analysis. This lead author picked out some piece of the puzzle, figured out how to solve it with the data we collected, designed and often carried out the analysis, drafted the article text, made countless revisions, and was the dedicated force that brought a study idea to publication in a journal. I thank the many lead authors for their rigor, leadership, and perseverance: E. Angel Aztlan-Keahey, Antonia Biggs, Karuna Chibber, Loren Dobkin, Caitlin Gerdts, Heather Gould, Laura Harris, Katrina Kimport, Jane Mauldon, Molly McCarthy, Sarah Miller, Heidi Moseson, Lauren Ralph, Sarah Roberts, Corinne Rocca, Gretchen Sisson, Ushma Upadhyay, and Katie Woodruff.

My system of referring to work by the lead author's name doesn't do justice to the major contributions of people who coauthored these papers by sharing sophisticated statistics expertise: Kevin Delucchi, Maria Glymour, Chuck McCulloch, John Neuhaus, Eric Vittinghoff, and Mark Wilson; by sharing knowledge of a new topic: Jessica Gipson, Daniel Grossman, Rachel Jones, Alissa Perrucci, E. Bimla Schwarz, Julia Steinberg, Laura Wherry; and by helping with analysis: Lyndsay Avalos, Michaela Ferrari, Minjeong Jeon, Sarah Raifman, Brenly Rowland, Goleen Samari, Danielle Sinkford, Alejandra Vargas-Johnson, and Elisette Weiss. Generous Chuck McCulloch taught a special customized longitudinal data analysis course for ANSIRH in preparation for the

321

analysis of these data. Behind the scenes, we were supported by our UCSF librarian, Jill Barr-Walker.

None of these people could be writing papers if the data hadn't been collected in the first place. It was not a small effort to recruit one thousand women from 30 abortion facilities over three years and interview them over five years. Here are the people who made it happen: Sandy Stonesifer was the project director for the first two years and helped me launch the study. Rana Barar was the force behind the study for the next ten years—directing staff, budgets, data sets, survey instruments, university processes, and consultants. The study would not have been such a success without her energy and organization. Heather Gould was vital to the entire process—from getting approval from the institutional review board to formalizing our protocols to designing and conducting the 31 in-depth interviews. Ten dedicated, patient, and hardworking interviewers worked from six a.m. to eight p.m. over years to conduct almost eight thousand interviews: Mattie Boehler-Tatman, Janine Carpenter, Jana Carrey, Undine Darney, Ivette Gomez, C. Emily Hendrick, Selena Phipps, Brenly Rowland, Claire Schreiber, and Danielle Sinkford. They have my eternal gratitude. Supporting the team and coordinating recruitment sites was an effort accomplished by Michaela Ferrari, Debbie Nguyen, Jasmine Powell, and Elisette Weiss. Jasmine Powell continues to direct and manage the study through its dissemination phase. Jay Fraser kept our electronic data collection system working, with help from Dirk Strasser. The smooth transition from paper surveys to electronic database was thanks to Cindy Barbee Adam and Michael Ip. Anna Spielvogel provided expert clinical advice for the rare cases of psychological distress.

Before any of the data collection began, I received invaluable advice about what survey questions to include from colleagues and mentors in the field: Nancy Adler, Geraldine Barrett, Kate Cockrill, Marcia Ellison, Philip Darney, Eleanor Drey, Cynthia Harper, Marie Harvey, Jillian Henderson, Stanley Henshaw, Signy Judd, Diane Morof, Lauri Pasch, Alissa Perrucci, Jan Rains, and

Nada Stotland. Kate Cockrill, Stanley Henshaw, Rachel Jones, and Susan Yanow helped me find possible recruitment sites. Jennifer Dunn, John Santelli, and Erin Schultz established the legal and public health case for including minors in the study. Parker Dockray, Lori Freedman, Katrina Kimport, Alissa Perrucci, Sarah Raifman, and Gretchen Sisson helped Heather Gould design the qualitative interview study guide and codes.

I am extremely grateful to the clinic staff at the 30 recruiting abortion facilities who reached out to eligible women and made a case for the study while juggling all their normal duties, and to the directors of these facilities who saw the value of research and made time for it in their busy practices.

UCSF is a fantastic place to conduct such a huge study. The Turnaway Study would not exist without Eleanor Drey voicing her concern for the well-being of women she could not serve. I thank Daniel Grossman and Tracy Weitz for leading my research group, ANSIRH. The fact that the study ever got off the ground is thanks to Dr. Weitz, who was director of ANSIRH at the time she encouraged me to pursue this research. She made the successful pitch to a foundation about the scientific importance of this study. I thank Jody Steinauer, Philip Darney, Claire Brindis, and Joe Speidel for their leadership of our umbrella organization, the UCSF Bixby Center for Global Reproductive Health; and Rebecca Jackson for her leadership of our division within the UCSF Department of Obstetrics, Gynecology and Reproductive Sciences. I am grateful for the support of Amy Murtha, chair of the department, and Nancy Milliken, director of the Center of Excellence in Women's Health. UCSF being fantastic doesn't mean it's easy. These people helped make the bureaucracy work for us: Michele Benjamin, Steve Dalton, Sarah Glass, Siobhan Hayes, John Rosin, and Jane Wong kept our finances in order; Kate Nolan helped us navigate the IRB; Mary Beth Blasnek, Dixie Horning, and Jane Meier advocated for social sciences. Molly Battistelli, Pat Anderson, Aura Orozco-Fuentes, and Clare Cook kept ANSIRH running. The Scholars Strategy Network, BerlinRosen, and my colleagues Jason Harless, Stephanie Herold, Rebecca Griffin, and Virali Modi-Parekh have made dedicated efforts to draw media attention to our scientific findings.

Taking a study and making a book was another large collaborative effort. I thank Sofia Resnick, editor, fact-checker, scene-setter, pseudonym-generator, and hyphen-adder, for her invaluable help. My deepest gratitude to Katie Watson for her thoughtful comments and careful review. Katrina Kimport, Carole Joffe, Renee Bracey Sherman, Amy Myrick, and Heather Gould provided helpful and important suggestions on earlier drafts. Chris Ahlbach searched the medical literature. I had a wonderful afternoon brainstorming abortion myths with Aileen Gariepy and with the women at Ibis Reproductive Health. Seth and Lorri Foster closely read my drafts and offered important edits. I am grateful to Shelly Kaller and Antonia Biggs for help with references and graphs. I thank Gail Ross and Dara Kaye of Ross Yoon Agency for their determination and vision in representing this book. A dedicated team at Scribner made it happen. I am grateful to my astute and enthusiastic editor Valerie Steiker, Nan Graham, Colin Harrison, Roz Lippel, Brian Belfiglio, Kate Lloyd, Ashley Gilliam, Sally Howe, Tamar McCollom, Dan Cuddy, and Laura Cherkas, as well as Jaya Miceli, who designed the cover.

I thank the many funders for their bravery in taking on the topic of abortion and their confidence in me to lead this study.

Above all, I thank the women who participated in this study—who picked up the phone and told us about their experiences and their feelings. I am particularly grateful to the 31 who completed our in-depth interviews and told us their experiences in full in their own words. Their generosity in sharing their stories deepened our understanding and provided important context for our statistics.

Finally, I thank my family, who got used to having to discuss abortion at nearly every gathering: Greenes, Fosters, van Renesses, Goldens, Katzes, and Fragers; and friends who have supported me and my family: Rosemarie, Mica, Kinkini, Margo, Jill, Mitch,

ACKNOWLEDGMENTS

Lisa, Nancy, Elizabeth, and Chris. Thanks to my sister Lesley for adapting the stories for a stage reading. I thank my brilliant and supportive husband, Seth; Noah and Kaia, who are the lights of my life; Lorri, Michael, Gail, and, in my heart, my dear father-in-law, Hague, and my beautiful mom, Anne.

References

Introduction

1 Upadhyay UD, Weitz TA, Jones RK, Barar RE, Foster DG. Denial of abortion because of provider gestational age limits in the United States. *Am J Public Health*. 2014 Sep;104(9):1687–1694. At least 4,000 women are turned away each year from abortion facilities and carry the pregnancy to term because they exceeded the gestational limit of accessible clinics. An unknown number, likely much larger, carry an unwanted pregnancy to term without ever making it to a clinic because they knew they were too far along, they could not raise the money, or they could not get there.

2 Most scientists put viability at 24 weeks, which marks the point at which 50% of babies born will survive, 17% of them with severe to moderate impairments. Source: American College of Obstetricians and Gynecologists. Periviable birth. *Obstetric Care Consensus*. 2017 Oct;6. https://www.acog.org/-/media/Obstetric-Care-Consensus-Series/occ006.pdf.

3 States with gestational limits for abortion. Kaiser Family Foundation. https://www.kff.org/womens-health-policy/state-indicator/gestational-limit-abortions/. Updated June 1, 2019.

4 Hutchings A, et al. Heartbeat bans. *Rewire.News*. May 30, 2019. rewire.news/legislative-tracker/law-topic/heartbeat-bans/.

5 Mike Pence campaign speech, July 28, 2016, via Reuters: https://www.reuters.com/video/2016/07/28/pence-prayer-and-a-pledge-to-end-roe-v-w?videoId=369417543. At the Values Voters Summit on September 10, 2016, he made similar comments about *Roe v. Wade*: "I'm pro-life; I don't apologize for it. I want to live to see the day that we put the sanctity of life back at the center of American law and we send *Roe versus Wade* to the ash heap of history, where it belongs." Mike Pence will send Roe v Wade to the ash heap of history, Washington, DC, 9/10/16. YouTube. https://www.youtube.com/watch?v=AILoMt8poYo. Posted September 10, 2016.

6 *Whole Woman's Health v. Hellerstedt*. 136 S. Ct. 2292 (2016). Decided June 27, 2016. https://www.supremecourt.gov/opinions/15pdf/15-274_new_e18f.pdf.

7 Raman S. Lawmakers urge Supreme Court to reexamine abortion decisions.

REFERENCES

Roll call. https://www.rollcall.com/news/congress/lawmakers-urge-su preme-court-to-reexamine-abortion-decisions. Updated January 2, 2020.

8 *Gonzales v. Carhart.* 127 S.Ct. 1610 (2007). Decided April 18, 2007. https://www.law.cornell.edu/supct/html/05-380.ZO.html.

9 Abortion surveillance 2016. Centers for Disease Control and Prevention. https://www.cdc.gov/reproductivehealth/data_stats/abortion.htm. Updated November 2, 2019.

10 Drey EA, Foster DG, Jackson RA, Lee SJ, Cardenas LH, Darney PD. Risk factors associated with presenting for abortion in the second trimester. *Obstet Gynecol.* 2006 Jan;107(1):128–135.

11 Lang J. What happens to women who are denied abortions? *New York Times.* June 12, 2013. www.nytimes.com/2013/06/16/magazine/study-women-de nied-abortions.html.

A Note about Statistics

1 The figures in this book show predicted probabilities from our statistical models rather than raw percentages. This allows us to account for any relevant differences in the study groups at baseline and loss to follow-up. In our analysis of the quantitative data, I excluded data from all women who sought abortions at one site that had a ten-week limit and where nearly all women denied an abortion got one elsewhere.

Chapter 1: The Turnaway Study

1 Remarks at a White House briefing for right-to-life activists, July 30, 1987. Ronald Reagan Presidential Library and Museum. https://www.reagan library.gov/research/speeches/073087a. Video available at https://www .youtube.com/watch?v=5mIJy5kLQmA.

2 Koop CE. *The Right to Live; The Right to Die.* Carol Stream, IL: Tyndale House; 1976.

3 Letter from Surgeon General C. Everett Koop to Ronald Reagan on the health effects of abortion on women. Just Facts. https://www.justfacts.com /abortion.koop.asp.

4 Jones RK, Jerman J. Population group abortion rates and lifetime incidence of abortion: United States, 2008–2014. *Am J Public Health.* 2017 Dec;107(12):1904–1909. doi:10.2105/AJPH.2017.304042. Foster DG. Dramatic decreases in US abortion rates: public health achievement or failure? *Am J Public Health.* 2017 Dec;107(12):1860–1862. PMID: 29116861. PMCID: PMC5678419.

5 Finkelstein A, Taubman S, Wright B, et al. The Oregon health insurance experiment: evidence from the first year. *Q J Econ.* 2012;127(3):1057–1106.

6 Upadhyay UD, Weitz TA, Jones RK, Barar RE, Foster DG. Denial of abor-

tion because of provider gestational age limits in the United States. *Am J Public Health*. 2014 Sep;104(9):1687–1694.

7 For insight into abortion providers' experiences of violence and harassment, read David Cohen and Krysten Connon's book *Living in the Crosshairs: The Untold Stories of Anti-Abortion Terrorism* (Oxford University Press, 2015).

8 Stack L. A brief history of deadly attacks on abortion providers. *New York Times*. November 29, 2015. https://www.nytimes.com/interactive/2015/11/29/us/30abortion-clinic-violence.html.

9 Foster DG, Kimport K, Gould H, Roberts SC, Weitz TA. Effect of abortion protesters on women's emotional response to abortion. *Contraception*. 2013 Jan;87(1):81–87. PMID: 23062524.

10 Smith K. Violence against abortion clinics hit a record high last year. Doctors say it's getting worse. *CBS News*, CBS Interactive. September 19, 2019. www.cbsnews.com/news/violence-against-abortion-clinics-like-planned-parenthood-hit-a-record-high-last-year-doctors-say-its-getting-worse/. Editorial Board. The doctors who put their lives on the line. *New York Times*. May 25, 2019. www.nytimes.com/2019/05/25/opinion/sunday/abortion-violence-protests.html.

11 Robb A. The making of an American terrorist. *New Republic*. December 19, 2016. newrepublic.com/article/138950/making-american-terrorist-robert-dear-planned-parenthood.

12 Jerman J, Jones RK, Onda T. Characteristics of U.S. abortion patients in 2014 and changes since 2008. Guttmacher Institute. www.guttmacher.org/report/characteristics-us-abortion-patients-2014. Published May 2016. Jatlaoui TC, Eckhaus L, Mandel MG, et al. Abortion surveillance—United States, 2016. *MMWR Surveill Summ*. 2019;68(SS-11):1–41. doi:10.15585/mmwr.ss6811a1.

13 For reference, roughly 13% of adult women in the country in 2018 lived below the poverty level, so those seeking abortion are four times as likely to be poor as women in the general population. United States Census Bureau. Current population survey. https://www.census.gov/cps/data/cpstablecreator.html. Accessed December 1, 2019.

14 Foster DG, Gould H, Kimport K. How women anticipate coping after an abortion. *Contraception*. 2012 Jul;86(1):84–90. PMID: 22176790.

15 Watson K. *Scarlet A: The Ethics, Law, and Politics of Ordinary Abortion*. New York: Oxford University Press; 2018.

Chapter 2: Why Do People Have Abortions?

1 The abortion war. *Fault Lines*. Al Jazeera English. August 29, 2012. https://www.aljazeera.com/programmes/faultlines/2012/08/20128288841399701.html.

2 Hutchings A, et al. Heartbeat bans. *Rewire.News*. May 30, 2019. rewire.news/legislative-tracker/law-topic/heartbeat-bans/.

3 Woodruff K. Coverage of abortion in select U.S. newspapers. *Women's Health Issues.* 2018 Oct. doi:10.1016/j.whi.2018.08.008.

4 Cowan SK. Secrets and misperceptions: the creation of self-fulfilling illusions. *Sociol Sci.* 2014 Nov 3. doi:10.15195/v1.a26.

5 Induced abortion in the United States. Guttmacher Institute. www.guttmacher.org/fact-sheet/induced-abortion-united-states. September 18, 2019.

6 Mauldon J, Foster DG, Roberts SC. Effect of abortion vs. carrying to term on a woman's relationship with the man involved in the pregnancy. *Perspect Sex and Reprod Health.* 2015 Mar;47(1):11–18. PMID: 25199435.

7 Upadhyay UD, Biggs MA, Foster DG. The effect of abortion on having and achieving aspirational one-year plans. *BMC Womens Health.* 2015;15(1):102. PMID: 26559911. Upadhyay UD, Angel Aztlan-James E, Rocca CH, Foster DG. Intended pregnancy after receiving vs. being denied a wanted abortion. *Contraception.* 2018 Sep 20. PMID: 30244161.

8 Foster DG, Biggs MA, Ralph L, Gerdts C, Roberts S, Glymour MM. Socioeconomic outcomes of women who receive and women who are denied wanted abortions in the United States. *Am J Public Health.* 2018 Mar;108(3):407–413. PMID: 29345993. PMCID: PMC5803812.

9 Pregnancy and drug use: the facts. National Advocates for Pregnant Women. http://advocatesforpregnantwomen.org/issues/pregnancy_and_drug_use_the_facts/.

10 Personhood. Rewire.News Legislative Tracker. https://rewire.news/legislative-tracker/law-topic/personhood/. Updated November 7, 2018.

11 Prahan R, Haberkorn J. Personhood movement loses twice. *Politico.* November 5, 2014. https://www.politico.com/story/2014/11/personhood-movement-north-dakota-colorado-112552.

12 Parental consent laws prevent minors from getting an abortion unless they have a parent's written consent. However, there are legal hoops a minor can jump through if she has a compelling reason not to involve a parent or guardian in this decision.

13 Finer LB, Frohwirth LF, Dauphinee LA, Singh S, Moore AM. Reasons U.S. women have abortions: quantitative and qualitative perspectives. *Perspect Sex Reprod Health.* 2005;37(3):110–118.

14 I Didn't Know I Was Pregnant. TLC. www.tlc.com/tv-shows/i-didnt-know-i-was-pregnant/.

15 Boklage CE. The survival probability of human conceptions from fertilization to term. *Int J Fertil.* 1990(35):75–94. Ammon Avalos L, Galindo C, Li DK. A systematic review to calculate background miscarriage rates using life table analysis. *Birth Defects Res A Clin Mol Teratol.* 2012;94(6):417–423.

16 Upadhyay UD, Weitz TA, Jones RK, Barar RE, Foster DG. Denial of abortion because of provider gestational age limits in the United States. *Am J Public Health.* 2014 Sep;104(9):1687–1694. PMID: 23948000.

17 Rocca CH, Kimport K, Gould H, Foster DG. Women's emotions one week after receiving or being denied an abortion in the United States. *Perspect Sex Reprod Health.* 2013 Sep;45(3):122–131. PMID: 24020773.

18 Twitter thread by Gabrielle Blair (@designmom). September 13, 2018. https://twitter.com/designmom/status/1040363431893725184. Also found

at: Blair G. My Twitter thread on abortion. *Design Mom.* September 13, 2018. https://www.designmom.com/twitter-thread-abortion.

19   Finer LB, Henshaw SK. Disparities in rates of unintended pregnancy in the United States, 1994 and 2001. *Perspect Sex Reprod Health.* 2006 Jun;38(2):90–96.

20   Hatcher, R. A., Trussell, J., Nelson, A. L., Cates, W., Stewart, F. H., & Kowal, D. (2007). Contraceptive technology (19th rev. ed.) New York: Ardent Media. Truong K. Here's the average amount of sex people are having at your age. *Refinery29.* September 1, 2017. www.refinery29.com/en-us /2017/08/168733/sex-frequency-age-average.

21   Moseson H, Foster DG, Upadhyay UD, Vittinghoff E, Rocca CH. Contraceptive use over five years after receipt or denial of abortion service. *Perspect Sex Reprod Health.* 2018 Mar;50(1):7–14. PMID: 29329494.

22   Wilcox AJ, Dunson DB, Weinberg CR, Trussell J, Baird DD. Likelihood of conception with a single act of intercourse: providing benchmark rates for assessment of post-coital contraceptives. *Contraception.* 2001 Apr;63(4):211–215.

23   Foster DG, Higgins JA, Karasek D, Ma S, Grossman D. Attitudes toward unprotected intercourse and risk of pregnancy among women seeking abortion. *Womens Health Issues.* 2012 Mar;22(2):e149–155. PMID: 22000817.

24   Moreau C, Cleland K, Trussell J. Contraceptive discontinuation attributed to method dissatisfaction in the United States. *Contraception.* 2007;76(4):267–272. Frost JJ, Singh S, Finer LB. Factors associated with contraceptive use and nonuse, United States, 2004. *Perspect Sex Reprod Health.* 2007;39(2):90–99. Mills A, Barclay L. None of them were satisfactory: women's experiences with contraception. *Health Care Women Int.* 2006;27(5):379–398.

25   Lessard LN, Karasek D, Ma S, et al. Contraceptive features preferred by women at high risk of unintended pregnancy. *Perspect Sex Reprod Health.* 2012 Sep;44(3):194–200. PMID: 22958664.

26   Jackson AV, Karasek D, Dehlendorf C, Foster DG. Racial and ethnic differences in women's preferences for features of contraceptive methods. *Contraception.* 2016 May;93(5):406-11. PMID: 26738619.

27   Roberts D. *Killing the Black Body: Race, Reproduction and the Meaning of Liberty.* New York: Pantheon Books; 1997.

Chapter 3: Access to Abortion in the United States

1   Grossman D, Grindlay K, Altshuler AL, Schulkin J. Induced abortion provision among a national sample of obstetrician-gynecologists. *Obstet Gynecol.* 2019 Mar;133(3):477–483. doi:10.1097/AOG.0000000000003110.

2   Myers C, Jones R, Upadhyay U. Predicted changes in abortion access and incidence in a post-*Roe* world. *Contraception.* 2019 Nov;100(5):367–373.

3   About Women's Right to Know Law. Louisiana Department of Health. http://ldh.la.gov/index.cfm/page/812. Act no. 411. HR 636 (La 2011). http://legis.la.gov/legis/ViewDocument.aspx?d=761700.

REFERENCES

4   Upadhyay UD, Weitz TA, Jones RK, Barar RE, Foster DG. Denial of abortion because of provider gestational age limits in the United States. *Am J Public Health*. 2014 Sep;104(9):1687–1694.

5   Roberts SC, Gould H, Kimport K, Weitz TA, Foster DG. Out-of-pocket costs and insurance coverage for abortion in the United States. *Womens Health Issues*. 2014 Mar–Apr; 24(2):e211–218. PMID: 24630423.

6   Restricting insurance coverage of abortion. Guttmacher Institute. www .guttmacher.org/state-policy/explore/restricting-insurance-coverage-abor tion. December 3, 2019.

7   State funding of abortion under Medicaid. Guttmacher Institute. www.gutt-macher.org/state-policy/explore/state-funding-abortion-under-medicaid. December 3, 2019. State funding of abortions under Medicaid. Henry J. Kaiser Family Foundation. June 21, 2019. www.kff.org/medicaid/state -indicator/abortion-under-medicaid/.

8   Jones RK, Upadhyay UM, Weitz TA. At what cost? Payment for abortion care by U.S. women. *Womens Health Issues*. 2013 May. www.sciencedirect .com/science/article/pii/S1049386713000224.

9   Abortion: judicial history and legislative response. Congressional Research Service. https://fas.org/sgp/crs/misc/RL33467.pdf. Updated December 7, 2018.

10 Henshaw SK, Joyce TJ, Dennis A, Finer LB, Blanchard K. Restrictions on Medicaid funding for abortions: a literature review. Guttmacher Institute. https://www.guttmacher.org/report/restrictions-medicaid-funding -abortions-literature-review. Published July 2009. Roberts SCM, Johns NE, Williams V, Wingo E, Upadhyay UD. Estimating the proportion of Medicaid-eligible pregnant women in Louisiana who do not get abortions when Medicaid does not cover abortion. *BMC Womens Health*. 2019 Jun;19(1):78.

11 State funding of abortion under Medicaid. Guttmacher Institute. www .guttmacher.org/state-policy/explore/state-funding-abortion-under-medic aid. December 3, 2019.

12 Upadhyay UD, Weitz TA, Jones RK, Barar RE, Foster DG. Denial of abortion because of provider gestational age limits in the United States. *Am J Public Health*. 2014 Sep;104(9):1687–1694.

13 Roberts SC, Gould H, Kimport K, Weitz TA, Foster DG. Out-of-pocket costs and insurance coverage for abortion in the United States. *Womens Health Issues*. 2014 Mar–Apr;24(2):e211–218. PMID: 24630423.

14 Dennis A, Blanchard K. Abortion providers' experiences with Medicaid abortion coverage policies: a qualitative multistate study. *Health Serv Res*. 2013;48:236–252. doi:10.1111/j.1475-6773.2012.01443.x.

15 Salganicoff A, Sobel L, Ramaswamy A. The Hyde Amendment and coverage for abortion services—Appendix. Henry J. Kaiser Family Foundation. https://www.kff.org/womens-health-policy/issue-brief/the-hyde-amend ment-and-coverage-for-abortion-services/. September 27, 2019.

16 Donovan MK, Guttmacher Institute. In real life: federal restrictions on abortion coverage and the women they impact. Guttmacher Institute. www .guttmacher.org/gpr/2017/01/real-life-federal-restrictions-abortion-cover age-and-women-they-impact. October 2, 2018.

17 Roberts SC, Gould H, Kimport K, Weitz TA, Foster DG. Out-of-pocket costs and insurance coverage for abortion in the United States. *Womens Health Issues*. 2014 Mar–Apr; 24(2):e211–218. PMID: 24630423.

18 Jerman J, Jones RK, Onda T. Characteristics of U.S. abortion patients in 2014 and changes since 2008. Guttmacher Institute. www.guttmacher.org /report/characteristics-us-abortion-patients-2014. Published May 2016.

19 Gerdts C, Fuentes L, Grossman D, et al. Impact of clinic closures on women obtaining abortion services after implementation of a restrictive law in Texas. *Am J Public Health*. 2016 May;106(5):857–864. doi:10.2105 /AJPH.2016.303134. Grossman D, White K, Hopkins K, Potter J. Change in distance to nearest facility and abortion in Texas, 2012 to 2014. *JAMA*. 2017;317(4):437–439. doi:10.1001/jama.2016.17026.

20 Upadhyay UD, Weitz TA, Jones RK, Barar RE, Foster DG. Denial of abortion because of provider gestational age limits in the United States. *Am J Public Health*. 2014 Sep; 104(9):1687–1694. PMID: 23948000.

21 Foster DG, Kimport K. Who seeks abortions at or after 20 weeks? *Perspect Sex Reprod Health*. 2013 Dec;45(4):210–218. PMID: 24188634.

22 Jones RK, Ingerick M, Jerman J. Differences in abortion service delivery in hostile, middle-ground and supportive states in 2014. *Womens Health Issues*. 2018 May–Jun;28(3):212–218. doi:10.1016/j.whi.2017.12.003.

23 Cohen D, Joffe C. *Obstacle Course: The Everyday Struggle to Get an Abortion in America*. Berkeley: UC Press; 2020. This book by my colleague Carole Joffe and Drexel University law professor David Cohen explores how these restrictions affect abortion providers.

24 Fletcher JC, Evans MI. Maternal bonding in early fetal ultrasound examinations. *N Engl J Med*. 1983;308:392–393.

25 Kimport K, Weitz TA, Foster DG. Beyond political claims: women's interest in and emotional response to viewing their ultrasound image in abortion care. *Perspect Sex Reprod Health*. 2014 Dec;46(4):185–191. PMID: 25209369.

26 Beusman C. A state-by-state list of the lies abortion doctors are forced to tell women. *Vice*. August 18, 2016. www.vice.com/en_us/article/nz88gx /a-state-by-state-list-of-the-lies-abortion-doctors-are-forced-to-tell -women.

27 American College of Obstetricians and Gynecologists. Induced abortion and breast cancer risk: ACOG Committee Opinion No. 434. *Obstet Gynecol*. 2009;113:1417–1418. Männistö J, Mentula M, Bloigu A, Gissler M, Heikinheimo O, Niinimäki M. Induced abortion and future use of IVF treatment: a nationwide register study. *PLoS ONE*. 2019 Nov;14(11):e0225162. doi:10.1371/journal.pone.0225162.

28 Daniels CR, Ferguson J, Howard G, Roberti A. Informed or misinformed consent? Abortion policy in the United States. *J Health Polit Policy Law*. 2016;41(2):181–209. Beusman C. A state-by-state list of the lies abortion doctors are forced to tell women. *Vice*. August 18, 2016. www.vice.com /en_us/article/nz88gx/a-state-by-state-list-of-the-lies-abortion-doctors -are-forced-to-tell-women.

29 Counseling and waiting periods for abortion. Guttmacher Institute. www

.guttmacher.org/state-policy/explore/counseling-and-waiting-periods -abortion. December 3, 2019.

30 Gould H, Foster DG, Perrucci AC, Barar RE, Roberts SC. Predictors of abortion counseling receipt and helpfulness in the United States. *Womens Health Issues.* 2013 Jul–Aug;23(4):e249–255. PMID: 23816155.

31 Munson ZW. *The Making of Pro-Life Activists: How Social Movement Mobilization Works.* Chicago: University of Chicago Press; 2008.

32 Kissling F. Abortion rights are under attack, and pro-choice advocates are caught in a time warp. *Washington Post.* February 19, 2011. www.washing tonpost.com/wp-dyn/content/article/2011/02/18/AR2011021802434.html.

33 Historical living arrangements of children. United States Census Bureau. www.census.gov/data/tables/time-series/demo/families/children.html . Updated October 10, 2019.

34 Parental involvement in minors' abortions. Guttmacher Institute. www .guttmacher.org/state-policy/explore/parental-involvement-minors-abor tions. December 3, 2019.

35 Henshaw SK, Kost K. Parental involvement in minors' abortion decisions. *Family Plann Perspect.* 1992;24(5):196–207, 213. Ralph L, Gould H, Baker A, Foster DG. The role of parents and partners in minors' decisions to have an abortion and anticipated coping after abortion. *J Adolesc Health.* 2014;54(4):428–434. doi:10.1016/j.jadohealth.2013.09.021.

36 However, a recent analysis shows no difference in complication rates for first- or second-trimester abortions by patient weight: Benson LS, Micks EA, Ingalls C, Prager SW. Safety of outpatient surgical abortion for obese patients in the first and second trimesters. *Obstet Gynecol.* 2016 Nov;128(5):1065–1070.

Chapter 4: Mental Health

1 Belluck P. Pregnancy centers gain influence in anti-abortion arena. *New York Times.* January 4, 2013. Kelly K. The spread of 'Post Abortion Syndrome' as social diagnosis. *Soc Sci Med.* 2014 Feb;102:18–25.

2 Foster DG, Gould H, Taylor J, Weitz TA. Attitudes and decision making among women seeking abortions at one U.S. clinic. *Perspect Sex Reprod Health.* 2012 Jun;44(2):117–124. PMID: 22681427.

3 Woodruff K, Biggs MA, Gould H, Foster DG. Attitudes toward abortion after receiving vs. being denied an abortion in the USA. *Sex Res Social Policy.* 2018;15:452–463. doi:10.1007/s13178-018-0325-1.

4 Joffe C. The politicization of abortion and the evolution of abortion counseling. *Am J Public Health.* 2013 Jan;103(1):57–65. doi:10.2105/AJPH.2012.301063.

5 Biggs A, Brown K, Foster DG. Perceived abortion stigma and psychological well-being over five years after receiving or being denied an abortion. *PLoS ONE* 15(1): e0226417. https://doi.org/10.1371/journal.pone.0226417

6 Schiller CE, Meltzer-Brody S, Rubinow DR. The role of reproductive

hormones in postpartum depression. *CNS Spectrums*. 2015;20(1):48–59. doi:10.1017/S1092852914000480.

7 Biggs A, Brown K, Foster DG. Perceived abortion stigma and psychological well-being over five years after receiving or being denied an abortion. PLoS ONE 15(1): e0226417. https://doi.org/10.1371/journal.pone.0226417.

8 However, I do know about support groups for people who have ended wanted pregnancies, for example https://endingawantedpregnancy.com/.

9 In a survey I did of over 5,000 women having an abortion at a Midwest clinic in 2008, 96.6% expected to cope well after their abortion. Among the 3.4% who anticipated poor coping were disproportionately women terminating wanted pregnancies for reason of fetal anomaly, women who did not have high confidence in their decision, women who had spiritual concerns about abortion, women with a history of depression, women who felt that they were pushed into their decision to have an abortion, and teenagers. Even so, the vast majority of women with these characteristics still anticipated coping well. Foster DG, Gould H, Kimport K. How women anticipate coping after an abortion. *Contraception*. 2012 Jul;86(1):84–90. PMID: 22176790.

10 Biggs MA, Upadhyay UD, McCulloch CE, Foster DG. Women's mental health and well-being 5 years after receiving or being denied an abortion: a prospective, longitudinal cohort study. *JAMA Psychiatry*. 2017 Feb 1;74(2):169–178. PMID: 27973641.

11 Substance Abuse and Mental Health Services Administration. 2015 National Survey on Drug Use and Health (NSDUH): Table 2.46B—Alcohol Use, Binge Alcohol Use, and Heavy Alcohol Use in Past Month among Persons Aged 12 or Older, by Demographic Characteristics: Percentages, 2014 and 2015. https://www.samhsa.gov/data/sites/default/files/NSDUH-Det Tabs-2015/NSDUH-DetTabs-2015/NSDUH-DetTabs-2015.htm#tab2-46b. Accessed January 18, 2017. Reeves, WC. Mental illness surveillance among adults in the United States. Centers for Disease Control and Prevention. https://www.cdc.gov/mmwr/preview/mmwrhtml/su6003a1.htm. Published September 2, 2011. Accessed September 12, 2019. Substance Abuse and Mental Health Services Administration. Results from the 2016 National Survey on Drug Use and Health: detailed tables. Center for Behavioral Health Statistics and Quality. https://www.samhsa.gov/data/sites/default/files/NSD UH-DetTabs-2016/NSDUH-DetTabs-2016.pdf. Published September 7, 2017. Accessed November 7, 2017. Bonomi AE, Anderson ML, Rivara FP, et al. Health care utilization and costs associated with childhood abuse. *J Gen Intern Med*. (2008)23:294. doi:10.1007/s11606-008-0516-1.

12 Biggs MA, Upadhyay UD, McCulloch CE, Foster DG. Women's mental health and well-being 5 years after receiving or being denied an abortion: a prospective, longitudinal cohort study. *JAMA Psychiatry*. 2017 Feb 01;74(2):169–178. PMID: 27973641.

13 Biggs MA, Gould H, Barar RE, Foster DG. Five-year suicidal ideation trajectories among women receiving or being denied an abortion. *Am J Psychiatry*. 2018 Sep 1;175(9):845-852 PMID: 29792049.

14 Roberts SCM, Foster DG, Gould H, Biggs MA. Changes in alcohol,

tobacco, and other drug use over five years after receiving versus being denied a pregnancy termination. *J Stud Alcohol Drugs*. 2018 Mar;79(2):293–301. PMID: 29553359.

15 Substance use during pregnancy causes a range of harms, including fetal alcohol spectrum disorders; tobacco use is linked to low birth weight, stillbirth, and SIDS; drug use during pregnancy can lead to low birth weight and preterm birth, as well as neurodevelopmental abnormalities.

16 I have to say *almost* nobody because I have learned that the organization We Testify (wetestify.org) has thrown abortion showers as part of their efforts to support people who share their abortion stories.

17 Biggs MA, Upadhyay UD, Steinberg JR, Foster DG. Does abortion reduce self-esteem and life satisfaction? *Qual Life Res*. 2014 Nov;23(9):2505–2513. PMID: 24740325.

18 Cohen S, Kamarck T, Mermelstein R. A global measure of perceived stress. *J Health Soc Behav*. 1983;24:385–396.

19 Harris LF, Roberts SC, Biggs MA, Rocca CH, Foster DG. Perceived stress and emotional social support among women who are denied or receive abortions in the United States: a prospective cohort study. *BMC Womens Health*. 2014;14:76. PMID: 24946971.

20 Dr. Biggs reran the analyses on the full five years of data and there were still no differences.

21 Biggs MA, Rowland B, McCulloch CE, Foster DG. Does abortion increase women's risk for post-traumatic stress? Findings from a prospective longitudinal cohort study. *BMJ Open*. 2016;6(2):e009698. PMID: 26832431.

22 Rocca CH, Kimport K, Gould H, Foster DG. Women's emotions one week after receiving or being denied an abortion in the United States. *Perspect Sex Reprod Health*. 2013 Sep;45(3):122–131. PMID: 24020773.

23 Barrett G, Smith SC, Wellings K. Conceptualisation, development, and evaluation of a measure of unplanned pregnancy. *J Epidemiol Community Health*. 2004;58(5):426–433.

24 Rocca CH, Samari G, Foster DG, Gould H, Kimport K. Emotions and decision rightness over five years following an abortion: an examination of decision difficulty and abortion stigma. *Soc Sci Med*. 2020 Jan 2:112704. doi:10.1016/j.socscimed.2019.112704.

25 Rocca CH, Kimport K, Roberts SC, Gould H, Neuhaus J, Foster DG. Decision rightness and emotional responses to abortion in the United States: a longitudinal study. *PLoS One*. 2015; 10(7):e0128832. PMID: 26154386.

26 Brief for Sandra Cano et al. as Amici Curiae in No. 05-380: 22–24.

27 Rocca CH, Samari G, Foster DG, Gould H, Kimport K. Emotions and decision rightness over five years following an abortion: an examination of decision difficulty and abortion stigma. *Soc Sci Med*. 2020 Jan 2:112704. doi:10.1016/j.socscimed.2019.112704.

28 Rocca CH, Gould H, Kimport K, Foster DG. Emotions and decisions rightness over five years after having an abortion in the United States. Annual Meetings of the American Public Health Association, Denver, CO, Nov 2016.

REFERENCES

29 Watson K. Reframing regret. *JAMA*. 2014;311(1):27–29. doi:10.1001/jama.2013.283739.

Chapter 5: Physical Health

1 Personal communication with Elizabeth Nash, senior state issues manager at the Guttmacher Institute. August 22, 2019.

2 Jones BS, Daniel S, Cloud LK. State law approaches to facility regulation of abortion and other office interventions. *Am J Public Health*. 2018;108(4):486–492. doi:10.2105/AJPH.2017.304278.

3 Sisson G, Kimport K. Facts and fictions: characters seeking abortion on American television, 2005–2014. *Contraception*. 2016 May;93(5):446–451. doi:10.1016/j.contraception.2015.11.015.

4 State funding of abortions under Medicaid. Henry J. Kaiser Family Foundation. www.kff.org/medicaid/state-indicator/abortion-under-medicaid/. June 21, 2019.

5 Upadhyay et al. Incidence of emergency department visits and complications after abortion. *Obstet Gynecol*. 2015 Jan;125(1):175–183.

6 Despite the relative safety of abortion, there have been, over the decades, a small number of high-profile rogue abortion providers responsible for maiming or, in a few cases, killing patients and, in the horrifying case of Kermit Gosnell, committing infanticide.

7 Raymond EG, Grimes DA. The comparative safety of legal induced abortion and childbirth in the United States. *Obstet Gynecol*. 2012;119:215–219.

8 Soma-Pillay P, Nelson-Piercy C, Tolppanen H, Mebazaa A. Physiological changes in pregnancy. *Cardiovasc J Afr*. 2016;27(2):89–94. doi:10.5830/CVJA-2016-021.

9 Centers for Disease Control and Prevention. Births: final data for 2017. *Natl Vital Stat Rep*. 2018 Nov 7;67(8):50. https://www.cdc.gov/nchs/data/nvsr/nvsr67/nvsr67_08-508.pdf.

10 Ananth CV, Keyes KM, Wapner RJ. Pre-eclampsia rates in the United States, 1980–2010: Age-period-cohort analysis. *BMJ*. 2013 Nov 7;347:f6564. https://www.ncbi.nlm.nih.gov/pubmed?term=24201165. Berg CJ, MacKay AR, Qin C, Callaghan WM. Overview of maternal morbidity during hospitalization for labor and delivery in the United States 1993–1997 and 2001–2005. *Obstet Gynecol*. 2009;113:1075–1081.

11 National Academies of Sciences, Engineering, and Medicine. The safety and quality of abortion care in the United States. Washington, DC: National Academies Press: 2018. doi:10.17226/24950.

12 Dilation and evacuation (D&E) is the surgical method of emptying the uterus after the first trimester of pregnancy.

13 Biggs MA, Gould H, Foster DG. Understanding why women seek abortions in the US. *BMC Womens Health*. 2013;13:29. PMID: 23829590.

14 A medication abortion involves taking two drugs: mifepristone stops the development of the pregnancy and misoprostol causes the uterus to contract and expel its contents. Taking misoprostol alone is common, especially

in countries where abortion is not legally available. Misoprostol alone is associated with a greater likelihood of incomplete emptying of the uterus than the combination of both drugs.

15 Safety and effectiveness of first-trimester medication abortion in the United States. ANSIRH issue brief. August 2016. https://www.ansirh.org/sites /default/files/publications/files/medication-abortion-safety.pdf. Mitka M. Some men who take Viagra die—why? *JAMA*. 2000:283(5):590–593. doi:10.1001/jama.283.5.590. Ostapowicz G, Fontana RJ, Schioødt FV, et al. Results of a prospective study of acute liver failure at 17 tertiary care centers in the United States. *Ann Intern Med*. 2002;137(12):947–954. https://www .ncbi.nlm.nih.gov/pubmed/12484709. McQuaid KR, Laine L. Systematic review and meta-analysis of adverse events of low-dose aspirin and clopi-dogrel in randomized controlled trials. *American J Med*. 2006;119(8), 624–638. doi:10.1016/j.amjmed.2005.10.039.

16 CDCs abortion surveillance system FAQs. Centers for Disease Control and Prevention. www.cdc.gov/reproductivehealth/data_stats/abortion .htm. Updated November 25, 2019.

17 Bartlett LA, Berg CJ, Shulman HB, et al. Risk factors for legal induced abortion-related mortality in the United States. *Obstet Gynecol*. 2004;103(4):729–737. doi:10.1097/01.AOG.0000116260.81570.60. Frick AC, Drey EA, Diedrich JT, Steinauer JE. Effect of prior cesarean delivery on risk of second-trimester surgical abortion complications. *Obstet Gyne-col*. 2010;115(4):760–764.

18 Lisonkova S, Joseph KS. Incidence of preeclampsia: risk factors and outcomes associated with early- versus late-onset disease. *Am J Obstet Gynecol*. 2013:209(6):544.e1–12. doi:10.1016/j.ajog.2013.08.019.

19 Gerdts C, Dobkin L, Foster DG, Schwarz EB. Side effects, physical health consequences, and mortality associated with abortion and birth after an unwanted pregnancy. *Womens Health Issues*. 2016 Jan–Feb;26(1):55–59. PMID: 26576470.

20 Ralph LJ, Schwarz EB, Grossman D, Foster DG. Self-reported physical health of women who did and did not terminate pregnancy after seeking abortion services: a cohort study. *Ann Intern Med*. 2019;171(4):238-247. doi: 10.7326/M18-1666.

21 What this means is that women who were denied an abortion and got an abortion elsewhere were grouped with the women who initially received an abortion, either in the first trimester or second depending on how many weeks along they were. And women who were just under the limit and received an abortion were placed into the first-trimester group as necessary (the overlap between the two groups occurred at clinics where the limit was within two weeks of the end of the first trimester).

22 DeSalvo KB, Bloser N, Reynolds K, et al. Mortality prediction with a sin-gle general self-rated health question: a meta-analysis. *J Gen Intern Med*. 2006;21:267–275. PMID: 16336622. Schnittker J, Bacak V. The increas-ing predictive validity of self-rated health. *PLoS One*. 2014;9:e84933. doi:10.1371/journal.pone.0084933.

23 Tooher J, Thornton C, Makris A, et al. Hypertension in pregnancy and long-

term cardiovascular mortality: a retrospective cohort study. *Am J Obstet Gynecol.* 2016;214(6):722.e1–6. https://www.ncbi.nlm.nih.gov/pubmed /26739795. Amaral LM, Cunningham MW, Cornelius DC, LaMarca B. Preeclampsia: long-term consequences for vascular health. *Vasc Health Risk Manag.* 2015;11:403–415.

24 Hjartardottir S, Leifsson BG, Geirsson RT, Steinthorsdottir V. Recurrence of hypertensive disorder in second pregnancy. *Am J Obstet Gynecol.* 2006;194(4):916–920. England L, Kotelchuck M, Wilson HG, et al. Estimating the recurrence rate of gestational diabetes mellitus (GDM) in Massachusetts 1998–2007: methods and findings. *Matern Child Health J.* 2015;19(10):2303–2313.

25 Pregnancy mortality surveillance system. Centers for Disease Control and Prevention. https://www.cdc.gov/reproductivehealth/maternalinfanthealth /pregnancy-mortality-surveillance-system.htm. Updated June 5, 2019. Accessed September 12, 2019.

26 Our study was not large enough or long enough to study breast cancer as an outcome. However, the relationship between abortion and breast cancer has been thoroughly debunked. American College of Obstetricians and Gynecologists. Induced abortion and breast cancer risk: ACOG Committee Opinion No. 434. *Obstet Gynecol.* 2009;113:1417–1418.

27 Pregnancy mortality surveillance system. Centers for Disease Control and Prevention. https://www.cdc.gov/reproductivehealth/maternalinfanthealth /pregnancy-mortality-surveillance-system.htm. Updated June 5, 2019. Accessed September 12, 2019.

28 McLemore MR. To prevent women from dying in childbirth, first stop blaming them. *Scientific American.* May 1, 2019. https://www.scientific american.com/article/to-prevent-women-from-dying-in-childbirth-first -stop-blaming-them/.

Chapter 6: Women's Lives

1 *Planned Parenthood of Southeastern Pa. v. Casey* (91-744), 505 U.S. 833 (1992) https://www.law.cornell.edu/supct/html/91-744.ZO.html.

2 Ginsburg RB. Some thoughts on autonomy and equality in relation to Roe v. Wade. *North Carol Law Rev.* 1985;63:375. https://scholarship.law.unc .edu/nclr/vol63/iss2/4.

3 Zabin LS, Hirsch MB, Emerson MR. When urban adolescents choose abortion: effects on education, psychological status and subsequent pregnancy. *Fam Plann Perspect.* 1989 Nov–Dec;21(6):248–255.

4 Upadhyay UD, Biggs MA, Foster DG. The effect of abortion on having and achieving aspirational one-year plans. *BMC Womens Health.* 2015;15:102. https://bmcwomenshealth.biomedcentral.com/articles/10.1186/s12905- 015-0259-1.

5 Gallup Historical Trends. Abortion. 2014. http://www.gallup.com/poll /1576/abortion.aspx. Gallup Historical Trends. Moral issues. 2014. http:// www.gallup.com/poll/1681/moral-issues.aspx. Smith TW, Son J. Trends in

public attitudes on abortion: general social survey 2012 final report. NORC at the University of Chicago. 2013. https://www.norc.org/PDFs/GSS%20 Reports/Trends%20in%20Attitudes%20About%20Abortion_Final.pdf.

6 Woodruff K, Biggs MA, Gould H, Foster DG. Attitudes toward abortion after receiving vs. being denied an abortion in the USA. *Sex Res Social Policy*. 2018;15:452–463. doi:10.1007/s13178-018-0325-1.

7 Saad, L. Americans' attitudes toward abortion unchanged. Gallup. 2016. http://news.gallup.com/poll/191834/americans-attitudes-toward-abortion -unchanged.aspx.

8 Rocca CH, Samari G, Foster DG, Gould H, Kimport K. Emotions and decision rightness over five years after abortion: an examination of decision difficulty and abortion stigma. *Soc Sci Med*. 2020 Jan 2:112704. doi:10.1016 /j.socscimed.2019.112704.

9 Woodruff K, Biggs MA, Gould H, Foster DG. Attitudes toward abortion after receiving vs. being denied an abortion in the USA. *Sex Res Social Policy*. 2018;15:452–463. doi:10.1007/s13178-018-0325-1.

10 Jerman J, Jones RK, Onda T. Characteristics of U.S. abortion patients in 2014 and changes since 2008. Guttmacher Institute. May 2016. https://www .guttmacher.org/report/characteristics-us-abortion-patients-2014#17.

11 The credit report study (discussed next) showed us that the two groups were actually very similar before the pregnancy was conceived, but we did not have this information at the time of this analysis of self-reported data. Even knowing what I know now, I would still do this analysis in this more conservative way, given the differences in self-reported outcomes at baseline.

12 Foster DG, Biggs MA, Ralph L, Gerdts C, Roberts S, Glymour MM. Socioeconomic outcomes of women who receive and women who are denied wanted abortions in the United States. *Am J Public Health*. 2018 Mar;108(3):407–413. PMID: 29345993. PMCID: PMC5803812.

13 Miller S, Wherry LR, Foster DG. The economic consequences of being denied an abortion. National Bureau of Economic Research working paper 26662. Published January 2020. http://www.nber.org/papers/w26662

14 Kearney MS, Levine PB. Why is the teen birth rate in the United States so high and why does it matter? *J Econ Perspect*. 2012;26(2):141–166.

15 Ralph LJ, Mauldon J, Biggs MA, Foster DG. A prospective cohort study of the effect of receiving versus being denied an abortion on educational attainment. *Womens Health Issues*. 2019 Nov–Dec;29(6):455–464. doi:10.1016 /j.whi.2019.09.004.

16 Laws requiring school districts to accommodate and not discriminate against lactating employees and students. Breastfeed LA. http://breastfeedla .org/wp-content/uploads/2015/10/BFLA-School-District-Laws-1.pdf.

17 Wells v. School districts prepared to accommodate breastfeeding teens. *Herald & Review*. January 6, 2018. herald-review.com/news/local/education /school-districts-prepared-to-accommodate-breastfeeding-teens/article _0567860b-9ea6-5243-ae86-7850169e4e9f.html. Breastfeeding rights. California Breastfeeding Coalition. http://californiabreastfeeding.org/breast feedingrights/breastfeeding-at-work/laws-that-protect-lactating-teens-at -school/.

18 Einhorn E. Teen pregnancy is still a problem—school districts just stopped paying attention. *Hechinger Report*. April 13, 2019. hechingerreport.org /teen-pregnancy-is-still-a-problem-school-districts-just-stopped-paying -attention/.

19 McCarthy M, Upadhyay UD, Ralph L, Biggs MA, Foster DG. The effect of receiving versus being denied an abortion on having and achieving aspirational five-year plans. *BMJ Sexual & Reproductive Health*. In press

Chapter 7: Children

1 Responsibility of the mother. BBC Ethics Guide. http://www.bbc.co.uk /ethics/abortion/philosophical/responsibility.shtml. Archived 2014. Penny L. The criminalization of women's bodies is all about conservative male power. *New Republic*. May 17, 2019. https://newrepublic.com/article/153 942/criminalization-womens-bodies-conservative-male-power.

2 Foster EM. How economists think about family resources and child development. *Child Dev*. 2002;73:1904–1914. Blake J. Family size and the quality of children. *Demography*. 1981;18:421–442. Downey D. When bigger is not better: family size, parental resources, and children's educational performance. *Am Sociol Rev*. 1995;60:15.

3 Joyce TJKR, Korenman S. The effect of pregnancy intention on child development. *Demography*. 2000;37:83–94. Barber JS, East PL. Children's experiences after the unintended birth of a sibling. *Demography*. 2011;48: 101–125.

4 Foster DG, Raifman SE, Gipson JD, Rocca CH, Biggs MA. Effects of carrying an unwanted pregnancy to term on women's existing children. *J Pediatr*. 2018 February 2019, Volume 205, Pages 183–189.e1 PMID: 30389101.

5 Jerman J, Jones RK, Onda T. Characteristics of U.S. abortion patients in 2014 and changes since 2008. Guttmacher Institute. 2016. www.guttmacher .org/report/characteristics-us-abortion-patients-2014.

6 Brothers KB, Glascoe FP, Robertshaw NS. PEDS: Developmental Milestones—an accurate brief tool for surveillance and screening. *Clin Pediatr (Phila)*. 2008;47:271–279.

7 World Health Organization. Report of a technical consultation on birth spacing. January 22, 2019. https://www.who.int/maternal_child_adolescent /documents/birth_spacing05/en/.

8 Further proof that the idea that one cannot become pregnant if one is still breastfeeding is a myth. Breastfeeding lowers the chance of conception, but not enough to recommend it as a primary method of contraception.

9 Hutcheon JA, Nelson HD, Stidd R, Moskosky S, Ahrens KA. Short interpregnancy intervals and adverse maternal outcomes in high-resource settings: an updated systematic review. *Paediatr Perinat Epidemiol*. 2019;33(1): O48–O59. https://onlinelibrary.wiley.com/doi/full/10.1111/ppe.12518.

10 Foster DG, Biggs MA, Raifman S, Gipson J, Kimport K, Rocca CH. Comparison of health, development, maternal bonding, and poverty among children born after denial of abortion vs after pregnancies subsequent to

REFERENCES

an abortion. *JAMA Pediatr.* Published online September 4, 2018. PMID: 30193363.

11 Federal poverty guidelines. Families USA. https://familiesusa.org/product/federal-poverty-guidelines.

12 We ask about male and female partners in our analyses of romantic relationships. But for cohabitation, we only have data on male partners.

13 Brockington IF, Fraser C, Wilson D. The Postpartum Bonding Questionnaire: a validation. *Arch Womens Ment Health.* 2006 Sep;9(5):233–242. https://link.springer.com/article/10.1007/s00737-006-0132-1.

14 The bonding measure we used was only for infants, so we do not know about feelings toward the child as s/he grows.

15 Crissey SR. Effect of pregnancy intention on child well-being and development: combining retrospective reports of attitude and contraceptive use. *Popul Res Policy Rev.* 2005 Dec;24(6):593–615. https://link.springer.com/article/10.1007/s11113-005-5734-1.

16 Sisson G, Ralph L, Gould H, Foster DG. Adoption decision making among women seeking abortion. *Womens Health Issues.* 2017 Mar–Apr;27(2):136–144. PMID: 28153742.

17 Foster DG, Biggs MA, Ralph L, Gerdts C, Roberts S, Glymour MM. Socioeconomic outcomes of women who receive and women who are denied wanted abortions in the United States. *Am J Public Health.* 2018 Mar;108(3):407–413. PMID: 29345993. PMCID: PMC5803812.

18 Armstrong E, et al. Intrauterine devices and implants: a guide to reimbursement: immediate post-abortion. University of California, San Francisco; http://larcprogram. ucsf.edu/immediate-post-abortion. Updated 2015. Cohen S. Repeat abortion, repeat unintended pregnancy, repeated and misguided government policies. *Guttmacher Policy Review.* 2007;10(2):8–12.

19 Gould H, Perrucci A, Barar R, Sinkford D, Foster DG. Patient education and emotional support practices in abortion care facilities in the United States. *Womens Health Issues.* 2012 Jul–Aug;22(4):e359–364. PMID: 22609254.

20 Moseson H, Foster DG, Upadhyay UD, Vittinghoff E, Rocca CH. Contraceptive use over five years after receipt or denial of abortion services. *Perspect Sex Reprod Health.* 2018 Mar;50(1):7–14. PMID: 29329494.

21 Prager SW, Steinauer JE, Foster DG, Darney PD, Drey EA. Risk factors for repeat elective abortion. *Am J Obstet Gynecol.* 2007 Dec;197(6):575.e1–6. PMID: 17904511.

22 Upadhyay UD, Aztlan-James EA, Rocca CH, Foster DG. Intended pregnancy after receiving vs. being denied a wanted abortion. *Contraception.* 2019 Jan; 99(1):42-47. PMID: 30244161.

23 Dr. Rachel Jones of the Guttmacher Institute tells me that of U.S. abortion patients in 2014, 30% already had kids and were done, 40% wanted a/another kid, 15% weren't sure if they wanted another kid, and 15% didn't have kids and didn't want them.

24 Upadhyay UD, Aztlan-James EA, Rocca CH, Foster DG. Intended pregnancy after receiving vs. being denied a wanted abortion. *Contraception.* 2018 Sep 20. PMID: 30244161.

25 Given the higher fertility post-abortion compared to post-birth, Dr. Goleen Samari of Columbia University and I have projected that a third of women having abortions have an "extra" child later that they would not have had if they had been denied that abortion. Abortion averts just two-thirds of one birth, in terms of average lifetime number of children born.

26 Aztlan EA, Foster DG, Upadhyay U. Subsequent unintended pregnancy among US women who receive or are denied a wanted abortion. *J Midwifery Womens Health*. 2018 Jan;63(1):45–52. PMID: 29377521.

Chapter 8: Men

1 Blair G. My Twitter thread on abortion. *Design Mom*. September 13, 2018. https://www.designmom.com/twitter-thread-abortion.

2 We did not ask the sexual identity of the person who the woman became pregnant with. We asked the woman about the "man involved," unfortunately failing to find out if any of the partners identified as a trans woman or nonbinary.

3 Rocca CH, Kimport K, Gould H, Foster DG. Women's emotions one week after receiving or being denied an abortion in the United States. *Perspect Sex Reprod Health*. 2013 Sep;45(3):122–131. PMID: 24020773.

4 Chibber KS, Biggs MA, Roberts SC, Foster DG. The role of intimate partners in women's reasons for seeking abortion. *Womens Health Issues*. 2014 Jan–Feb;24(1):e131–138. PMID: 24439939.

5 See the justification for California's ballot measure: California Proposition 73, Parental Notification for Minor's Abortion (2005). Ballotpedia. https://ballotpedia.org/California_Proposition_73,_Parental_Notification_for_Minor%27s_Abortion_(2005).

6 Foster DG, Gould H, Taylor J, Weitz TA. Attitudes and decision making among women seeking abortions at one U.S. clinic. *Perspect Sex Reprod Health*. 2012 Jun;44(2):117–124. PMID: 22681427.

7 Finer LB, Frohwirth LF, Dauphinee LA, Singh S, Moore AM. Reasons U.S. women have abortions: quantitative and qualitative perspectives. *Perspect Sex Reprod Health*. 2005;37(3):110–118.

8 Roberts SC, Biggs MA, Chibber KS, Gould H, Rocca CH, Foster DG. Risk of violence from the man involved in the pregnancy after receiving or being denied an abortion. *BMC Med*. 2014;12:144. PMID: 25262880.

9 Mauldon J, Foster DG, Roberts SC. Effect of abortion vs. carrying to term on a woman's relationship with the man involved in the pregnancy. *Perspect Sex Reprod Health*. 2015 Mar;47(1):11–18.

10 Upadhyay U, Foster DG, Biggs MA. Effects of abortion on women's intimate relationships: findings from a prospective 5-year longitudinal cohort study. Under review.

11 Note that abortion is not associated with infertility. However, as Jada points out, if one puts off trying to become pregnant until one's midthirties or early forties, it can be more difficult to conceive.

REFERENCES

Chapter 9: Reactions to and Reflections on the Turnaway Study

1   Biggs MA, Upadhyay UD, McCulloch CE, et al. Women's mental health and well-being 5 years after receiving or being denied an abortion: a prospective, longitudinal cohort study. *JAMA Psychiatry*. February 2017;74(2):169–178. https://jamanetwork.com/journals/jamapsychiatry/fullarticle/2592320.

2   Rocca CH, Kimport K, Roberts SC, Gould H, Neuhaus J, Foster DG. Decision rightness and emotional responses to abortion in the United States: a longitudinal study. *PLoS One*. 2015;10(7):e0128832. PMID: 26154386.

3   Foster DG, Biggs MA, Ralph L, Gerdts C, Roberts S, Glymour MM. Socioeconomic outcomes of women who receive and women who are denied wanted abortions in the United States. *Am J Public Health*. 2018 Mar;108(3):407–413. PMID: 29345993. PMCID: PMC5803812. Foster DG, Biggs MA, Raifman S, Gipson J, Kimport K, Rocca CH. Comparison of health, development, maternal bonding, and poverty among children born after denial of abortion vs after pregnancies subsequent to an abortion. *JAMA Pediatr*. 2018;172(11):1053-1060. PMID: 30193363. Foster DG, Raifman SE, Gipson JD, Rocca CH, Biggs MA. Effects of carrying an unwanted pregnancy to term on women's existing children. *J Pediatr*;205:183-9 February 2019 Volume 205, Pages 183–189.e1. PMID: 30389101. Gerdts C, Dobkin L, Foster DG, Schwarz EB. Side effects, physical health consequences, and mortality associated with abortion and birth after an unwanted pregnancy. *Womens Health Issues*. 2016 Jan–Feb;26(1):55–59. PMID: 26576470. Ralph LJ, Schwarz EB, Grossman D, Foster DG. Self-reported physical health of women who did and did not terminate pregnancy after seeking abortion services: a cohort study. *Ann Intern Med*. 2019;171(4):238-247. PMID: 31181576.

4   Foster DG, Kimport K. Who seeks abortions at or after 20 weeks? *Perspect Sex Reprod Health*. 2013 Dec;45(4):210–218. PMID: 24188634.

5   Abortion surveillance 2016. Centers for Disease Control and Prevention. https://www.cdc.gov/reproductivehealth/data_stats/abortion.htm. Updated November 25, 2019.

6   Amaral G, Foster DG, Biggs MA, Jasik CB, Judd S, Brindis CD. Public savings from the prevention of unintended pregnancy: a cost analysis of family planning services in California. *Health Serv Res*. 2007 Oct;42(5):1960–1980. PMID: 17850528. Foster DG, Rostovtseva DP, Brindis CD, Biggs MA, Hulett D, Darney PD. Cost savings from the provision of specific methods of contraception in a publicly funded program. *Am J Public Health*. 2009 Mar;99(3):446–451. PMID: 18703437.

7   Frost JJ, et al. Publicly supported family planning services in the United States: likely need, availability and impact. Guttmacher Institute. https://www.guttmacher.org/fact-sheet/publicly-supported-FP-services-US. Published October 2019.

8   Foster DG, Parvataneni R, de Bocangegra HT, Lewis C, Bradsberry M, Darney P. Number of oral contraceptive pill packages dispensed, method continuation, and costs. *Obstet Gynecol*. 2006 Nov;108(5):1107–1114. PMID: 17077231. Foster DG, Hulett D, Bradsberry M, Darney P, Policar M. Num-

ber of oral contraceptive pill packages dispensed and subsequent unintended pregnancies. *Obstet Gynecol.* 2011 Mar;117(3):566–572. PMID: 21343759.

9   Insurance coverage of contraceptives. Guttmacher Institute. https://www .guttmacher.org/state-policy/explore/insurance-coverage-contraceptives. Updated February 1, 2020.

10 Fifteen percent of women who agreed to be in the study did not complete the first interview and are not included among the 956 who gave self-reported data. But they are included in our death record searches (chapter 5) and our analysis of credit reports (chapter 6).

11 History of the Nurses' Health Study. Nurses' Health Study. https://www .nurseshealthstudy.org/about-nhs/history. Morton LM, Cahill J, Hartge P. Reporting participation in epidemiologic studies: a survey of practice. *Am J Epidemiol.* 2006;163(3):197–203.

12 Dr. Loren Dobkin, then a nursing doctoral student, evaluated all of our strategies to increase participation rates and found that repeatedly visiting the recruiting clinic had the most impact. See Dobkin LM, Gould H, Barar RE, Ferrari M, Weiss EI, Foster DG. Implementing a prospective study of women seeking abortion in the United States: understanding and overcoming barriers to recruitment. *Womens Health Issues.* 2014 Jan–Feb;24(1):e115–123. PMID: 24439937.

13 Foster DG, Higgins JA, Karasek D, Ma S, Grossman D. Attitudes toward unprotected intercourse and risk of pregnancy among women seeking abortion. *Womens Health Issues.* 2012 Mar;22(2):e149–155. PMID: 22000817. Lessard LN, Karasek D, Ma S, et al. Contraceptive features preferred by women at high risk of unintended pregnancy. *Perspect Sex Reprod Health.* 2012 Sep;44(3):194–200. PMID: 22958664.

14 Foster DG, Gould H, Taylor J, Weitz TA. Attitudes and decision making among women seeking abortions at one U.S. clinic. *Perspect Sex Reprod Health.* 2012 Jun;44(2):117–124. PMID: 22681427.

15 Munk-Olsen T, Laursen TM, Pedersen CB, Lidegaard O, Mortensen PB. Induced first-trimester abortion and risk of mental disorder. *N Engl J Med.* 2011;364(4):332–339. Munk-Olsen T, Laursen TM, Pedersen CB, Lidegaard O, Mortensen PB. First-time first-trimester induced abortion and risk of readmission to a psychiatric hospital in women with a history of treated mental disorder. *Arch Gen Psychiatry.* 2012;69(2):159–165. Steinberg JR, Laursen TM, Adler NE, Gasse C, Agerbo E, Munk-Olsen T. The association between first abortion and first-time non-fatal suicide attempt: a longitudinal cohort study of Danish population registries. *Lancet Psychiatry.* 2019 Dec;6(12):1031–1038. doi:10.1016/S2215-0366(19)30400-6. Van Ditzhuijzen J, Ten Have M, de Graaf R, Van Nijnatten C, Vollebergh WAM. Long-term incidence and recurrence of common mental disorders after abortion: a Dutch prospective cohort study. *J Psychiatric Research.* 2018 Jul;102:132–135. Gomez AM. Abortion and subsequent depressive symptoms: an analysis of the National Longitudinal Study of Adolescent Health. *Psychol Med.* 2018 Jan;48(2):294–304. doi:10.1017/S0033291717001684. Steinberg JR, Becker D, Henderson JT. Does the outcome of a first pregnancy predict depression, suicidal ideation, or lower self-esteem? Data from the National

REFERENCES

Comorbidity Survey. *Am J Orthopsychiatry*. 2011;81(2):193–201. Warren JT, Harvey SM, Henderson JT. Do depression and low self-esteem follow abortion among adolescents? Evidence from a national study. *Perspect Sex Reprod Health*. 2010;42(4):230–235.

16 Gilchrist AC, Hannaford PC, Frank P, Kay CR. Termination of pregnancy and psychiatric morbidity. *Br J Psychiatry*. 1995;167(2):243–248.

17 Pregnancy mortality surveillance system. Centers for Disease Control and Prevention. https://www.cdc.gov/reproductivehealth/maternalinfanthealth/pregnancy-mortality-surveillance-system.htm. Updated June 5, 2019. Accessed September 12, 2019.

18 Petersen EE, Davis NL, Goodman D, et al. *Vital Signs:* pregnancy-related deaths, United States, 2011–2015, and strategies for prevention, 13 states, 2013–2017. *MMWR Morb Mortal Wkly Rep*. 2019;68:423–429. doi:10.15585/mmwr.mm6818e1.

19 Jones RK, Jerman J. Abortion incidence and service availability in the United States, 2014. *Perspect Sex Reprod Health*. 2017 Mar;49(1):17–27. doi:10.1363/psrh.12015. Sedgh G, Bearak J, Singh S, et al. Abortion incidence between 1990 and 2014: global, regional, and subregional levels and trends. *Lancet*. 2016 Jul 16;388(10041):258–267. I assume that current rates hold steady for 25 years of trying to avoid pregnancy. But abortion rates have been declining and so these lifetime estimates would have been higher in the past.

Chapter 10: The Turnaway Study and Abortion Policy

1 Nash E, Benson RG, Mohammed L, Cappello O. Policy trends in the states, 2017. Guttmacher Institute. https://www.guttmacher.org/article/2018/01/policy-trends-states-2017. Published January 2, 2018.

2 Jones RK, Jerman J. Abortion incidence and service availability in the United States, 2014. *Perspect Sex Reprod Health*. 2017 Mar;49(1):17–27. doi:10.1363/psrh.12015. Jones RK, Witwer E, Jerman J. Abortion incidence and service availability in the United States, 2017. Guttmacher Institute. September 2019. https://www.guttmacher.org/report/abortion-incidence-service-availability-us-2017.

3 Foster DG. Dramatic decreases in US abortion rates: public health achievement or failure? *Am J Public Health*. 2017 Dec;107(12):1860–1862. PMID: 29116861. PMCID: PMC5678419.

4 Women who have given birth in the past year make up 2% of the population living below the federal poverty level. Source: Tables S1701 and B13010 available at https://data.census.gov/cedsci/.

5 Okeowo A. Fighting for abortion access in the south. *New Yorker*. October 4, 2019. https://www.newyorker.com/magazine/2019/10/14/fighting-for-abortion-access-in-the-south. What is reproductive justice? SisterSong Women of Color Reproductive Justice Collective. https://www.sistersong.net/reproductive-justice. For an excellent primer on the reproductive justice framework, see *Reproductive Justice: An Introduction* by Loretta Ross and Rickie Solinger (University of California Press, 2017).

REFERENCES

6 Petersen EE, Davis NL, Goodman D, et al. *Vital Signs*: pregnancy-related deaths, United States, 2011–2015, and strategies for prevention, 13 states, 2013–2017. *MMWR Morb Mortal Wkly Rep*. 2019;68:423–429. doi:10.15585/mmwr.mm6818e1.

7 Roberts D. *Killing the Black Body: Race, Reproduction and the Meaning of Liberty*. New York: Vintage Books; 1999.

8 Prather C, Fuller TR, Jeffries WL IV, et al. Racism, African American women, and their sexual and reproductive health: a review of historical and contemporary evidence and implications for health equity. *Health Equity*. 2018 Sep 24;2(1):249–259. doi:10.1089/heq.2017.0045.

9 Dehlendorf C, Diedrich J, Drey E, Postone A, Steinauer J. Preferences for decision-making about contraception and general health care among reproductive age women at an abortion clinic. *Patient Educ Couns*. 2010;81(3):343–348.

10 Grossman D, White K, Hopkins K, Potter JE. Change in distance to nearest facility and abortion in Texas, 2012 to 2014. *JAMA*. 2017;317(4):437–439. doi:10.1001/jama.2016.17026.

11 Foster DG. Testimony for the Senate Judiciary Committee hearing. March 15, 2016. https://www.judiciary.senate.gov/imo/media/doc/03-15-16%20 Foster%20Testimony.pdf.

12 Erika Christensen and her husband, Garin Marschall, have written a beautiful letter advocating on behalf of later-abortion patients with links to many of their stories, which can be found at https://www.abortionpatients.com.

13 Late-term abortion: protecting babies born alive and capable of feeling pain: full committee hearing [video]. Committee on the Judiciary. https:// www.judiciary.senate.gov/meetings/late-term-abortion_protecting-babies -born-alive-and-capable-of-feeling-pain. Time stamp 1:32:00.

14 Berry S. Pro-abortion witness testifies it's acceptable to deny medical care to baby born alive after abortion. *Breitbart*. March 19, 2016. https://www .breitbart.com/politics/2016/03/19/pro-abortion-witness-testifies-its-ac ceptable-to-deny-medical-care-to-baby-born-alive-after-abortion/.

15 *Planned Parenthood of the Heartland v. Reynolds ex rel. State*, 915 N.W.2d 206, 218 (Iowa 2018).

16 Tribunal Constitucional de Chile. Rol No 3729-(3751)-17-CPT. August 28, 2017. https://www.camara.cl/sala/verComunicacion.aspx?comuid=36761.

17 Murtagh C, Wells E, Raymond EG, Coeytaux F, Winikoff B. Exploring the feasibility of obtaining mifepristone and misoprostol from the internet. *Contraception*. 2018 Apr;97(4):287–291. doi:10.1016/j.contraception. 2017.09.016. Grossman D. Why 2020 presidential candidates should support over-the-counter access to abortion pills. *USA Today*. December 18, 2019. https://www.usatoday.com/story/opinion/2019/12/18/abortion-pills -safe-could-ease-access-crisis-women-column/2665854001/.

18 Rowan A. Prosecuting women for self-inducing abortion: counterproductive and lacking compassion. Guttmacher Institute. *Guttmacher Policy Review*. 2015 Sep 22;18(3). https://www.guttmacher.org/gpr/2015/09 /prosecuting-women-self-inducing-abortion-counterproductive-and-lack ing-compassion.

19 Council on Scientific Affairs, American Medical Association. Induced termination of pregnancy before and after Roe v Wade: trends in the mortality and morbidity of women. *JAMA*. 1992 Dec 9;268(22):3231–3239.

Chapter 11: Next Steps for Science

1 Government of Nepal. Muluki Ain (Eleventh Amendment), 2059 No 28(a), Chapter on Life (unofficial translation on file with Center for Reproductive Rights) 2002. *Kathmandu University Medical Journal*. 2003;2(7):177–178.

2 Alkema L, et al. Global, regional, and national levels and trends in maternal mortality between 1990 and 2015, with scenario-based projections to 2030: a systematic analysis by the UN Maternal Mortality Estimation Inter-Agency Group. *Lancet*. 2016;387(10017):462–474.

3 Puri M, Singh S, Sundaram A, Hussain R, Tamang A, Crowell M. Abortion incidence and unintended pregnancy in Nepal. *Int Perspect Sex Reprod Health*. 2016 Dec 1;42(4):197.

4 Devkota MD, Adhikari RK, Upreti SR. (2016) Stunting in Nepal: looking back, looking ahead. Maternal & Child Nutrition, 12: 257–259. doi: 10.1111/mcn.12286.

5 Puri M, Vohra D, Gerdts C, Foster DG. "I need to terminate this pregnancy even if it will take my life": A qualitative study of the effect of being denied legal abortion on women's lives in Nepal. *BMC Women's Health* (2015) 15:85 DOI 10.1186/s12905-015-0241-y.

6 For more on the experience of being a provider, read David Cohen and Krysten Connon's *Living in the Crosshairs: The Untold Stories of Anti-Abortion Terrorism* (Oxford University Press, 2015).

7 A sepsis ward was a ward of a hospital where doctors and nurses cared for women when an infection had reached their bloodstream. Sepsis was almost always lethal prior to antibiotics, but even now, mortality rates for people with sepsis (from any cause, not just abortion) is 40%. Sepsis. Mayo Clinic. https://www.mayoclinic.org/diseases-conditions/sepsis/symptoms-causes/syc-20351214. Council on Scientific Affairs, American Medical Association. Induced termination of pregnancy before and after Roe v Wade: trends in the mortality and morbidity of women. *JAMA*. 1992 Dec 9;268(22):3231–3239. https://www.ncbi.nlm.nih.gov/pubmed/1433765.

8 About trust women. Trust Women. http://www.trustwomenpac.org/about/.

9 Joffe C. The legacy of George Tiller. Beacon Broadside. https://www.beaconbroadside.com/broadside/2009/06/carole-joffe-the-legacy-of-george-tiller.html. Published June 4, 2009.

10 Ginsburg RB. Some thoughts on autonomy and equality in relation to Roe v. Wade. *North Carol Law Rev*. 1985;63:375. https://scholarship.law.unc.edu/nclr/vol63/iss2/4.

REFERENCES

Afterword

1 Fuentes L, Jerman J. Distance traveled to obtain clinical abortion care in the United States and reasons for clinic choice. *Journal of Women's Health*. 2019 Dec;28(12):1623–1631. doi:10.1089/jwh.2018.7496.

2 Cartwright AF, Karunaratne M, Barr-Walker J, Johns NE, Upadhyay UD. Identifying national availability of abortion care and distance from major US cities: systematic online search. *J Med Internet Res*. 2018 May;20(5):e186. doi:10.2196/jmir.9717.

3 Jones RK, Lindberg L, Witwer E. COVID-19 abortion bans and their implications for public health. *Perspect Sex Reprod Health*. 2020 May;52(2):65–68. doi:10.1363/psrh.12139. Novack S. Abortion clinics in Texas rely on traveling doctors. Coronavirus is keeping some of them home, *Texas Observer*. March 20, 2020. https://www.texasobserver.org/abortion-access-coronavirus/.

4 Roberts SCM, Schroeder R, Joffe C. COVID-19 and independent abortion providers: findings from a rapid-response survey. *Perspect Sex Reprod Health*. 2020 Dec;52(4). doi:10.1363/psrh.12163.

5 Sobel S, Ramaswamy A, Frederiksen B, Salganicoff A. State action to limit abortion access during the COVID-19 pandemic. Kaiser Family Foundation. August 10, 2020. https://www.kff.org/coronavirus-covid-19/issue-brief /state-action-to-limit-abortion-access-during-the-covid-19-pandemic/. Bayefsky MJ, Bartz D, Watson KL. Abortion during the Covid-19 pandemic— ensuring access to an essential health service. *N Engl J Med*. 2020;382(19):e47. doi:10.1056/NEJMp2008006.

6 Keating D, Tierney L, Meko T. In these states, pandemic crisis response includes attempts to stop abortion. *Washington Post*. April 21, 2020. https:// www.washingtonpost.com/nation/2020/04/21/these-states-pandemic-crisis -response-includes-attempts-stop-abortion/?arc404=true. Donley G, Chen BA, Borrero S. The legal and medical necessity of abortion care amid the COVID-19 pandemic. *J Law Biosci*. 2020;7(1):a013. doi:10.1093/jlb/lsaa013.

7 Najmabadi S. Texas clinics resume abortion services as state acknowledges ban is no longer in place. *Texas Tribune*. April 22, 2020. https://www.texas tribune.org/2020/04/22/texas-abortions-coronavirus-ban/.

8 White K, Kumar B, Goyal V, Wallace R, Roberts SCM, Grossman D. Changes in abortion in Texas following an executive order ban during the coronavirus pandemic. *JAMA*. Published online January 4, 2021. doi:10.1001 /jama.2020.24096.

9 Mifeprex REMS Study Group. Sixteen years of overregulation: time to unburden Mifeprex. *N Engl J Med*. 2017;376:790–794. doi:10.1056/NE JMsb1612526. US Food and Drug Administration. Mifeprex risk evaluation and mitigation strategy (REMS) program. Updated March 2016. https:// www.accessdata.fda.gov/drugsatfda_docs/rems/Mifeprex_2016-03-29_ REMS_document.pdf. Accessed February 3, 2021.

10 Coleman J. Judge waives requirement for in-person visit to get abortion pill during pandemic. *The Hill*. July 13, 2020. https://thehill.com/policy

REFERENCES

/healthcare/507158-judge-waives-requirement-for-inperson-visit-to-get
-abortion-pill-during. Accessed February 3, 2021. Kunzelman M. Federal
judge rules women can get abortion pill without doctor visits. July 13, 2020.
https://www.pbs.org/newshour/health/federal-judge-rules-women-can
-get-abortion-pill-without-doctor-visits. Accessed February 3, 2021.

11 Upadhyay U, Schroeder R, Roberts SCM. Adoption of no-test and telehealth
medication abortion care among independent abortion providers in response
to COVID-19. *Contracept X*. 2020;2:100049. doi:10.1016/j.conx.2020.100049.

12 American College of Obstetricians and Gynecologists. Joint statement on
abortion access during the COVID-19 outbreak. March 18, 2020. https://
www.acog.org/clinical-information/physician-faqs/~/link.aspx?_id=43
CF073F75B0407882567D8C250A2A76&_z=z. Accessed February 3, 2021.
National Abortion Federation. Abortion & COVID-19. 2020. https://pro
choice.org/abortion-covid-19/. Accessed February 3, 2021. Raymond EG,
Grossman D, Mark A, et al. Commentary: no-test medication abortion: a
sample protocol for increasing access during a pandemic and beyond. *Contraception*. 2020 Jun;101(6):361–366. doi:10.1016/j.contraception.2020.04.005.

13 Ginsburg RB. Some thoughts on autonomy and equality in relation to Roe
v. Wade. *North Carol Law Rev*. 1985;63:375. https://scholarship.law.unc
.edu/nclr/vol63/iss2/4.

14 Barnes R. Supreme Court restores requirements for medication abortions,
siding with Trump administration. *Washington Post*. January 12, 2021. https://
www.washingtonpost.com/politics/courts_law/supreme-court-medication
-abortion/2021/01/12/3720192c-4617-11eb-a277-49a6d1f9dff1_story.html.

15 Williams J. The case for accepting defeat on Roe. *New York Times*. September 29, 2020. https://www.nytimes.com/2020/09/29/opinion/abortion-roe
-supreme-court.html.

16 Eighty percent of Americans want abortion to be legal in at least some circumstances. Abortion. Gallup. https://news.gallup.com/poll/1576/abortion
.aspx. Accessed February 3, 2021.

17 Kim S, Young N, Lee Y. The role of reproductive justice movements in
challenging South Korea's abortion ban. *Health and Human Rights Journal*. 2019 Dec; 21(2):97–107. https://www.ncbi.nlm.nih.gov/pmc/articles
/PMC6927381/. Politi D and Londoño E. Argentina legalizes abortion, a
milestone in a conservative region. *New York Times*. December 30, 2020.
https://www.nytimes.com/2020/12/30/world/americas/argentina-legalizes
-abortion.html.

18 In the past 25 years, nearly 50 countries liberalized their abortion laws. The
world's abortion laws. Center for Reproductive Rights. https://reproductive
rights.org/worldabortionlaws. Accessed February 3, 2021.

19 Abortion policy in the absence of Roe. Guttmacher Institute. Updated February 1, 2021. https://www.guttmacher.org/state-policy/explore/abortion
-policy-absence-roe. Accessed February 3, 2021.

20 Jerman J, Jones RK, Onda T. Characteristics of U.S. abortion patients in
2014 and changes since 2008. Guttmacher Institute. www.guttmacher.org
/report/characteristics-us-abortion-patients-2014. Published May 2016.

Index

INDEX

INDEX

denial of abortion (*cont.*)
  ban on public funding and, 69
  comparison of receipt of abortion
    with. *See* comparison of receipt or
    denial of abortion
  contraceptive use after, 210, 211, 212
  dignity of risk and, 128–29
  domestic violence and, 22, 232–33,
    290, 307
  economic well-being after, 174–75
  emotional response to, 120–23
  employment after, 175
  future intended childbearing after,
    213–14
  gestational limit and, 2
  happiness of mothers with children
    after, 121, 204, 207, 220, 221, 224
  health insurance coverage after, 211
  life course after, 165–66
  low-income women and, 6, 278
  maternal bonding and, 207–8
  maternal mortality after, 259
  mental health effects of, 103, 108, 109,
    110, 120–23
  morality of abortion attitudes and, 171
  obesity and, 87
  ongoing relationship with men after,
    234–35, 238–39
  post-traumatic stress disorder after,
    118, 119, 120
  poverty levels after, 22, 37, 165, 176,
    202, 280
  risks in, 144, 147–49, 148 (figure)
  self-esteem and life satisfaction after,
    115
  stress after, 116–17
  study women's reactions to, 126–27,
    209
  suicidal ideation after, 112
denial of pregnancy, 45, 242
denial of services
  obese women and, 87
Denmark, 81, 82, 258
depression
  after abortion, 4, 39, 76, 101, 104,
    109–10, 110 (figure), 127, 307,
    335n9
  mothers of study women and, 188,
    196
  study women with, 39, 83–84, 99, 106,
    107, 108, 109, 111–12, 127, 137, 172,
    173, 190, 192, 220–21, 245

  suicidal thoughts related to, 113
  unintended pregnancy and, 105, 108,
    109, 120
Destiny (study participant), 38–39,
  184–85
dignity of risk, 128–29
divorce
  domestic violence and, 167
  of parents of study women, 89
  study women and, 59, 167–68
Dobkin, Loren, 146
doctors. *See* abortion physicians
Dr. Tiller Patient Assistance Fund, 70
domestic violence, 230–33
  abortion-rights advocates on, 24
  children's removal due to, 235–36
  comparison of receipt or denial of
    abortion and, 232–33, 238
  denial of abortion and, 22, 232–33,
    290, 307
  divorce and, 167
  financial dependence and, 276
  gestational limits and, 249
  later abortions and, 84
  mental health harm from, 106, 107
  possible *Roe* overturn and higher
    exposure to, 288
  as primary reason for seeking an
    abortion, 231
  study women and, 40, 59, 168,
    230–32, 235–36, 264, 267–68, 270,
    276, 290
  teenagers and, 86
  Turnaway Study analysis of, 118–19,
    231
  women's fear of, 231
Drey, Eleanor, 4–5, 19
drinking behavior. *See* alcohol use
drug use
  comparison of receipt or denial of
    abortion and, 113, 127
  early versus later abortions and, 82
  fetal health and, 40–41
  impact of denial of abortion on, 127,
    205
  impact on pregnancy of, 336n15
  lack of pregnancy preparation and, 144
  later abortions and, 83–84
  men's use of, 189, 193, 194–95, 237, 238
  by parents of study women, 119, 187,
    196
  as reason for abortion, 40–42

guilt
  after abortions, 7, 75, 84, 102, 105,
    120, 122, 123, 196–97
  about adoption, 209
Guttmacher Institute, 72, 251, 254

happiness
  after abortions, 24, 28, 29, 121, 122
  of adopted children after placement,
    262, 271, 272, 298, 301
  with being pregnant, 75, 121, 185,
    201, 294
  of birth mothers after adoption
    process, 298, 301
  after birth of children, 23
  of mothers with children after denial
    of abortion, 121, 204, 207, 220, 221,
    224
  study women and, 120, 121, 122, 224,
    245, 294, 298
Harris, Laura, 116
health care institutions. *See also*
    abortion clinics
  contraception availability in, 54
health effects of abortion. *See also*
    mental health; physical health
  myth about abortion risk and, 305–6
  Surgeon General Koop's report on, 14
health insurance, 16
  abortion coverage under, 66–69, 211
  contraception coverage under, 49, 53
  lack of, and abortion costs, 64, 257
  study women with, 20, 85, 133,
    242–43, 246
health of children born before abortion,
    as reason for abortion, 38
health of fetus. *See* fetal development
health of women
  abortion restrictions based on
    protection of, 39, 282–83
  alcohol, tobacco, or drug use and, 40
  concerns about, as reason for
    abortion, 37, 39–40, 144
  earlier studies on abortion and, 6
  impact of denied abortions on, 21–22
  as justification for banning abortions,
    4, 39
  need for reliable data on abortion
    and, 4
  pregnancies with risks for, 39–40
  as reason for abortion, 35 (table), 37,
    40

study women's problems in, 40, 56–58
  support for abortion rights and, 24
  terminating a pregnancy due to,
    20–21
heartbeat bills, 31–32
Hispanic women. *See* Latina women
hormonal changes
  after abortion, 104, 134–35
  during pregnancy, 44, 143
hormonal contraceptives, 44, 51, 212,
    273
hotlines, 70, 78
human life amendment proposal, 13

I Didn't Know I Was Pregnant
    (television series), 44
income level. *See also* low-income
    women; poverty
  abortion-related expenses and, 67
  age of mothers having children and,
    181
  child-rearing costs and, 176
  comparison of receipt or denial of
    abortion and, 23, 174, 176, 177
    (figure), 178, 202
  denial of abortion and, 39
  study women on working and, 267,
    273
  study women's dependence on men
    for, 83, 168, 269
  subsequent children and, 206
informed consent law, 78
informed referral, 63–64
intrauterine devices (IUDs), 49, 50
    (table), 51, 97, 211, 212, 273, 274
isolation, feelings of, 23, 99, 104, 290

Jackson, Andrea, 54
Jada (study participant), 45, 68, 164, 239,
    241–46, 343n11
Jessica (study participant), 15, 37, 40, 54,
    55–62, 63–65, 66, 73, 78, 103, 151,
    164, 167, 200, 225–26, 229, 231, 232,
    234, 278
jobs. *See* employment
Julia (study participant), 203
June Medical Services v. Russo, 287

Kamali (study participant), 103
Kavanaugh, Brett, 3, 283
Kaya (study participant), 124
Kennedy, Anthony, 4, 100–101, 108, 124

INDEX

INDEX

INDEX

Stonesifer, Sandy, 17
stress. *See also* post-traumatic stress
    disorder (PTSD)
    abortion and, 15, 108, 116–17, 119
    study women and, 132, 134, 135, 150,
        189, 267
substance use. *See* drug use
Sue (study participant), 79, 170, 175,
    176, 204, 205, 209
suicidal ideation, 277
    abortion aftermath and, 4, 76, 101–2,
        151
    myth about abortion and, 307
    predictors of, 113
    study women and, 108, 110–13, 127
support. *See* social support
Supreme Court
    congressional members' letter on
        abortion restrictions to, 3
    June Medical Services v. Russo, 287
    Kennedy's comment on abortion and
        women's health in, 4, 100–101
    new judge picks and possible *Roe*
        overturn by, 3, 283, 319
    Roe v. Wade decision in. *See Roe v.
        Wade* decision
    state restriction laws and, 2, 281–83
Sydney (study participant), 106, 227

Tamara (study participant), 183
teenagers
    abortions and, 20, 65, 167, 335n9
    discovery of pregnancy by, 86–87
    education level of, 167
    gestational limits and, 249
    impact of abortion and early
        childbearing on, 181
    later abortions and, 83, 85–86
    parental-involvement laws and, 42, 86,
        124, 330n12
    parents' insurance for abortions by,
        67–68
    state restrictions on, 86
    suicidal thoughts and, 101–2
    in Turnaway Study, 55, 187–89,
        265–66
Texas
    counseling booklets in, 76
    gestational limits law in, 3
    impact of closing of clinics in, 71
    Supreme Court's striking down of
        laws in, 3, 281–83

third-trimester abortions, 248, 306, 312
Tiller, George, 70, 312–13
tobacco use
    impact on pregnancy of, 336n15
    as reason for abortion, 40–42
trans men, 9, 279, 289
trans women, 279, 289, 343n2
travel to clinics, as barrier, 64, 71–73
Trump, Donald
    defunding of family clinics with
        contraceptive services and, 53
    Roe v. Wade pledge of, 3
    Supreme Court judge picks and
        possible *Roe* overturn and, 3,
        283
tubal ligations, 51, 57, 191, 212
Turnaway Study
    abortion for fetal anomalies excluded
        from, 20–21, 40, 122–23
    abortion policy and, 277–90
    anti-abortion journalists and activists'
        interest in, 248–49
    background to, 5–8
    changing the conversation about
        abortion through, 308–9
    court citations of research from, 286
    criticisms of, 250, 252, 255, 256
    earlier report from Surgeon General
        Koop on effects of abortion and,
        14–15
    factors in design of, 15–16
    findings summary for, 21–22
    first to compare women receiving
        abortions and those turned away, 6
    focus of survey questions in, 7–8
    initial motivation in, 100
    interview process in, 6, 16–17, 19
    issues in pregnancy decision-making
        and, 5–6
    launch of, 17–19
    media attention to, 247–48
    methodology of, 256
    naming of, 5–6
    national studies of abortion compared
        with, 254–55
    as natural experiment, 15–16
    number of women recruited for, 6–7,
        16, 253
    objectivity of, 250–51
    participation rate in, 252–54
    pilot before, 17
    purpose of, 256–58

366

INDEX

THE
TURNAWAY
STUDY

Diana Greene Foster, PhD

This reading group guide for The Turnaway Study *includes an introduction, discussion questions, and ideas for enhancing your book club. The suggested questions are intended to help your reading group find new and interesting angles and topics for your discussion. We hope that these ideas will enrich your conversation and increase your enjoyment of the book.*

Introduction

What happens when a woman seeking an abortion is turned away? To answer this question, Diana Greene Foster assembled a team of scientists—psychologists, epidemiologists, demographers, nurses, physicians, economists, sociologists, and public health researchers— to conduct a landmark ten-year study. They followed a thousand women from across America, some of whom received abortions, some of whom were turned away. The results were thorough and astonishing.

As the national debate around abortion intensifies, *The Turnaway Study* offers the first in-depth, data-driven examination of the negative consequences for women who cannot get abortions and provides incontrovertible evidence to refute the claim that abortion harms women. Interwoven with the study findings are ten first-person narratives. Candid, intimate, and deeply revealing, the stories bring to life the women behind the science. *The Turnaway Study* is a must-read for anyone who cares about the impact of abortion and abortion restriction on people's lives.

Topics and Questions
for Discussion

1. As Dr. Foster writes, the term "turnaway" "resonates with a whole set of issues that surround women's decision making around pregnancy" (page 5). What are some of the issues she identifies? In your opinion, why might it be important to consider the many ways people and society "turn away" when it comes to abortion?

2. Unlike previous studies that compared women who received abortions to women who carried wanted pregnancies to term, the Turnaway Study studied women with unwanted pregnancies and compared those who received to those who were denied the abortions they sought. Why is this distinction important? How does Dr. Foster describe the advantages of the Turnaway Study's methodology?

3. According to Dr. Foster, Amy's in-depth interview (beginning on page 25) shows how "abortion can be a normal part of planning a family and living a meaningful life." Dr. Foster suggests that stories like Amy's, which are largely missing from abortion discourse, are essential to consider. Describe how Amy's circumstances informed her decision to seek an abortion. How does a story like Amy's contribute to a broader conversation about abortion?

4. Refer to Figure 1 on page 46. For many women who receive later abortions (20 weeks or later), difficulties finding and getting to a clinic are significant factors in delaying their care. Identify challenges and impediments to receiving care that are

unique to second- and third-trimester abortions. What effect might these obstacles have on the person seeking care?

5. Dr. Foster discusses the Hyde Amendment, which restricts federal funds from paying for an abortion. What challenges does the Hyde Amendment pose to women seeking an abortion? What do you think of a restriction on abortion that only affects low-income women?

6. In the Turnaway Study, researchers asked women to rate their emotions (regret, anger, sadness, guilt, happiness, relief) with regard to their unwanted pregnancies and separately, their abortions. Women were asked about each emotion individually, allowing, for example, participants to report feeling high levels of both relief *and* anger. Why is it important that the questions were asked in this way?

7. The Turnaway Study found that women denied abortions had higher anxiety and lower self-esteem in the first six months but did not find differences in mental health between women who received or were denied an abortion in the long run. Were you surprised by any of the findings regarding mental health outcomes? If yes why, and what informed your prior belief?

8. Dr. Foster discusses a person's "right to make their own personal decisions, even decisions that they might regret," or what Katie Watson has called the "dignity of risk" (page 128). According to Dr. Foster, how is this an important concept to consider when talking about abortion, especially in light of the Turnaway Study's findings that mental health is not adversely affected by receiving an abortion?

9. The Turnaway Study found that a woman's existing and—should she choose to have them—future children benefit across multiple metrics when she is able to receive a wanted abortion. How does this finding add nuance to discussions of children's well-being, with regard to abortion?

10. In chapter 9, Dr. Foster points out that, even in the wake of the Turnaway Study, "we are still talking about whether abortion harms women and not whether lack of abortion harms

women and children." In your opinion, how could reframing the question in this way affect the discourse around abortion?

11. How does Brenda's story (beginning on page 265) of being denied an abortion illustrate the Turnaway Study's finding that women's concerns about having a child tend to come about, if they are made to carry the pregnancy to term?

12. In chapter 10, Dr. Foster writes, "There are more restrictions on abortion in 2020 than there were in 1973, when the U.S. Supreme Court first affirmed access to abortion as a constitutional right in *Roe v. Wade.*" What are some reasons she cites for this increase in restrictions?

13. As Dr. Foster points out, "many of us are alive today because our mothers and grandmothers were able to avoid carrying a prior unwanted pregnancy to term" (page 263). How does her own family history illustrate this point?

14. How is the term "reproductive justice" defined on page 280? Why is it important to specifically address the needs of marginalized persons and communities? How do abortion rights fit into a reproductive justice framework?

15. Findings from the Turnaway Study have already made their way into the courtroom, resulting in evidence-based testimony about abortion that would have been impossible before the study was published. In your opinion, and in light of the Turnaway Study's findings, how might your state's abortion laws be made to better serve people seeking abortions?

16. Of the ten personal stories shared in the book, which was most impactful, eye-opening, or challenging for you and why?

Enhance Your Book Club

To further enhance your book club, please consider the following materials and resources:

Continued Reading

- Dr. Meera Shah's *You're the Only One I've Told*
- Annie Finch's *Choice Words*
- Dorothy Roberts's *Killing the Black Body*
- Katie Watson's *Scarlet A: The Ethics, Law, and Politics of Ordinary Abortion*
- David Cohen and Carole Joffe's *Obstacle Course: The Everyday Struggle to Get an Abortion in America*

Screening Suggestions

- *Dirty Dancing* (1987)
- *The Cider House Rules* (1999)
- *Obvious Child* (2014)
- *Grandma* (2015)
- *Little Woods* (2019)
- *Never Rarely Sometimes Always* (2020)
- *Saint Frances* (2020)
- *Unpregnant* (2020)

Documentaries

- *12th & Delaware* (2010)
- *After Tiller* (2013)
- *Ours to Tell* (2020)